Mind-Melding Unity and Blender for 3D Game Development

Unleash the power of Unity and Blender to create amazing games

Spencer Grey

BIRMINGHAM—MUMBAI

Mind-Melding Unity and Blender for 3D Game Development

Copyright © 2021 Packt Publishing

Group Product Manager: Rohit Rajkumar
Publishing Product Manager: Aaron Tanna
Senior Editor: Hayden Edwards
Content Development Editor: Aamir Ahmed
Technical Editor: Saurabh Kadave
Copy Editor: Safis Editing
Project Coordinator: Ajesh Devavaram
Proofreader: Safis Editing
Indexer: Subalakshmi Govindhan
Production Designer: Aparna Bhagat

First published: December 2021

Production reference: 1261121

Published by Packt Publishing Ltd.
Livery Place
35 Livery Street
Birmingham
B3 2PB, UK.

ISBN 978-1-80107-155-0

www.packt.com

For mom and her all-encompassing love. For dad, I hope you're watching. For A and A, my inspiration and motivation. Ad astra per aspera.

– Spencer Grey

Contributors

About the author

Spencer Grey is a native New Yorker who started making games by typing in source code from magazines (that used to be a thing!). Once upon a time, he was creative director of Sesame Street's digital group where he would boss around Elmo and Big Bird. After that, he cofounded Electric Funstuff and for 15 years developed game ideas for companies such as Scholastic, Sony, and Lego. Spencer has been a teacher, programmer, writer, and producer in the games industry. Mr. Grey is definitely not related to the grey aliens stored in Area 51. Definitely not. No way.

Many thanks to the excellent team at Packt who made this an efficient and pleasant process. Thank you, Pratik, Aaron, Hayden, Aamir, Divij, Saurabh, and the others I haven't met. Thanks also to the human race for being such complex and amusing creatures.

About the reviewers

Stefan van der Vyver lives in Cape Town, South Africa. He was born in 1975 and started coding in 1987. Coding experience involved Turbo Pascal, Python, Visual Basic, C#, .Net, .ASP, PHP, HTML5, Javascript, AngularJS, and REACTJS. Stefan started working on Blender 3D in 2003. He worked on professional 3D animation, in conjunction with software development for more than a decade before eventually focusing on software development.

Unity 3D was used as the primary development platform for an educational virtual world development in South Africa from 2011 to 2014 where Stefan was developer and product lead. Stefan is passionate about education and the role of technology in education. As a Senior Software Developer he is heavily involved in developing new products and coming up with innovative architecture solutions.

Being involved with book reviews allows him to keep his skills up to date, and to give back to the community.

Sungkuk Park is a Berlin-based game developer. He majored in art studies at Hongik University in Seoul but turned into a software engineer in the gaming industry. His interests cover almost everything about gaming. Now he has started a career as a technical artist.

Publications:

- Author of *Seamless Society*, July 21, 2020, in collaboration with the online exhibition platform *DDDD*

- Author of *Wallpeckers: Breaking down the barriers between media*, an article in Korean Art magazine *Misulsegye*, March 2019

- Author of *The Possibility of the Impossibility of the "Art Games"*, an article in Korean Art magazine *Misulsegye*, February 2017

- Translator and editor of *Game Level Generation Using Neural Networks*, a featured post of Gamasutra

Table of Contents

Preface

Section 1: There and Back Again – An Asset Roundtrip with Unity and Blender

1
Melding Unity and Blender

What is Unity?	4	Knowledge Prerequisites	10
Top 12 Reasons for Using Unity	5	Software Prerequisites	11
		Hardware Prerequisites	12
What Is Blender?	7	How to Read This Book	12
Top 8 and a Half Reasons for Using Blender	8	**Getting Additional Help**	12
Requirements for this Book	10	**Summary**	13

2
Gathering Our Resources

Technical Requirements	16	**Using the Asset Store**	23
Creating Our Unity Project	16	What is the Asset Store?	23
The Unity Hub	17	Searching the Asset Store	25
Selecting a Project Template	18	**Using the Package Manager**	27
Your new project	19	**Getting ready for Blender**	32
Creating the project folders	20	Installing the FBX Exporter package	32
Defining Our Mini-Game Level	22	Exporting the turret	34
Mini-Game Gameplay Mechanics	22		

Additional Assets to Download   35
Audio Assets   36

Textures   37
Summary   37

3

Entering the Blender Zone for the First Time

Technical Requirements   40
Introducing Blender   40
The Toolbar (Area 1)   42
Editor, mode selection, and mode
menus (Area 2)   44
Pivot, Snap, and Proportional Editing
(Area 3)   44
Header menu bar (Area 4)   45
View modes and tools (Area 5)   46
Axes Gizmo (Area 6)   46
Zoopancamper! (Area 7)   47
The Outliner Panel (Area 8)   48
The Properties Panel (Area 9)   48
The Status Bar (Area 10)   50

**Monkeying Around with the
Monkey Head**   50
Translation: Moving the Monkey   52
Rotation: Twirling the Monkey   53
Scaling: Mushing the Monkey   53
The Sidebar   54
Applying your transforms   55
Getting ready to move on   56

Entering Edit Mode   57
Creating a Monkey-corn   59

Altering the Turret   63
Carving Out a Lid   64
Creating the launch tube   67
Creating the Struts   70
Fixing a flaw   72

Summary   73

4

Asset Assimilation: Returning to Unity

Technical Requirements   76
**Preparing the Turret for
Gameplay**   76
Importing the Turret   76
Restructuring the Turret   79
Texturing the turret   81
Creating a material for the missile tube 82
Applying the material to the tube   82
Planning the turret behavior   83
Adding in iTween   84

Scripting the Turret   85
Setting up turret actions   87
Tag, you're it! Creating a placeholder
player hero   92
Finally, Scanning!   93
Testing the ScanAction   96
Preparing for the ShootAction   98
Creating the ShootAction   100
Testing the ShootAction: Pew! Pew!
Pew!   104

Preparing for the LaunchAction   105
Creating the LaunchAction   106
Testing the LaunchAction   110

Code Checklist for the Chapter   110
The Ultimate Advanced Unity Tip   111

Summary   112

Section 2: The Right Stuff: Scenery, Props, and Characters

5

On the Level: Making Modular Scenery

Technical Requirements   116
Understanding Modular Level Design   116
Setting our Goals   118
The Humble Floor   119
Walls and corners   119

Blocking Out our Level   120
A Quick Recap of our Blender Know-How   121
Navigation and hot-keys   121
Knowing Your Numpad   122

Creating Floors   123

Creating a Wall   126
Creating a wall corner   130

Texture Mapping, UV Mapping/ Unwrapping, and Materials   132
UV Mapping 101   132
UV Unwrapping 101   133
Materials 101   136
Unwrapping and texturing the Wall   136
Working in the UV Editing Workspace   137
Unwrapping and texturing the wall corner   142

Summary   145

6

Living It Up: Adding Fun with Animation

Technical Requirements   148
Understanding Basic Animation Concepts   148
Keyframes   148

Animating in Blender   149
Frame rate   153
Working with Keyframes   154
Auto-keying   157
Markers   157

Creating Animated Blastdoors   158
Blastdoor creation scheme   158
Creating the Blastdoor Doorframe   159
Creating the Simple Door   164
Animating the Simple Door   165
Creating the Complex Door   166
Animating the complex door   173

Texturing the Blastdoors 178
Texturing the Doorframe 178
Texturing the Simple Door 180

Texturing the Complex Door 181

Exporting Your Goodies 183
Summary 184

7

Prep Work: Materials, Grids, and Snapping

Technical Requirements 186

Getting Our Act Together: Collecting Our Great Stuff in Unity 186
Importing into Unity 187

Living in a Material World: Materials for Walls, Doors, and Floors 193

Creating our new materials 196

Snapping and the Scene Grid 200
Changing the color of the grid lines 204
Vertex Snapping 206

Summary 207

8

Laying Out the Level

Technical Requirements 210
Laying Out the Level 210
Level Layout Tips 211
Areas A and B 212
Area C 213
Area C2 213
Area D 214
Area E 214

Area F 215
Area G 216

The Sky's the Limit: Adding a Skybox 217
Sounds Like Trouble: Adding some Audio Effects 219
Summary 221

9

Secret Weapon #1: Deploying ProBuilder

Technical Requirements 224
An Introduction to ProBuilder 225
ProBuilder vs. Blender 225

History of ProBuilder 225

Installing ProBuilder 226
Exploring The ProBuilder Toolbar 232
Orange-Colored Options – Tools and Editors 233

Creating Objects with ProBuilder 234
Blue Colored Options: Selection
Modifiers and Actions 238
Green Colored Options: Object
Editing Tools 240
Red-Colored Options: Element Editing

Tools 242
Other ProBuilder options 245

**Bridgework – Making Movable
Scenery** 246
Summary 251

10

Secret Weapon #2: Animating with Timeline

Technical Requirements 254
Introducing Timeline 254
When to use Timeline for animation 255
Timeline Tracks 256

**Prepping the Prism: Getting our
asset ready to animate** 257
Creating the Prism Prefab 261

**Captain to the Bridge!—
Animating our Bridge
with Timeline** 263

Creating a Timeline 263
Creating an Animation Track 265
The Plan for the Bridge 267
Recording an Infinite Clip 268
Animating the prism walkway 268
Previewing your Animation 270
Finishing the bridge animation 271
Adding Audio 274

Summary 277

11

We Could Be Heroes: Blender Character Modeling

Technical Requirements 280
Blender Command Review 280
3D View Commands 280
Miscellaneous 3D View Commands 282
Edit Mode Commands 282
Pro Tip: Faster Command Access 283

Prepping for the marine 284
Organizing the objects in your scene 285
Randomizing Colors 286

Modeling the Marine 287
Head 288
Torso 297
The Arm 306
The Hand 308
The Leg 312

The Boot 315
Touchups 316
Parenting 317
Finalizing the Model and the File 317

Summary 319

12

It Was Rigged!: Character Rigging

Technical Requirements	322	Processing the Hands	338
Just One Thing...	322	Processing the Legs	339
UV-Unwrapping and Texturing		Processing the Feet	340
the Marine	322	Rigging the Marine	342
UV Unwrapping Refresher	322	Exporting the marine	343
Loading the texture image into the UV		Getting started with Mixamo	344
space	324	Doing excellent things with the	
Getting started with the Marine	325	marine	348
Processing the Head	326	Downloading Animations	348
Processing the Torso	334	Summary	351
Processing the Arms	337		

Section 3: Assets Assemble! Putting It All Together

13

Animation and Movement In-Game

Technical Requirements	356	Marine movement and Camera	
Getting the marine ready for		Control	371
duty	356	Camera Tracking with Secret Weapon	
Creating and applying the marine		#4: Cinemachine	375
material	357	Animating the Scenery	378
Creating the marine prefab	359	Animating the Blast doors	378
Animating the Marine	362	Animating the Bridge	383
Adding lights to the level	369	Summary	385

14

Endgame: Adding Spit and Polish

Technical Requirements	**388**	Debugging the Mayhem	409
Make with the shooting already	**388**	**Creating a Main Menu**	**410**
		Changing the menu text	411
Preparing to Shoot	388	Adding audio to the menu	413
Adding Sound to the shooting	390	Setting Up Scene Loading	416
Scripting the Shooting, Part I	391		
Scripting the Shooting, Part II	394	**Adding Post Processing**	**417**
A Marine Checklist	397	**Creating the Final Room**	**420**
Making the Turrets Go Boom	**399**	**Summary**	**422**
A Checklist for the Turret and Missile	405		

Other Books You May Enjoy

Index

Preface

Space. The final frontier.

Don't you just wish you could fill it up with amazing video games that you make yourself? The Unity game engine by itself is a great tool for achieving this, but if you are an indie game developer, hobbyist, or student, you may feel limited because quality assets that make your game shine cost M-O-N-E-Y. Or do they?

The Blender 3D/2D modeling application removes this obstacle. Blender is a free, open source, battle-tested, and sophisticated tool that allows you to create an infinite number of visual assets for your games, limited only by your imagination and how much effort you want to invest.

This book takes you on a whirlwind tour of both Unity and Blender, teaching you to use both of them in a complementary fashion and touching on some of the most powerful features of each.

By the end of the book, we will wind up with a mini-game level for which we will have created most of the assets—animated scenery and an animated character—ourselves from scratch. We will also touch on ways to add polish to your games, such as audio, lighting, and post-processing. More importantly, the knowledge acquired in this book can be applied to just about any project in any game genre. Strap yourself in, it's gonna be a heck of a ride…

Who this book is for

I am imagining that you are an eager indie game developer, hobbyist, or student. Or perhaps you are a savvy industry professional who recognizes that this book is bound to become a collector's item and are looking to cash in.

At any rate, this book assumes that you have just a smattering of Unity knowledge, with the following at a minimum:

- Understand how all your assets live in your Project View
- Understand the Scene View and how to navigate around

- Understand how game objects appear in the Hierarchy

- Understand how to examine an object in the Inspector

- Understand how to add components and C# scripts to an object and run your game

Honestly, if you don't already have these skills, you can acquire them in about 20 minutes from one of the gazillion YouTube videos or books that cover them. This book assumes you have *no* prior knowledge of Blender. If you do, please sign up for a mind-wipe first.

What this book covers

Chapter 1, Melding Unity and Blender, achieves lift off in a very gentle fashion. We first take a quick look at Unity, its capabilities, its history, and why you might choose it over competing game engines. Next, we do the same with Blender. Finally, we cover the knowledge, software, and hardware prerequisites for using this book (there are very few!).

Chapter 2, Gathering Our Resources, begins by talking about project setup and provides a light backstory for our minigame. We move on to explore the Asset Store and the Package Manager and conclude by learning to export assets from Unity, getting them ready for Blender.

Chapter 3, Entering the Blender Zone for the First Time, introduces the Blender interface and some of the key tools (out of the many, many, *many* available) we will be using. Next, we spend time learning to alter a pre-existing asset and getting ready to return it to Unity.

Chapter 4, Asset Assimilation: Returning to Unity, delivers on the promise of the previous chapter. We take our modified asset, texture it, animate it, and script it. We make it an apocalyptic (almost) weapon that can shoot with audio and visual effects.

Chapter 5, On the Level: Making Modular Scenery, starts by defining what all this "modular" business is about. Then we get into some good stuff, creating sci-fi scenery from scratch and learning to UV-unwrap it (we also define UV-unwrapping!).

Chapter 6, Living It Up: Adding Fun with Animation, delves further into Blender. We learn some basic animation techniques, creating more scenery, animating it, and texturing it.

Chapter 7, Prep Work: Materials, Grids, and Snapping, returns to Unity for further work on our new assets. We improve their materials and also learn about Grid and Snap settings for level layout.

Chapter 8, Laying Out the Level, continues building on the last chapter. We actually lay out our minigame level and then we add a little pizzazz with a Skybox and ambient sound and music.

Chapter 9, Secret Weapon #1: Deploying ProBuilder, examines an under-utilized and relatively recent addition to Unity: ProBuilder. We learn when you might want to use ProBuilder instead of Blender and we get our feet wet by starting to craft one of the final areas of the game.

Chapter 10, Secret Weapon #2: Animating with Timeline, shows us another animation tool in Unity that confusingly has the same name as a Blender tool. We learn when you might want to use one rather than the other and we animate what we created in the previous chapter.

Chapter 11, We Could Be Heroes: Blender Character Modeling, covers our most complex Blender modeling challenge yet: a space marine! We will get lots of practice with previous Blender tools and learn new ones along the way.

Chapter 12, It Was Rigged!: Character Rigging, covers what character rigging is, why it is important, and then—by golly—we go ahead and miraculously rig our character.

Chapter 13, Animation and Movement In-Game, covers all sorts of great stuff: we get our marine moving with sound effects, we follow the marine's movement with a Cinemachine virtual camera, we add lights to the level, and we animate our blast doors and the bridge. This chapter has everything but the kitchen sink!

Chapter 14, Endgame: Adding Spit and Polish, brings everything to a close, and yet it is just the beginning. How paradoxical. We teach the marine to both shoot and die. We teach the turret how to explode in spectacular fashion. The missile too! We create a main menu and learn to build our game. Then we add some post-processing visual effects and a final area to conclude the game. Mission accomplished!

To get the most out of this book

As I mentioned earlier, there are very few requirements for this book. You do not need *any* Blender knowledge, and you need about 20-minutes-worth of Unity knowledge that you can glean from any number of readily available free sources, or—heck!—you could even crack open the Unity manual and teach yourself!

Software/hardware covered in the book	Operating system requirements
Unity Editor	Windows, macOS, or Linux
Blender	Windows, macOS, or Linux

If you are using the digital version of this book, we advise you to type the code yourself or access the code from the book's GitHub repository (a link is available in the next section). Doing so will help you avoid any potential errors related to the copying and pasting of code.

Download the example code files

You can download the example code files for this book from GitHub at `https://github.com/PacktPublishing/Mind-Melding-Unity-and-Blender-for-3D-Game-Development`. If there's an update to the code, it will be updated in the GitHub repository.

We also have other code bundles from our rich catalog of books and videos available at `https://github.com/PacktPublishing/`. Check them out!

Code in Action

The Code in Action videos for this book can be viewed at `https://bit.ly/30yLR5Q`.

Download the color images

We also provide a PDF file that has color images of the screenshots and diagrams used in this book. You can download it here: `https://static.packt-cdn.com/downloads/9781801071550_ColorImages.pdf`.

Conventions used

There are a number of text conventions used throughout this book.

`Code in text`: Indicates code words in text, database table names, folder names, filenames, file extensions, pathnames, dummy URLs, user input, and Twitter handles. Here is an example: "Mount the downloaded `WebStorm-10*.dmg` disk image file as another disk in your system."

A block of code is set as follows:

```
void Update() {
    // todo cast a ray forward
    // if it hits something, do the following...
    return;  // not very exciting, I know
}
```

When we wish to draw your attention to a particular part of a code block, the relevant lines or items are set in bold:

```
void InitSpaceport() {
  InitPerimeterDefenses();
  OrderHyperlunchForStaff();
  RunGarbageDisposalDiagnostics();  // it's been acting up
  RelocateTeleporterPad();
}
```

Bold: Indicates a new term, an important word, or words that you see onscreen. For instance, words in menus or dialog boxes appear in **bold**. Here is an example: "Select **Vaporize Intruders** from the **Defensive Countermeasures** panel."

Tips or Important Notes

Appear like this. One good tip is to read all the tips. You might learn something new.

Get in touch

Feedback from our readers is always welcome.

General feedback: If you have questions about any aspect of this book, email us at customercare@packtpub.com and mention the book title in the subject of your message.

Errata: Although we have taken every care to ensure the accuracy of our content, mistakes do happen. If you have found a mistake in this book, we would be grateful if you would report this to us. Please visit www.packtpub.com/support/errata and fill in the form.

Piracy: If you come across any illegal copies of our works in any form on the internet, we would be grateful if you would provide us with the location address or website name. Please contact us at copyright@packt.com with a link to the material.

If you are interested in becoming an author: If there is a topic that you have expertise in and you are interested in either writing or contributing to a book, please visit authors.packtpub.com.

Share Your Thoughts

Once you've read *Mind-Melding Unity and Bender for 3D Game Development*, we'd love to hear your thoughts! Scan the QR code below to go straight to the Amazon review page for this book and share your feedback.

https://packt.link/r/1-801-07155-1

Your review is important to us and the tech community and will help us make sure we're delivering excellent quality content.

Section 1: There and Back Again – An Asset Roundtrip with Unity and Blender

In a very speedy excursion, we export an asset from Unity, import it into Blender, perform a simple modification, and then import it back into Unity.

This section comprises the following chapters:

- *Chapter 1, Melding Unity and Blender*
- *Chapter 2, Gathering Our Resources*
- *Chapter 3, Entering the Blender Zone for the First Time*
- *Chapter 4, Asset Assimilation: Returning to Unity*

1
Melding Unity and Blender

"The journey of 1,000 parsecs begins with a single thruster burn."
– The AutoSage of Rigel VI

Hello, Earthling! How would you like unlimited cosmic power? That is essentially what you get when you use the ultra-versatile **Unity** game engine in combination with the awesome assets you can create with the **Blender** graphics toolkit. "Wait a minute," you say with worry, "that much power sounds expensive." Well, worry not! All that power can be had for the low, low price of... *nothing*!

(Full disclosure: if you start making more than $100,000 a year with Unity, you need to start paying a licensing fee. You should be so unlucky!)

This book starts you on the path to that unlimited power. Once begun, it is a never-ending journey bounded only by your effort and imagination. Unity and Blender go together like some of the most famous human combinations:

- Peanut butter and jelly
- Pen and paper
- Thelma and Louise

On our journey, we will learn how to create, alter, texture, animate, and script 3D objects in Unity and Blender and exchange them between the two programs in our pursuit of making breath-taking, mind-altering, fun-inducing, superlative-worthy video games.

This chapter lays the groundwork for what lies ahead. We will cover the following:

- What is Unity and why choose it?
- What is Blender and why choose it?
- What software, hardware, and knowledge should you have to make this journey?

What is Unity?

Unity is a paradox. It is a **video game engine** that is not a video game engine, or rather, it is so much more than that.

Firstly, what's a video game engine? Aww, come on. Are you really reading this book and asking that? Okay, you are forgiven. Maybe you are recovering from a mind-wipe. A video game engine is a software tool that helps you to create a video game. One example of an incredibly famous video game engine would be... Unity!

Unity was first released in 2005. It was available only on Mac and could only publish games for Mac. That very quickly changed and now, over a decade later, Unity is a mature and capable (though not yet sentient) piece of software. Unity is available for use on Windows, macOS, and Linux. As of this writing, Unity can create 3D *and* 2D games for more than 25 different platforms! These platforms include Windows, macOS, and Linux as well as WebGL, PlayStation, Xbox, Nintendo Switch, various virtual reality and augmented reality platforms, and more!

Here is an example of a made-in-Unity, first-person-shooter:

Fig. 1.1 – Escape from Tarkov. Developer: Battlestate Games

And here is an example of a retro 2D arcade game:

Fig. 1.2 – Cup Head. Developer: Studio MDHR

When I say Unity can "create games," I don't actually mean it can *only* "create games." That's just the tip of the planetoid. Unity is currently used to create many different kinds of experiences in areas and industries besides video games, including the fields of virtual/augmented/extended reality (VR/AR/XR), simulation, real-time cinema, film pre-visualization, and automotive design and marketing. Oh yeah, let's not leave out construction, architecture, art installations, engineering, and research data visualization. Got all that? For those of you sitting in the back, there may be a pop quiz later.

Now, it's true that there are other powerful game engines out there, such as **Unreal**, **Godot**, and so on. So why should Unity be your go-to game engine of choice?

Top 12 Reasons for Using Unity

These are the top reasons for using Unity as your game engine of choice:

1. *Versatility*: If you can dream it, you can build it, all the way up to AAA titles. Unity has an amazing toolset that allows you to create 2D and 3D games ranging from the very simple to the very complex. It can be your go-to choice whether you are re-making Pong or creating the next best MMORPG.

2. *Ease of Learning*: To be clear, Unity development can get very complex. But to get started with Unity and produce something surprisingly fun and advanced can take as little as 15 minutes. And Unity caters to different learning styles, with visual scripting available for those who prefer that to code editing.

3. *Portability*: With little to no modification, you can get your latest masterpiece running on a number of the many platforms Unity supports, including desktop, web, mobile, and XR!

4. *Community*: You are not alone. Unity has a development community of over 1.5 million people. You read that right, 1.5 million humans. Of course, that is insignificant on a galactic scale, but from your limited perspective, it is quite impressive. This means that if you run into a problem or need advice, the answers are out there in cyberspace. The Unity developer community is very friendly and encouraging as well.

5. *Learning support*: Unity has excellent documentation as well as an extensive, dedicated, free learning site: `https://learn.unity.com`. This is not to mention the hundreds of high-quality tutorial videos on YouTube as well as the many excellent how-to books available (such as this one!).

6. *Customizability*: Every developer and every project is different. The Unity editor is tremendously configurable and even programmable. You can create in-editor custom tools to make working on your specific game much easier. And if you need a certain special visual quality for your game? Even the rendering pipeline Unity uses for graphics is programmable and customizable.

7. *Price*: **Free!** Did I mention that already? You only need to start paying a fee if your games start making gobs of money. Gobs.

8. *Reach*: You have certainly played a Unity-made game before whether you knew it or not. As of the writing of this book, Unity games have reached over 500 million gamers and the Unity engine is responsible for creating 34% of free mobile games on the market. Unity games reach every game market there is.

9. *Assets*: 3D models, 2D art, visual effects, sound effects, GUIs, tools, templates, and much more. Back in the bad old days of game development, there were some powerful game engines and development technologies available (anyone remember Microsoft's XNA?) but, as an indie developer or hobbyist, there was nothing to put *into* your game unless you created it yourself or paid (or mind-controlled) a talented artist. It cannot be overstated how valuable the Unity Asset Store is, whether for assets to use in prototyping or in your final release. And some very high-quality assets are available for free. In fact, on our journey, we will use multiple free assets in addition to the ones we create.

10. *Development Support Tools*: Unity includes tools for integration with different code editors/IDEs, version control systems, asset creation tools (such as Photoshop), and it supports collaborative team development as well.

11. *Monetization-Friendliness*: Unity *wants* you to profit from your efforts! Built-in packages such as **Unity Ads** and **In-App Purchases** make it easy to build revenue opportunities into your game. And the Unity **Analytics** tools allow you to discover and make use of insights about how players play your game. Even minor game changes can greatly boost the success of your game.

12. *Maturity*: Unity has been around long enough that most of its sharp edges have been smoothed. Over and over, every day the engine proves itself to be stable, effective, and reliable.

With Unity explained away, let's take a look at the other focus of this book…

What Is Blender?

Well, firstly, Blender is *not* a kitchen appliance. If you try to make a game with Unity and *that* kind of blender, the results could be interesting, but it sounds rather dangerous and messy.

Blender is described as a "computer graphics software toolset." It was first and foremost designed to create sophisticated 3D graphics when it was released in 2002 but now is capable of producing spectacular 2D creations as well.

Blender is free and (unlike Unity) open source. It is used every day for creating assets and animations for computer games and visualizations. In addition, it can create animated films, visual effects, and artwork, models for 3D printing, simulations of fluid, smoke, and soft bodies, and it also does video editing and compositing. Did I mention it's *free*? As in, costing no money.

So, what's the catch?

It's a *beast*.

When you first experience Blender, especially if you have had no previous experience with 3D creation software, you may get dizzy and get a nosebleed and want to pilot your ship into the heart of a quasar. But fear not! That will pass!

As intimidating as Blender may seem at first, it *can* be mastered. The secret is to tackle it a little bit at a time, learning bits of related functionality, and to understand and believe that there *is* a method to Blender's glorious madness. As an open source project it has grown in different directions with its community and it has its own particular way of doing things. At some point, you will just "get it."

If you are brave and determined and attentive, you will achieve great success. You get out of it what you put into it (in that sense, it *is* like the kitchen appliance!).

Here is some Blender "wow":

Fig. 1.3 – A Party Tug at 6:00 A.M., by Ian Hubert

As with Unity, there are many powerful, competing **Digital Content Creation** (DCC) programs available, two of the biggest being **3DS Max** and **Maya**. So why would we use Blender over one of those?

Top 8 and a Half Reasons for Using Blender

Although this list isn't as long as the one for Unity, many of the reasons to use Blender are the same and they are no less important.

The top reasons to use Blender are:

1. *Free and open source*: Other industry-standard 3D applications (such as 3DS Max, Houdini, and Maya) cost thousands of dollars. Blender gives you AAA graphics capabilities for nothing. The fact that Blender is open source might not seem like an immediate benefit to non-programmers, but it actually has tremendous benefits. See *Extensibility*, below.

2. *Versatility*: This book will focus on using Blender for modeling, texturing, and animation, but Blender is a treasure trove of functionality. Unlike other proprietary modeling programs, Blender is more of a "one-stop shop", with capabilities that include powerful 2D graphics creation and animation, motion tracking, and video compositing, among others.

3. *Community*: Blender has a huge user base, with some estimates putting it at around three million Earthlings. Like the Unity community, it is very friendly and helpful, providing support and inspiration.

4. *Learning Support*: In addition to the official Blender documentation, there are hundreds of excellent YouTube videos to help you learn, not to mention highly valuable resources available in book form (ahem!).

5. *Fast Workflow*: Once you get comfortable with Blender's preferred mouse-and-keyboard work process, you will see your productivity soar. It is arguably faster than the more menu-oriented workflows of other programs.

6. *Customizability*: Blender is nothing if not highly customizable. You can change just about everything in the UI and input system to your heart's content. Beyond that, the application is programmable via the popular Python language.

7. *Lightweight and Multi-Platform*: Blender easily runs on Mac, Windows, and Linux. In addition, compared to other top 3D applications, Blender is tiny. It can easily fit on a thumb drive you take with you and run anywhere.

8. *Extensibility*: Blender has a huge number of existing plugins, ranging from the very general to the super-specific (for example, there's one just for creating rocks). Because Blender is open source, it's not limited by the size of an in-house development team. This means that developers from all over the world are constantly working on new features and creating plugins.

9. *Built-in Monkey*: Unlike other programs that augment their standard palette of 3D primitives (cube, sphere, and so on) with a teapot, Blender comes with its own 3D mascot, Suzanne the monkey.

Show me the monkey!

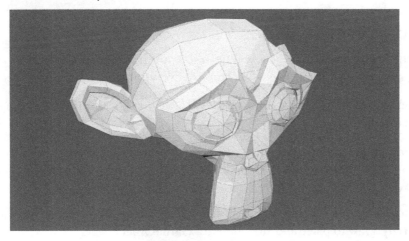

Fig. 1.4 – Suzanne. Another future overlord?

We have now identified our two primary tools for achieving cosmic power. But what do you need to use them?

Requirements for this Book

We are boldly going where a lucky few have gone before.

In this book, we will get comfortable using Unity and Blender hand in hand, specifically learning how to create new assets in Blender—and modify existing ones—and then incorporate them into a simple sci-fi Unity mini-game project. We will learn how to create materials and do animation in both Unity and Blender, and we will learn best practices for when to use each tool.

By the end of this book, we will have covered an incredible amount of ground (or space?). You will have created, animated, and scripted some science-fiction themed props, scenery, and characters that you can reuse in your future games.

The following sections outline the bare minimum in terms of knowledge, hardware, and software that you will need in order to have a pleasant and productive experience with this book.

Modeling versus Sculpting

Blender has two primary 3D creation methods: polygonal modeling and sculpting. Polygonal modeling focuses on creation by assembling polygons such as quads and triangles, whereas sculpting treats your creation more as if you were shaping something out of clay. The two creation methods have different workflows and tools. This book will focus on polygonal modeling in Blender.

Knowledge Prerequisites

I'll say this: the braver you are, the less you need to know heading into this book. If you follow along closely, you will be able to accomplish everything we set out to do.

That said, there are just a few basic things that will keep your head from exploding and your blood from boiling:

- You should have a rough familiarity with 3D concepts such as x, y, and z coordinates and transformations within that space: translating, rotating, and scaling. It helps if you have heard of vectors, but no knowledge of 3D math is assumed.
- You should have a basic knowledge of using the Unity editor's **Scene View** and **Hierarchy View** to place and manipulate a **GameObject**.

- You should understand how to examine and manipulate the properties of a **GameObject** in the **Inspector** window. You should also understand how to add a **Component** to your **GameObject** in this window.

- You are able to create a new C# script, add it to a **GameObject**, and edit it in the code editor of your choice. In this book, we will use Visual Studio. A basic understanding of C# will be helpful to complete the projects, but the code that is included is clearly explained. The majority of this book is not very code-heavy; it is only toward the end of this book, when we start to bring together all the assets we have created, that we will make the most use of scripting.

- You should know the basics of using an image-editing program such as Photoshop. This knowledge will only be necessary for sections on texturing assets.

If it has not been made clear, you do *not* need to have any prior experience with Blender.

Software Prerequisites

At a bare minimum, you will need copies of both Unity and Blender installed, updated to the current version of each. As of this writing, the latest version of Unity is version 2020.3.21 and the latest version of Blender is version 3.0.0..

Both programs are cross-platform and available for macOS, Windows, and Linux.

The latest version of Unity can be found at `https://unity3d.com/get-unity/download`.

It is *strongly* recommended that you install the **Unity Hub** software, which helps you manage your projects, your editor installations, and also provides access to key learning materials.

The latest version of Blender can be found at `https://www.blender.org/download/`.

In addition to Unity and Blender, you should have access to an image-editing program. **Photoshop** is the industry standard but comes with a price tag. A free alternative is **GIMP**, which can be downloaded here: `https://www.gimp.org/downloads/`.

Blender itself has some image-editing capability. Although we will not delve into it, you may want to explore that if you don't use other alternatives.

Hardware Prerequisites

Software needs a place to run, doesn't it? So how do we decide between a desktop computer versus a laptop versus a tablet?

Well, the tablet question is easy to answer. Blender will not run on a tablet. So a desktop or laptop it is then. The particular hardware requirements for Unity and Blender can be found at these locations:

- Unity: `https://unity3d.com/get-unity/download`
- Blender: `https://www.blender.org/download/requirements/`

In general, you should do fine with a system that is younger than 5 years old and has DX10 (shader model 4.0) capabilities with a full HD display.

Using a 3-Button Mouse

Yes, you can technically use Blender and Unity without a 3-button mouse. But that is like saying that technically you can survive in outer space without a spacesuit. Those 10-15 seconds you would survive would be pretty painful. In other words, use a 3-button mouse. Your sanity will thank you.

How to Read This Book

Now, I understand that many of you are going to be naughty and flit about between chapters like an over-caffeinated hummingbird.

Personally, I believe you will get the best learning experience from this book by reading it in chapter order and—although I make efforts to have chapters be as self-contained as possible—I specifically try to have later tasks and concepts build on earlier ones. That said, it is still quite possible to jump around the chapters willy-nilly, like the aforementioned hummingbird. Your eventual punishment for doing so will not be too severe.

Getting Additional Help

One book, even one as awesome and mighty as this one, cannot cover everything, especially when it deals with two complex programs.

Thus, I encourage you to use this book as a launchpad and when you invariably encounter new situations where you need additional help, to make full use of the ample free resources available at your (virtual) fingertips.

The official Unity Support page is at `https://unity.com/support-services` and the extensive community forums are at `https://forum.unity.com`.

The official Blender support page is at `https://www.blender.org/support/`.

There are many other unofficial high-quality support sites if you do a little Google searching.

As mentioned, **YouTube.com** has a vast array of tutorial and showreel videos.

Packt Publishing also has an extensive line of books for Unity and Blender that delve into many specific topics in much more detail than we can go into here. A complete list can be found by searching at `https://www.packtpub.com/`.

Summary

Let's review. In this chapter:

We've identified key capabilities of both Unity and Blender and looked at why you should choose these programs over their competitors.

Also, I've flagged that you do not need any prior experience with Blender, but it will help greatly if you have a modest familiarity with Unity.

Besides that essential up-front knowledge, we've looked at what software you will need installed and what hardware will get the job done with the least amount of pain.

We've foreshadowed the mini-game level we will develop in this book, which will give you the skills and confidence necessary to go on and create bigger and bolder things in your other projects.

Coming up next, we will gather the necessary resources for our journey, becoming familiar with the Unity Asset Store and setting up the project where all the action will take place.

Ready to become a master of time and space? I hear your engines firing up and I have received your request to launch. Permission granted.

3... 2... 1... lift off!

2
Gathering Our Resources

"Proper preparation prevents poor performance."
– An Anonymous Alliteration Advocate

Hello again! I am glad to see we didn't lose you as we exited the stratosphere. You look a little blue though. In your species, that means you're either nauseous or molting.

Before we enter deep space, we are going to stock up on some things we will need for our journey. Although we will make several of our own 3D creations, in order to make our final mini-game level extra-awesome, we require not only some additional 3D models, but some sound effects and music, some 2D artwork for textures and our **user interface** (**UI**), along with some visual effects.

Where will we acquire these things? From the trusty Unity Asset Store, of course, where many amazing assets can be found for absolutely free. If you want additional supplies such as bean dip and extra towels, you must supply those yourself.

As we pause to stock up, we will cover some interesting topics in this chapter:

- How to create and set up the Unity project for this book
- Defining our mini-game story and features
- How to use the Asset Store to find and download assets
- How to use the Package Manager to install and import assets
- How to install the FBX Exporter package
- How to export a Game Object for use in Blender

Ready for all that? Let's go!

Technical Requirements

To follow along with this chapter you will need a copy of Unity installed, which you can get from this link: `https://unity3d.com/get-unity/download`.

The supporting files for this chapter can be found here: `https://github.com/PacktPublishing/Mind-Melding-Unity-and-Blender-for-3D-Game-Development/tree/main/Chapter02`

Creating Our Unity Project

I'm assuming this is not the first time you have created a Unity project, so this will be a super-quick refresher. (If it is your first time, kudos for your bravery. Go slow and see *Chapter 1*, *Melding Unity and Blender*, for all the places you can turn to if you get stuck or confused.)

To begin, launch the **Unity Hub**.

You did install the Hub, didn't you? It just makes life so much easier. If you don't have it installed, stop resisting my mind control and go get the Hub from here: `https://unity3d.com/get-unity/download`.

The Unity Hub

With the Hub installed and launched you should see something that looks like this:

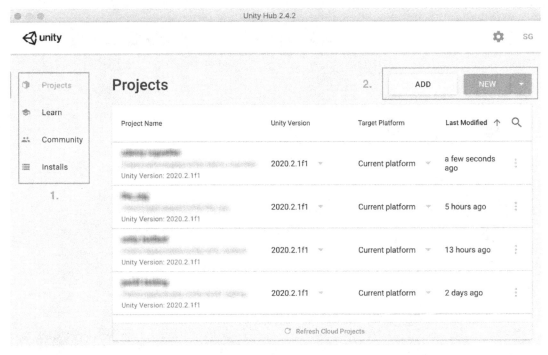

Fig. 2.1 – The Unity Hub

In previous projects you may have zoomed past the Hub window, but I just wanted to draw attention to all of the functionality that is packed into this launcher app. If you look at the area labeled *1.* in the preceding screenshot, you can see the following four choices you can choose from:

- **Projects**: By far, this is what you will most often choose when you launch the Hub. If you look in area *2.*, you'll see that you can **Add** an existing project or choose to create a **New** one.

- **Learn**: These are quick links to Unity-provided projects and tutorials. They are excellent quality and can provide you with polished assets to use, as well as showing you professional ways to structure your projects and code.

- **Community**: Again, these are quick links to the Unity Blog, Forums, and so on.

- **Installs**: Here, you can see all the different versions of the Unity editor you have installed, and you can find and install new versions, as well as remove old versions.

Let's go ahead and create a new project. Click **New** in area *2.*

Selecting a Project Template

You should now see the options for creating a new project. Go ahead and choose the **3D** project option.

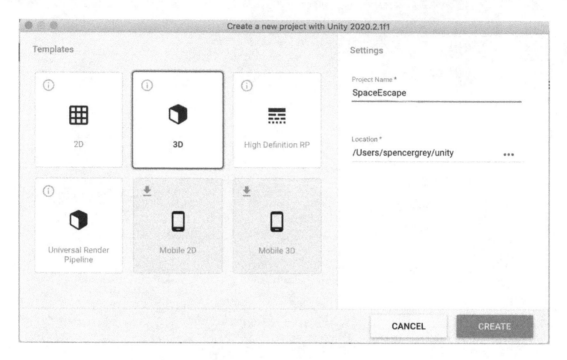

Fig. 2.2 – Project Template options

Next, give your project a name, such as **SpaceEscape**. Use any name you like, but really SpaceEscape is great, highly descriptive, and a sign of having an advanced intellect. If you want to choose an inferior name, go right ahead.

You may be wondering what some of the other project templates are. More information can be found in the following tip, as well here: `https://docs.unity3d.com/Manual/ProjectTemplates.html`.

> **URP and HDRP Pipelines**
>
> The **Universal Rendering Pipeline** (**URP**, formerly known as the **Lightweight Render Pipeline**, or **LWRP**) and the **High Definition Rendering Pipeline** (**HDRP**) ship with Unity. They are each an example of a **Scriptable Render Pipeline**, which is a means of having very fine control over the frame-rendering process via C#. URP provides great scalable performance across Unity platforms, while HDRP provides very high-end graphics and needs appropriate hardware to back it up. Unity's default pipeline is currently known as the **Built-In Render Pipeline** and is good, but more limited than the scriptable ones. Eventually URP will become the default. In this book we will use the built-in pipeline as we want to skip the additional complexity of working with URP. You can learn more about working with URP at `https://learn.unity.com/tutorial/introduction-to-urp`. Information about HDRP can be found at `https://learn.unity.com/tutorial/introduction-to-hdrp-2019`.

Once you have selected the 3D template, click on **Create** and wait for the Unity editor to launch.

Your new project

We have arrived at docking station Unity! A major milestone! Presumably, you've been here before. In fact, you may have altered the application so much as to make it unrecognizable. My opening editor screen looks like this:

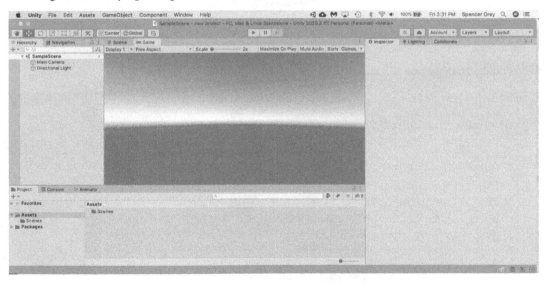

Fig. 2.3 – My initial screen layout

If yours looks different, let's be sure we are all starting out from the same place. In the upper right of the screen click **Layout** and choose **Default**.

The default layout is not necessarily the best one—it really depends on the task you are trying to do—but it is a good general-purpose layout and gives us a common reference point. Depending on your personal preference and your comfort level with working in the editor, you can experiment with the other layouts or even create your own specialized layout.

Creating the project folders

Let's do something very simple, but very necessary: creating folders to organize our mini-game. We won't be using most of these until later in the book, but forewarned is four-armed, er, forearmed, I mean.

Right-click within your **Project** window and create the following folders:

- Animation
- Audio (also create three subfolders: SFX, Soundtrack, and UI)
- Materials
- Models (also create a Textures subfolder)
- Prefabs
- Scripts (also create an Editor subfolder)
- Sprites
- UI

Go ahead and do that now. I will wait.

Spencer waits awhile

Okay, be honest. You didn't do it, did you? If not, the following tip is for you…

> **Tip: Don't be lazy!**
>
> Develop good organizational habits early! You may say, "I'll come back and clean things up later." **Wrong!** "Later" never happens and as your project grows, it will become a mess and your head will explode! "Just do it," as the sneaker people say. Your future self will thank you.

There are many different ways to structure your project. You will encounter other ways as you are exposed to other people's projects. The way we do it here is, of course, superior, but you will only realize that by seeing inferior ways of organization.

The more important thing is to be consistent. That way, when you revisit a project in the future or if, hopefully, you share the project with someone else, the structure is predictable, and you won't have to rely on the search bar for everything.

One additional tip is to decide whether to view your project assets as icons or textual labels. If you look at the **Project** detail pane, by default, Unity displays your files as medium-size icons:

Fig. 2.4 – The Project assets view

In the lower right is a slider. If you drag the slider to the right, the icons will become bigger, but time and space as we know it will end because no one needs icons that big.

If you drag the slider to the left, the icons will shrink until they eventually become much more reasonable text labels:

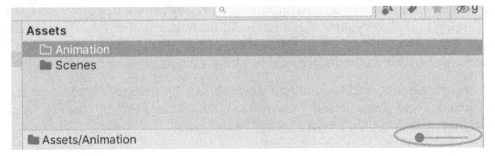

Fig. 2.5 – A superior view of your project, showing text labels!

I prefer the compact label view. But it's your planet (for the time being), so you decide. Now, let's pause and think about the Big Picture.

Defining Our Mini-Game Level

If we don't know where we are ultimately heading, we are liable to navigate right into a black hole or worse. Let's add some definition to what we want our mini-game level to be like by the end of the book.

First, we'll come up with a backstory. Although not strictly necessary, this will add flavor to the vision in our minds. It will influence the choices we make about the assets we acquire and the ones we create, as well as influence the choices we make about the game mechanics and layout. Plus, of course, the fact that this backstory has the ring of truth to it...

> *(Darken theater. Cue music.)*
>
> *Not very long ago, in a nearby galaxy...*
>
> *An ancient splinter colony of technologically advanced humans came across the sinister plans of a shape-shifting alien race to infiltrate a small blue planet orbiting a yellow sun. The benevolent humans took it upon themselves to warn their brethren and they captured the aliens' invasion plans.*
>
> *After a fierce battle, a lone space marine found himself (herself?) with the last remaining chance to get the plans off the planet. To do so, the brave marine would have to overcome the automated defenses of the aliens' starport facility. The odds were slim, but space marines eat slim odds for breakfast. Along with donuts.*

Sound good? I'll leave it to you to decide who will star in the movie.

Mini-Game Gameplay Mechanics

We are going for simple here, since the thrust of the book is about assets, not coding, but we still have a huge number of options open to us, especially considering how easy Unity makes developing different genres of games. One of the most popular is the **first-person shooter** (**FPS**) style, but we are *not* going to choose that. Why? Because we will be creating our own hero character model and we want to get a good look at them.

Similar to some old-school RPGs, our mini-game will be a 3D over-the-shoulder game where you move your character with the arrow keys. Interactions such as opening doors and activating the telescoping bridge asset will be automatic.

Again, just to drive the point home, we are going for simple. Clearly, we are targeting a desktop/laptop with this control scheme, but everything we are learning about assets and animation in this book is completely generic and could equally be applied to touch games on mobile devices or controller-driven console games. Packt offers several books on mobile development. To find them, you can go to `https://www.packtpub.com/` and search for **Unity mobile**.

Ready to start bringing everything to life? Let's gear up.

Using the Asset Store

Okay, so far in our project we have some empty folders. Very exciting. Let's start filling them up at one of any Unity developer's favorite websites: the Unity Asset Store!

What is the Asset Store?

The Asset Store is an indie dev's dream: it is a digital marketplace offering quality content of every type imaginable, but it is also a bargain bin filled with hidden treasures available at little to no cost. How do you get to this place of wonders? Well, one way is from the Unity editor. In the top menu bar, choose **Window > Asset Store**.

Doing this will pop open a new window. But what's this? Where *is* the Asset Store?

Fig. 2.6 – The Asset Store moved! Where'd it go?

Fear not! The Asset Store *used* to be accessible from within the Unity editor but is now only usable via a browser. This is because of Unity's effort to improve editor performance. It's no big deal.

Notice there is a checkbox that will have your browser open automatically if you choose the menu option. Tick the box and click the **Search online** button. Your browser should launch. If for some reason it does not, or if you simply want to navigate directly to the store in the future, surf over to `https://assetstore.unity.com/`.

The landing page for the Asset Store changes almost every day, but you should see something similar to this:

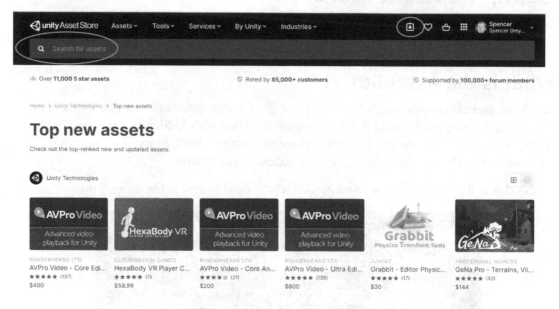

Fig. 2.7 – Asset Store homepage

The important things of note are the search bar in the upper left of the window, used for searching of course, and the down-arrow-in-a-box in the upper right, used for accessing the assets you own in your **My Assets** collection.

Searching the Asset Store

When you perform a search, you will get a page that has three main areas:

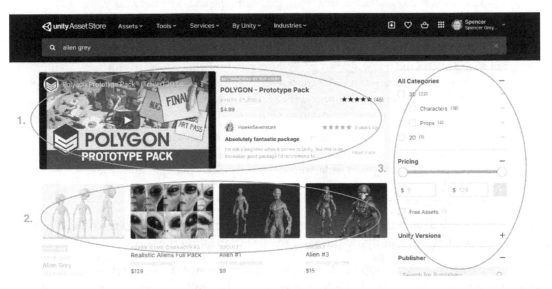

Fig. 2.8 – Results after performing a search

Area *1* (not to be confused with Area 51 in Nevada!) is an Asset Store promotion. Area *2* shows the search results based on the search term you typed in the bar, and the settings you have set for the search filters are in Area *3*.

The filters provide many useful ways to refine your search, ranging from the very basic asset categories, to the price range, editor version, publisher, ratings, platform availability, and release date.

If you are looking for any of the many free assets Unity releases for its tutorials, search for **Unity Technologies** under the **Publisher** filter.

> **A Cornucopia of Content**
>
> It's easy to assume that the Asset Store is mostly focused on providing 3D models and 2D artwork for games, but that is just the beginning and does not nearly cover the breadth of what is available. In addition to all manner of 3D characters, props, and scenery, there are texture, animation, and motion capture packs to jazz them up. There are a huge number of jaw-dropping visual effects, vast libraries of sound effects and music, and an astonishing variety of editor tools to enhance your development process in every conceivable way. Lastly, there are many template kits for different game genres (FPS, 2D turn-based strategy, platformer, RTS, and so on) to give you a headstart in your game.
>
> Spend some time searching for your favorite topics and randomly follow links that catch your eye. Explore the home pages of artists whose work you admire. See what else they have. It's a wide, wild asset world. See what's possible. You'll be amazed!

The first asset we will acquire is the one we use to take a quick round-trip from Unity into Blender and back again, modifying the asset to our liking along the way.

In the Asset Store search bar, type in **Robo's turret (free sample)**. The asset we want is a sci-fi blaster turret and it should be first in your search results. You can click that, or if you really enjoy typing, go ahead and point your browser to `https://assetstore. unity.com/packages/3d/environments/sci-fi/robo-s-turret-free- sample-147413`.

You should see the turret asset home page:

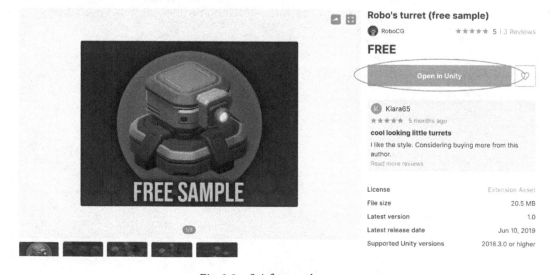

Fig. 2.9 – Sci-fi turret homepage

Initially, the circled blue button will say **Add to My Assets**. Click that and in a moment the button will change to read **Open in Unity**. Go ahead and click that, which will lead us directly into our next topic, using the Package Manager.

Using the Package Manager

Having clicked to open the asset in Unity, you will see a floating window that looks similar to this:

Fig. 2.10 – The Package Manager window

Don't worry if it looks a bit different or if it's docked instead of floating. If it says **Package Manager** on the top tab you are in the right place.

A **package** is a digital container that holds any combination of assets, shaders, textures, plug-ins, icons, and scripts. (So basically, anything Unity can handle.) Unity has a number of 'official' packages that come with the editor. The assets you get in the Asset Store come in their own packages. You can even create your own packages to share. The **Package Manager** helps you deal with all this awesomeness. You can see everything available and what, in particular, has already been installed in your project. It also allows you to install new packages, update existing ones, and remove those you don't need.

If you want to open the Package Manager directly from within the editor, from the top menu, choose **Window > Package Manager**.

If you are going to use the Package Manager a lot (as we will shortly) it might be convenient to dock the window on your screen. Click and drag the **Package Manager** tab and drop it next to your **Game** view (or anywhere you prefer):

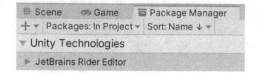

Fig. 2.11 – Give yourself convenient access to the Package Manager

The Package Manager window has some notable areas:

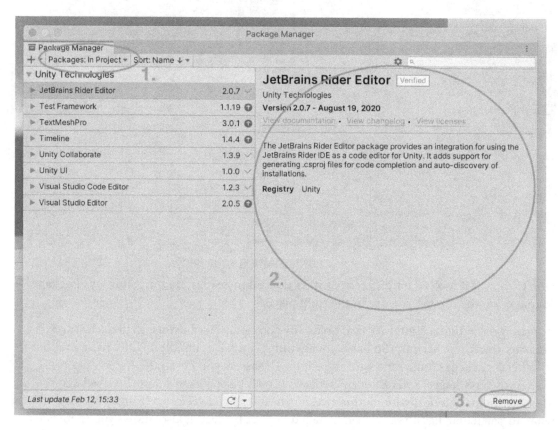

Fig. 2.12 – Important Package Manager areas

Area *1* is a filter for which packages you are viewing. We will come back to this in a moment.

Area *2* is the details pane for the currently selected package. These details include the following:

- The package display name and author
- The version number and release date
- The link to open the package documentation page
- The link to open the package change log
- A brief description and often a link for more information

Area *3* will show a different button depending on the status of the package. It may say **Install**, **Download**, **Update**, **Import**, or **Remove**.

The filter in Area *1* has four options:

Fig. 2.13 – Package filter options

The filters can be used to sort in the following ways:

- **Unity Registry**: Unity keeps a central registry of its 'official' packages that are available for distribution. This shows all of them, regardless of whether you have them installed.
- **In Project**: A list of packages installed in the current open project.
- **My Assets**: This is a list of all the fantastic stuff you own, whether it is installed in the project or not. This list may get large and not display all at one time, so you will want to make use of the search bar in the upper-right to narrow down the list.
- **Built-in**: Displays only built-in Unity packages, which represent some of the core Unity features.

Package Manager list loading lag

When it opens, the Package Manager loads a list of packages defined by the current filter. Sometimes for unknown reasons, or possibly due to solar flare activity, this can take a long time. The list area will display **Fetching Packages** and at the bottom, you will see an animated icon with the label **Refreshing Packages**. If it seems like this is taking much too long, save your project and restart the editor. That should solve the problem.

So, where were we? Ah, yes. You had been to the Asset Store and had chosen to open the sci-fi turret in Unity. That should have opened the **Package Manager** window and the button in the lower right should now read **Download**.

Click **Download** and when the download completes, the button will change to read **Import**. When you click that, you will get a pop-up window asking you which files from the package you want to import. By default, everything will be selected and that is what we want. Go ahead and click **Import**, and soon the turret model and its supporting files will appear in your project in their own folder.

In the **Robo's Turret** folder, open up the **Scenes** subfolder and double-click **Demo Scene**. Voila! You should know enough about Unity scenes to know how to zoom in a little and examine our first prize…

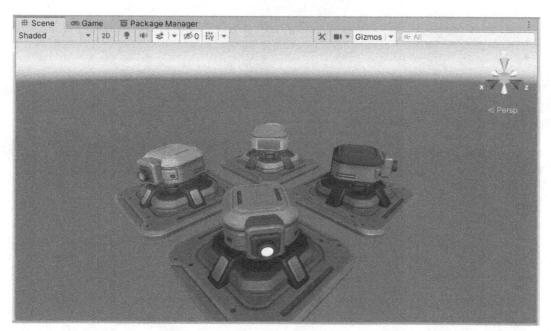

Fig. 2.14 – Blaster turrets – the perfect defense?

These beauties certainly look like they are up to the task of shooting a space marine full of energy bolts, yes? Yes.

(Note: It is okay if you make little 'Pew! Pew! Pew!' shooting noises.)

Select a turret in the Hierarchy and double-click to examine it closely.

The turret is almost perfect.

Almost, except that it should really be able to fire missiles too.

You see that panel on the top that practically screams "I am so cool that I pop up and fire a missile"?

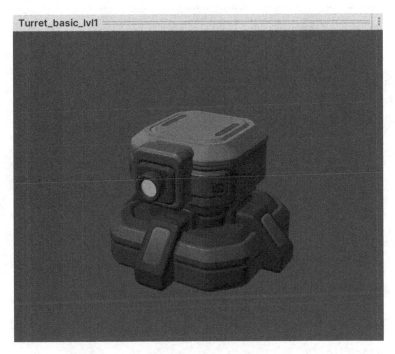

Fig. 2.15 – Oh, handsome turret, you have let me down

Well, it doesn't. The turret model is only composed of two meshes: the base and the top. This means that we can have the top rotate and shoot, but it falls short in the pop-open-and-expel-projectile category.

"Cursed fate!" you shout to the heavens as you gnash your teeth and rend your garments. "I just want one stupid little missile launcher and life would be perfect!"

Well, if this were any other book, that would be the end of the story. But no! We are learning to bend assets to our will. All we have to do is get our turret into Blender to work our techno-magic.

Getting ready for Blender

Okay, we're getting to the moment we have been building toward: getting an existing asset from Unity into Blender. So how do we do that? With Unity's **FBX Exporter** package of course!

File formats

If you don't already know, **.fbx** is one of the most common types of 3D file formats, along with **.obj**, **.3ds**, **.dae**, and others. This format can store a lot of information besides 3D geometry and materials. Among other things, it can store animation information too.

So, let's get that puppy installed.

Installing the FBX Exporter package

Open the **Package Manager** window (or tab), select **Unity Registry** in the filter box, and type **fbx** in the search bar.

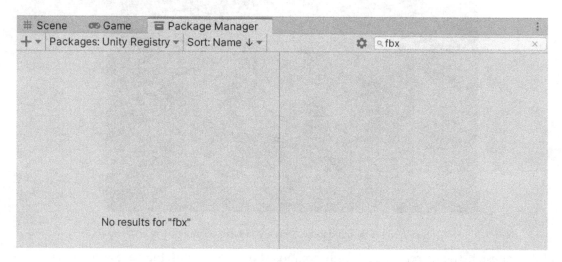

Fig. 2.16 – Fail!

If you see the package, great, skip ahead to installing it. If you don't see the package, don't panic. It could be you are using a version of Unity where it is still a **Preview Package**. These are packages that are highly functional but don't quite yet have a release level of polish and testing. Some of them are very experimental. Others, like the FBX Exporter, are reliable but have been in preview a long time.

To see Preview Packages we need to enable them in the **Project Settings**. In the editor's top menu, go to **Edit > Project Settings > Package Manager**. Tick the box that says **Enable Preview Packages**.

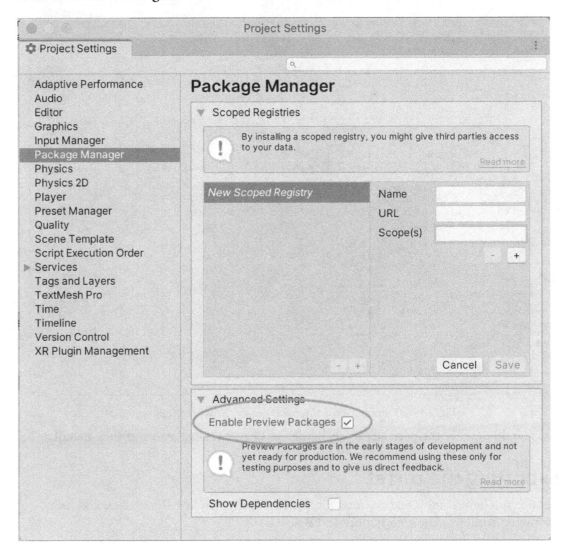

Fig. 2.17 – Unlocking Unity's hidden secrets

That's it. After that, close the window. Back in the **Package Manager** window, try searching for **fbx** again:

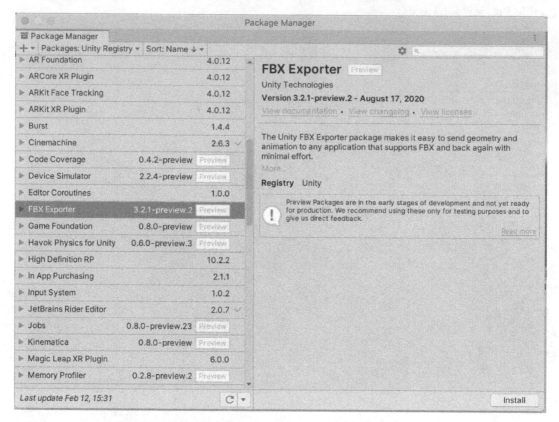

Fig. 2.18 – There's that missing package info. Now we're talking!

You should now see the package, boldly labeled as **Preview**. Go ahead and click **Install**.

Exporting the turret

Be sure you have a *single* turret selected in the **Hierarchy** window. Right-click, and from the popup window choose to **Export To FBX**.

You will next see a popup window named **Export Options**:

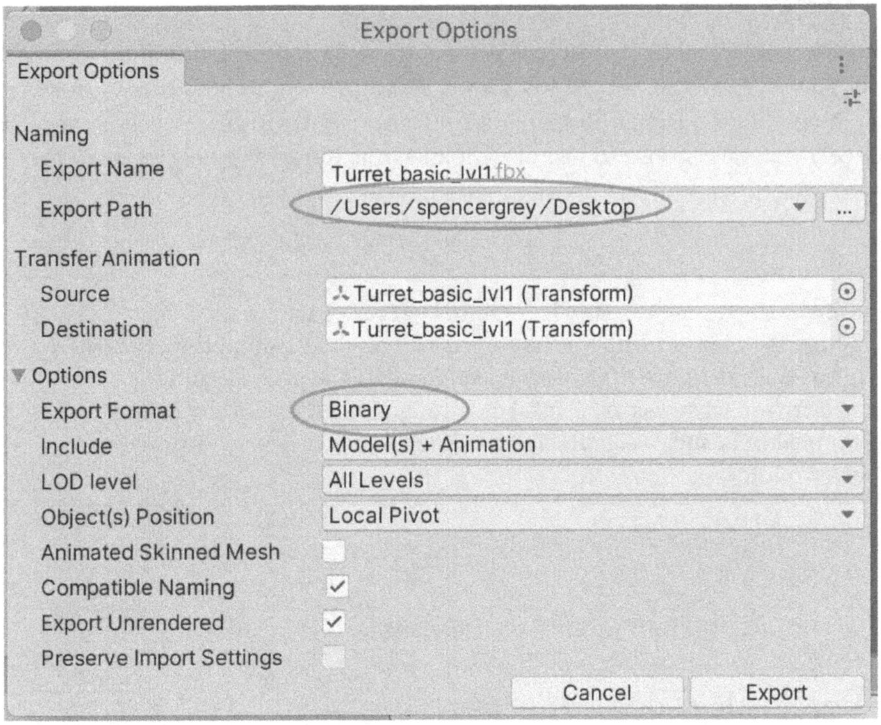

Fig. 2.19 – FBX Export settings

There are two settings you need to change. Most importantly, change the **Export Format** to **Binary** so Blender can read it. Secondly, change the **Export Path** to someplace you will remember outside of your Unity project. If you feel like it, you can change the name of the exported file. Leave everything else as is and click **Export**.

Bye-bye. The next time you see the turret will be in Blender!

Before that though, since you are now an Asset Store expert, we have a shopping list of things that will enhance our mini-game…

Additional Assets to Download

Let's get more F-R-E-E, free stuff! In the lists that follow, I have made some recommendations based on my taste. Let your own tastes and imagination decide what you use, but the assets we will use in this book will all come from the primary recommended choices.

Search for the names in bold in the following list or type in the given URL to find each package in the **Asset Store**.

I realize there is a *lot* listed here—there is just so much to choose from. It's like being in a candy store! You do *not* need everything downloaded immediately to continue following along in the next chapter. Depending on your internet bandwidth/speed (and your level of impatience!) you can choose to just download assets libraries when we need them. It's entirely up to you.

> **Tip: Third-party package folders**
>
> For the most part, it's safest to leave third-party packages in the folder structure they import with. This is because if you drag around the assets there may be issues in future if you ever need to update the package and the folder names are not what was expected. For packages that are basically collections of simple assets, such as audio files, it's generally safe to move those assets to your own folders.

Audio Assets

I have broken audio down into several subcategories:

SFX – General Foley Sound Effects

- **Sci-Fi SFX Package**: A wide selection of good effects including servos, footsteps, doors, and UI elements. `https://assetstore.unity.com/packages/audio/sound-fx/sci-fi-sfx-package-184029`.

- **Ash Valley Cybernetics Lite**: Another good selection. `https://assetstore.unity.com/packages/audio/sound-fx/ash-valley-cybernetics-lite-108327`.

Weapons

- **Futuristic Gun Soundfx**: Bang bang! Err, more like zap zap! `https://assetstore.unity.com/packages/audio/sound-fx/weapons/futuristic-gun-soundfx-100851`.

Music

- **Sci-fi Music Pack 1**: I like the tension some of these tracks evoke. `https://assetstore.unity.com/packages/audio/music/sci-fi-music-pack-1-105576`.

Ambient Sound

- **Sci-fi Ambience**: Very atmospheric and lonely. `https://assetstore.unity.com/packages/audio/ambient/sci-fi/sci-fi-ambience-112553`.

UI Sound Effects

- **GUI Audio Package**: All the blips, bloops, and beeps we will need. `https://assetstore.unity.com/packages/audio/sound-fx/gui-audio-package-164401`.
- **Sci-Fi UI Sound FX**: Okay, just a few more blips, bloops, and beeps. `https://assetstore.unity.com/packages/audio/sound-fx/scifi-ui-sound-fx-27282`.

Textures

- **Sci-fi Texture Pack 2**: The name says it all. `https://assetstore.unity.com/packages/2d/textures-materials/sci-fi-texture-pack-2-42026`.
- **EU Sci-fi Textures Set Volume 1**: Very gritty, quality textures. `https://assetstore.unity.com/packages/2d/textures-materials/eu-sci-fi-textures-set-volume-1-135089`.

Okay, whew! That's it for now. Are you sick of the Asset Store yet? I hope not. We'll be back for a few more useful things later on. I suggest you spend some time exploring your new acquisitions. Many of them have their own demo scenes, or, for assets such as sound effects, you can play them right from the **Inspector** window. I'm sure your investigations will spark your imagination and get you thinking about all the possibilities that lie ahead.

Summary

So that's it. *Chapter 2* is a wrap. We learned about the Unity Hub, we got the structure of our project set up, and we defined a backstory and gameplay for our mini-game. We downloaded a ton of cool free stuff by using the Asset Store in conjunction with the Package Manager. Lastly, we learned how to get assets out of Unity by installing and using the FBX Exporter.

Not bad, considering the limits of human concentration.

We are now well equipped. Prepare yourself for what lies ahead on our wondrous journey. We are about to enter the Blender zone, where you will start to master creating and altering objects in 3D space!

3
Entering the Blender Zone for the First Time

"Don't Panic!" — A very famous book on hitchhiking the galaxy

Brace yourself. We are heading through what might be a rough patch of time-space distortion. Learning Blender, especially without any previous experience with 3D modeling, can seem overwhelming, but trust me, go slow, grasp the fundamentals, and you'll get there.

In this chapter, we will introduce some of the Blender fundamentals, gain some practice with them, and then tackle modifying the sci-fi turret we downloaded in the last chapter.

Specifically, we will boldly cover:

- Exploring the default Blender interface
- Manipulating objects in Object Mode
- Manipulating vertices, edges, and faces in Edit Mode
- Altering the sci-fi turret geometry
- Exporting the turret for a triumphant return to Unity

By the end of this chapter, you will have taken some important steps towards 3D omnipotence, you will have learned some of the most basic and critical Blender tools, and you will be two-thirds complete in the Unity-Blender roundtrip tour we are taking the turret asset on.

I am aware humans are fragile. Please do not burst with excitement.

Technical Requirements

For this chapter we will focus exclusively on Blender, so that is all you need to have installed. Again, using the latest version is recommended. As of this writing, the latest version is 3.0.0. You can download it here: `https://www.blender.org/download/`.

The supporting files for this chapter can be found here: `https://github.com/PacktPublishing/Mind-Melding-Unity-and-Blender-for-3D-Game-Development/tree/main/Chapter03`

The code in action video for this chapter can be found here: `https://bit.ly/3CteLBM`.

Introducing Blender

The great Chinese general Sun Tzu once said, "Know thy enemy." If you just replace "enemy" with "amazing 3D program that will open up new worlds for you," you will get what we are aiming for here. It's time to expand your horizons and capabilities, and the best way to begin is to start, so here we go without further ado.

Go ahead and launch Blender. You should see the following screen:

Fig. 3.1 – Oops, not Blender. Definitely ignore. Especially since you don't read
the Standard Galactic Alphabet

Ahem. Correction, if you launch the *proper* Blender application you will get a splash
screen very similar to this one:

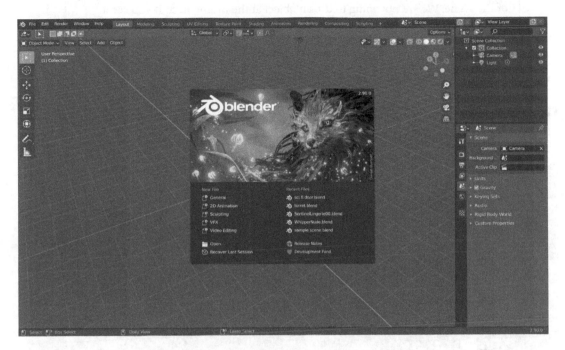

Fig. 3.2 – The actual Blender splash screen

The splash screen allows you convenient access to recent files and older files, as well as
allowing you to create a new file pre-configured for various different types of workflows.
Additionally, you can browse the Blender release notes or donate money if you're into
that sort of thing, and lastly, you can recover your work from your last Blender session
if something, for some reason, went horribly, horribly wrong.

If you don't want any of that splash screen goodness, press *Esc* or just click pretty much
anywhere that looks like it's not clickable. You can keep the screen from displaying on
startup by unchecking the checkbox under **Edit | Preferences | Interface | Splash Screen**.

Once the pop-up window is gone you will be staring at the default **Layout** workspace,
a three-dimensional space in a perspective projection very similar to the **Scene View**
in Unity. You should have a basic familiarity with 3D space from Unity.

> **Clearing the way**
>
> Depending on your Blender version you may see a default cube in the middle
> of the scene. We are not going to use an object at the moment, so if you see a
> cube, left-click it to select. It should get an orange outline. Press **X** to pull up
> a pop-up prompt asking you to confirm deletion. Click **Delete**. All gone.

You should now see something very similar to this:

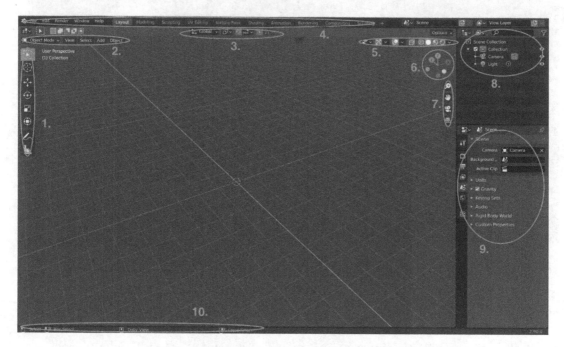

Fig. 3.3 – There are a lot of options in the Layout workspace. Don't panic!

Holy Crab Nebula! This screen has a lot going on. I've grouped the options into ten (!)
areas. What I want to do is take a quick look at each area, so you get some idea of what's
out there. Just get the lay of the land. Do not worry about memorizing anything just yet.
Relax. We are skimming. Let whatever information that sticks with you stick, and for now,
don't worry about the rest.

The area numbers in the titles below refer to the numbered areas in *Fig 3.3*.

The Toolbar (Area 1)

The Toolbar on the left-side provides quick onscreen access to some of the most-used
functionality in whatever mode you are in. We start off in Object Mode, so we see Object
Mode tools. Some tools will reveal further options if you click and hold on them:

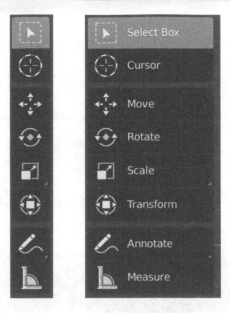

Fig. 3.4 – The Toolbar—icon view and expanded icon plus text view

You can change the display of the toolbar by moving your mouse to its right edge until it becomes a bar with arrows facing left and right. If you click and drag to the right, the toolbar will first change to a dual column of icons and then it will switch to a verbose icon-and-text view.

From top to bottom the tools are:

- **The Selection tool**: This is how we pick things to work on in 3D space. There are several different ways to select things and we will look at them later.

- **The 3D cursor**: Much like a text cursor can show you where you are about to perform an edit, the 3D Cursor shows you where you will perform an operation such as object creation, and so on.

- **The Move tool**: The Move tool translates an object on the x, y, z axes.

- **The Rotate tool**: This tool spins an object on the x, y, z axes.

- **The Scale tool**: This tool enlarges or shrinks an object on the x, y, z axes.

- **The (Combined) Transform tool**: This wacky tool lets you use all three of the previous tools at once. No one in their right mind would do this, of course, but it does place an interesting-looking gizmo around your object.

- **The Annotation tool**: Sometimes it is useful to write notes to yourself, especially before a mindwipe. This tool lets you scribble reminders directly in the 3D scene.

- **The Measurement tool**: When you are modeling real-world objects that need precise measurements you can draw onscreen rulers to help you.

We will get practice using some of these tools further along in this chapter.

As mentioned, the Toolbar changes depending on what mode you are in. So that leads us into…

Editor, mode selection, and mode menus (Area 2)

Above the Toolbar you will see this area:

Fig. 3.5 – Editor and Mode selection area

In the upper left, the **Editor Type** dropdown allows you to choose which editor you are working with (the icon for this looks like a grid with a sphere on it, however, hover your mouse for a tooltip if you are not sure which icon it is). Blender has many different types of editors depending on what you're working on. Besides the 3D editor view, these include an animation timeline, a UV editor, and many more.

We will leave the editor as **3D Viewport**. The viewport has two modes we are interested in: **Object Mode** and **Edit Mode**. Object Mode allows you to perform operations (such as rotation) on an entire object such as a cube, a monkey head, or an Orion-class Starstriker. Edit Mode allows you to manipulate all the bits that go into making the object: the vertices, edges, and faces. You will learn more about this in the *Entering Edit Mode section*.

Next to Object Mode there are four choices: **View**, **Select**, **Add**, and **Object**. These are the drop-down menus associated with Object Mode. If you were in Edit Mode, these menu choices would be different.

Pivot, Snap, and Proportional Editing (Area 3)

Moving to the middle top of the screen, we see:

Fig. 3.6 – Pivot, Snap, and Proportional Editing. Yes, I know you are saying "Whaaaa?"

We won't spend time here now. Pivot options give you different choices for what/where to rotate and move around. Snap gives you fine control by letting you transform objects by set increments instead of free movement. Proportional Editing is a cool but advanced tool we won't cover.

Header menu bar (Area 4)

Across the top of the screen, you should see:

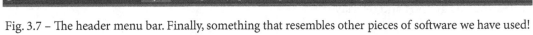

Fig. 3.7 – The header menu bar. Finally, something that resembles other pieces of software we have used!

You should have a fairly good idea of what you can expect from the five dropdown menus. Only the key features are mentioned in the following list:

- **File**: You will often use this option to save, load, create, import, and export files.
- **Edit**: Edit offers **Undo** and **Redo** among other functionality and it gives us access to the very important **Preferences** section.
- **Render**: Render gives access to Blender's awesome rendering power, although we will not be using this because Unity will render our creations.
- **Window**: This dropdown gives some self-explanatory choices, including taking a screenshot, toggling the status bar visibility, and navigating your workspaces.
- **Help**: Here you will find links to the Blender manual, tutorials, and other useful resources.

The remaining choices on the right are the names of the default Blender **workspaces**. A workspace is a collection of windows/panels that is pre-configured with tools and views that are most relevant to particular types of Blender workflows. For example, the tools you most often use when making a 2D animation are very different than those you most use when making a 3D sculpture.

We will begin by using the **Layout** and **Modeling** workspaces and use others later. When you are advanced, you can create your own workspaces to suit your particular needs.

> **Customizing Workspaces**
>
> Blender's user interface is *highly* customizable, which means you can modify the workspaces to suit your every devious purpose. The controls take a little getting used to but wind up making sense. To learn tons more about the Blender interface start here: https://www.blender.org/features/interface/.

View modes and tools (Area 5)

Moving across the top of the screen to the right we have these options:

Fig. 3.8 – View modes and tools

Without going into detail now, these choices allow you to filter what is displayed, how it is displayed (for example, shaded, wireframe, and so on), and whether to show helper features such as gizmos and overlays.

Axes Gizmo (Area 6)

Speaking of gizmos, below those view tools you have this multi-colored marvel:

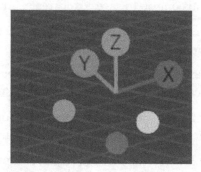

Fig. 3.9 – The x, y, z axes orientation gizmo thingamabob

This shows the current orientation of your scene camera. Clicking a colored dot changes the orientation to that axis. Clicking and dragging within the axes area *but not on a dot* will rotate the view freely.

Ex, Why, and Zee Axes

First of all, *axes* is the plural of *axis* and does not refer to medieval weapons. There are three axes in the 3D world: x, y, and z. Some humans insist that the name of the third 3D axis be pronounced "zed." This is clearly wrong and must be stopped. There is actually incontrovertible proof of why "zee" is the proper pronunciation. It lies in the industry-wide mnemonic device that helps you remember the color-coding for the axes: "ex," "why," "zee" rhymes with "arr," "gee," "bee" (RGB, or red, green, blue). "Ex," "why," "zed" is an exquisite failure as a rhyme. Case closed. *Mic drop.*

Zoopancamper! (Area 7)

Huh? Sounds like someone sneezed. Gesundheit! What are these four icons below the Axes Gizmo?

Fig. 3.10 – This icon group is a bit strange. Why the heck are these here?

There may be an official name for this grouping and there may be an official reason these tools are presented together, but I think the official name and reason are forever lost in time.

Using my superior intellect, I call the group *Zoopancamper*, which cleverly combines bits of the names of the four tools: **Zoom**, **Pan**, **Camera View**, and **Perspective View**. Their reason for being actually becomes clear the more you use Blender. There are times when you want to manipulate your view entirely with your mouse and no keyboard input.

The magnifying glass icon is a way to control zooming without the mouse-wheel. Simply click on the magnifying glass and drag up or down to zoom in and out.

In a related manner, the hand allows you to pan your view. Click the hand and drag to do that.

The camera icon is a toggle. If you have a virtual camera in your scene (and you do, by default), clicking the icon will switch to and from what the camera is viewing. We will not be using this tool.

The grid icon is also a toggle. It is an alternative to the 5 key on your Numpad and it switches your scene view back and forth between perspective and orthographic views.

> **Perspective and Orthographic Views**
>
> You are likely familiar with the idea of perspective and orthogonal projection from Unity. Perspective is the idea that parallel lines converge with increased distance. Imagine you are standing on a long set of straight train tracks. The tracks below your feet are parallel. If you look far off, the train tracks seem to come together. Yet if you walked all the way to where you were looking, you would find the tracks are still parallel, but looking back where you came from, those tracks now seem to converge! It's one of many optical illusions that fool human senses. Humans are easy to fool. Trust me on this one.

The Outliner Panel (Area 8)

Okay, we've almost gotten through the ten areas of the Blender Layout workspace. In the upper right of the workspace is the Outliner Panel, which is similar in concept to Unity's **Hierarchy View**:

Fig. 3.11 – The Outliner Panel. I have nothing clever to say about this

The Outliner Panel gives you an overview of all the objects that exist in your scene. It allows you to organize your objects into convenient groups called **Collections** and it gives you fine control over what is visible and manipulatable/editable within your scene. In one sense, you can think of a Collection like an empty Game Object in the Unity **Hierarchy View** that is just used for organization.

The Properties Panel (Area 9)

Below the Outliner Panel is the Properties Panel. *Everything* in Blender (objects, scenes, tools, and so on) has properties you can adjust. This panel is the main place you can do that. Each tab down the left side is a different group of related properties, for example, *Fig 3.12* shows the **Scene** properties. Among other things, if you were creating a simulation, you might want to toggle gravity on or off in the scene.

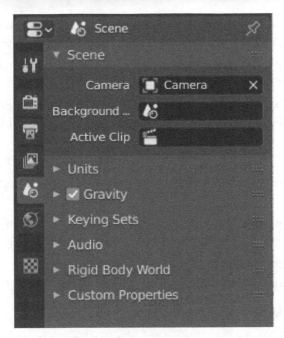

Fig. 3.12 – The Properties Panel. These are not even close to all the tabs available

You select a group of related properties by choosing a tab on the left. The tabs can change depending upon the workspace context. Here is a quick rundown of the default tabs:

- **Active Tool**: Change properties of the tool you have selected from the toolbar.

- **Render Properties**: Change properties related to 3D rendering, including which rendering engine to use. We will only use Blender rendering for quick checks of our 3D models.

- **Output Properties**: Here you can change things related to dimension, color, frame rate, and so on. We will leave most of these settings alone.

- **View Layer Properties**: View layers allow you to break up complex renders into different parts to speed up production. We will not use this.

- **Scene Properties**: These properties allow you to specify things such as default unit scales and physics defaults.

- **World Properties**: The world defines the environment that the scene is in. The surface shader sets the background and environment lighting. Volume shaders affect the entire scene with volumetric effects, such as mist.

- **Object Properties**: This tab gives you easy access to many aspects of a selected object. Some properties, such as the Transformations (Rotation, Location, and so on) are redundant ways to change things besides onscreen and hot-key tools.

- **Modifier Properties**: Object **modifiers** allow amazing non-destructive transformations to objects. We will make good use of these in the future!

- **Particle Properties**: Blender can do extremely sophisticated particle simulations, but we will not be using these capabilities in this book.

- **Physics Properties**: Blender can also do very sophisticated physics simulations. We will likewise not be covering these in this book, but check out online demo videos. Truly amazing.

- **Object Constraint Properties**: Constraints allow you to define limits to how objects behave relative to each other. A simple example would be two rectangles acting as a hinge joint.

- **Object Data Properties**: These properties allow access to many fine details of an object, including UV Maps and Normals. We will revisit this tab often.

- **Material Properties & Texture Properties**: The last two tabs let us set details about the visual surface appearance of our objects. We will come back to these often too.

That's it for the Properties Panel. Lastly, we have to briefly mention…

The Status Bar (Area 10)

By default, at the bottom of your screen you will see:

Fig. 3.13 – The Status Bar. Highly useful for things like checking your status

The Status Bar displays contextual information such as keyboard and mouse shortcuts, result or warning messages, and statistical information. 'Nuff said. I think you get it.

Wow! That's it! We made it through the ten areas of the Layout workspace, the default screen! Can you even remember the first one?

Okay, enough overviewing. Let's play with stuff!

Monkeying Around with the Monkey Head

Poor Suzanne, she is going to be our assistant as we explore some of the Blender tools we have learned about. But really, a monkey is so much more interesting than playing with a cube. So, let's get started.

Create a new Suzanne by pressing *Shift + A* to open the **Add** pop-up window and choosing **Mesh | Monkey**. You can also accomplish this by going to the onscreen **Add** menu at the upper left and choosing **Mesh | Monkey** from the drop-down menu.

It's possible you've shifted the viewport. If you're not looking at Suzanne's face, change to the **Front** view by pressing the period (.) on the Numpad or from the **View** menu choose **Viewport | Front**:

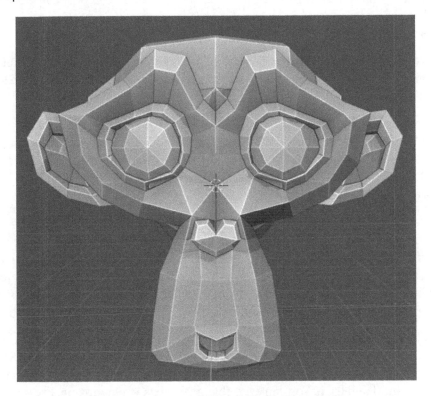

Fig. 3.14 – Front view. There's that gorgeous girl

Now, in rapid succession, try to get used to rotating, panning, and zooming your *view* (we are not yet *altering* the model/mesh). Remember, it's the middle mouse button to rotate (also called "tumble"), shift + the middle mouse button to pan, and the mouse-wheel to zoom. You can also zoom and pan using the "zoopancamper" tools. Go ahead and play around a bit until you are comfortable with these controls.

Redundancy thy name is Blender and Blender is thy name

In Blender, you will often find that it seems like there are 17 different ways to accomplish the same thing. While this might seem confusing at first, it's actually a good thing. Ultimately the most productive and fastest way to use Blender is with a two-handed combination of mouse controls and keyboard shortcuts. But there are *so* many keyboard shortcuts that, until you master a bunch of them, you can access many of the most common functions with onscreen tools or drop-down/pop-up menus.

Translation: Moving the Monkey

As mentioned, we have been changing the view of the camera, *not* altering the properties of the model itself. But now let's learn how to change the model. You probably know from Unity the three basic transformations: translating (that is, moving), rotating, and scaling. Blender lets us do the same.

Make sure you have Suzanne selected. She should have an orange outline. If not, left-click anywhere on her head to select her. (To deselect you can left-click anywhere in the scene that's not an object.)

Now then, to move objects you *could* use the translation tool icon on the Tool Bar but you want to become a Blender pro, right? The pros use hot-keys to work at blinding speed. So, what hot-key would you choose for movement? Perhaps, *T* for translate? Nope. That toggles the Toolbar. Maybe *M* for move? Wrong. That moves things into Outliner Collections (see *Area 8*, in the preceding section). Give up? Blender has made the somewhat less memorable choice of *G*, which you can think of as "G is for grab."

With Suzanne selected, press *G* and move your mouse. You will see Suzanne move around the screen. If you like where you've moved her, left-click to commit your transform and release the object from the mouse. If you change your mind, right-click and the object position will revert, undoing your change. Many Blender commands work in this same "left-click commit, right-click revert" manner.

There is a secret awesome trick that you should learn right away. If you only press *G* you will move Suzanne about freely, but there is a way to get greater precision. After pressing *G*, if you immediately press *X*, *Y*, or *Z* you will restrict the model's movement along the axis you chose. Go ahead and try it. You can even change the axis while moving. Press *G*, then *X*. Suzanne will be constrained to move along the X axis. Then, while you are moving, press *Y*. The movement constraint will change and Suzanne will only move along the Y axis.

Excluding an Axis

If you are feeling especially tricky you can learn how to do transforms on two axes at a time by *excluding* a single axis. The key (so to speak) is the *Shift* key. Pressing *Shift* and *X*, *Y*, or *Z* will exclude that axis. So, for example, if you wanted to disallow movement on the X axis, you could press *G* then *Shift + X* and translation would *only* happen on the Y and Z planes.

Want even more precision? You got it. You can use the number keys to specify how many **Blender Units** to position your object along a given axis. So, for example, to put Suzanne three units up in the air, you can select her head and press *G*, then *Z*, then *3*. This even works with negative numbers. To position her below the origin, select her and then press *G*, then *Z*, then - (the minus key), then *3*. Try it.

Sometimes—especially when you are starting out with Blender—you can "lose" objects in your 3D space. Here are two solutions, depending on whether your object is selected or not. If you happen to lose track of where Suzanne is, you can press . on the Numpad or choose **View | Frame Selected**. It's possible that Suzanne is both out of view *and* not selected. If that's the case, first select her by going to the Outliner window at the upper right and highlighting the line that says **Suzanne**. Then you can choose **Frame Selected**.

Blender Units

The units of measurement in 3D programs are arbitrary, but there are standards, and we are in luck when it comes to agreement between Unity and Blender. A Blender Unit is the amount of space taken up by a single grid square in the default Blender 3D viewport. By default, this is meant to represent one meter. Unity makes the same assumption. You can change the measurement of the default unit in both Blender and Unity, but it is best to have a good idea of what you are doing and a good reason before you do so. Changing the default from one meter can mess up things having to do with the physics systems and can cause you problems with having the scale of different objects being inconsistent.

If you now understand how translation (grabbing/moving) works in Blender, the next two transformations will be a piece of cake.

Rotation: Twirling the Monkey

Rotation in Blender works very similarly to translation and it even has a hot-key that's easier to remember. You guessed it. It's *R*!

The same modifiers apply as well. So, after pressing *R* you can press *X*, *Y*, or *Z* to constrain rotation along those axes. After the axes, you can again enter a number. This number represents the *number of degrees* of rotation around the axis. So, for example, if you wanted to look at Suzanne from the side you could rotate her one quarter turn (90 degrees) around the vertical (Z) axis by typing *R, Z, 90*. Did you do it? See? You're becoming a Blender speed demon!

Scaling: Mushing the Monkey

Scaling holds no surprises. Scaling can adjust the size of your object individually along each axis (you'll often do all three at once). A scaling factor of 1 means that the object is at 100% of its default size (the size it was modeled at). For various reasons, you might want to make it larger or smaller, thinner, thicker, and so on. To change the object scale, press *S* to scale, then press *X*, *Y*, or *Z* to select an axis, and finally choose a number to represent the scaling factor (not a percentage!). For example, if you wanted Suzanne to be eight times as tall, you would type *S, Z, 8*. Then you'd have a mega-monkey.

The Sidebar

As with all things Blender, there are alternate ways to accomplish things. If you would like to simply, directly, and exactly enter translation values, you can do so in the **Sidebar**. Press *N* and the Sidebar will insert itself between the Axes Gizmo and the Outliner window:

Fig. 3.15 – The Sidebar is a direct way to enter exact transformations

You can remember the hot-key for the Sidebar by thinking *N* stands for "*No* idea why this is the Sidebar hot-key." You can also toggle access to the Sidebar by choosing **View > Sidebar**.

One handy feature of the Sidebar that is not available from hot-keys or onscreen icons is the **Dimensions** input fields. These let you precisely control the size of your object along each axis. Specifying dimensions is most useful for primitives or simple objects where the boundaries are clear. You can specify dimensions for more complex objects, but you will be specifying the dimensions of the object's bounding box, which is the smallest possible cube that contains all of the object's geometry.

Applying your transforms

In Object Mode it is important to remember that the transformations you make are *on top of* your object's default/base configuration. You are *not* actually changing the base state. But what if you want to permanently change the base configuration? So, for example, you don't want Suzanne to appear in your scene with a Z-scale factor of 2, you want her to actually be twice as tall by default with a scaling factor of 1 (that is, the normal size at 100%). Or what if you created a cylinder that was supposed to be a pipe and you wanted it to be lying on its side (rotated) by default? In this case, you need to **Apply** your transformations.

Applying your transformations will change the base object and reset all the transforms to their defaults: whatever translation you had assigned will become the new 0, 0, 0 position of your object, the rotations will become the default 0, 0, 0 rotations, and the scaling will become the default 1, 1, 1 scaling. Applying your transformations can become especially important later on when you apply special, powerful Modifiers that might be using the base object configuration. Forgetting to apply your transformations when you actually mean to can be a source of aggravation for beginners.

To apply transformations to your object, go to the Object drop-down menu at the upper left and choose **Apply**. You will have the choice of which transforms to apply or all of them as well as several advanced options we will not cover. The shortcut to apply your transforms is *Control / Command + A*.

Transformations are the essential fundamentals of 3D modeling. You will see in *Entering Edit Mode* that they apply not just to objects but the component parts that make up objects. But there's just one more thing before we get there…

Getting ready to move on

You should really be fairly comfortable with making basic transformations before we move on. Here is a little challenge to test your understanding. Let's create a cube of cubes: we will create eight cubes and position them at the corners of a virtual cube in 3D space:

Fig. 3.16 – This arrangement is what we are going for

Ready? To create a new cube, press *Shift* + *A* and choose **Mesh | Cube**. You can do this eight times or, if you're feeling sassy, you can use *Shift* + *D* to **Duplicate** an existing cube. The x, y, z (zee!) coordinates of the cubes should be as follows:

- Cube 1: 0, 0, 0
- Cube 2: 0, 4, 0
- Cube 3: 0, 4, 4
- Cube 4: 0, 0, 4

- Cube 5: 4 , 0 , 0
- Cube 6: 4 , 4 , 0
- Cube 7: 4 , 0 , 4
- Cube 8: 4 , 4 , 4

Go ahead and use hot-keys or the Sidebar to position the cubes at the right coordinates. If you make mistakes remember to use *Control / Command + Z* to undo and/or *Shift + X* to delete.

It's important that you gain confidence by practicing. If you skip this challenge, your sun will go super-nova (well, eventually anyway). Do the challenge now.

Minutes pass. Muzak plays. The invasion clock counts down.

Could you do it? If so, major congrats! But I know how Blender can make your head spin! If you couldn't quite do it, don't panic! Go back and review, then try again. When you get it, you're ready to move on and learn how to exercise even more control over your object in Edit Mode.

Entering Edit Mode

Now we really get to cause trouble. You may recall from when we were surveying the Layout screen view that at the upper left, we can see we are in Object Mode by default:

Fig. 3.17 – Get ready to leave Object Mode!

Edit Mode will allow us to completely reshape or otherwise contort and polymorph our object. Make sure (poor unsuspecting) Suzanne is selected. Then you can switch modes by choosing the drop-down menu or pressing the *Tab* key to toggle between Object and Edit modes. (Note: You must have an object selected to enter Edit Mode—otherwise nothing happens!)

When you are in Edit Mode, the options to the right change:

Fig. 3.18 – Edit Mode. New button icons and more drop-down menus

The three icon buttons are hugely important and should be grasped before anything else. These buttons, in order, allow you to edit *vertices*, *edges*, and *faces*, the fundamental building blocks of your 3D object:

- A **vertex** is, simply put, a point in 3D space. It has an x, y, and z coordinate. The plural of vertex is the ridiculous word, *vertices*. (Should the human race happen to be subjugated in the near future, the plurals of the words *vertex* and *index* will be declared *vertexes* and *indexes* immediately.) A vertex by itself is not very interesting, which leads us to edges.

- An **edge** is a connection between two vertices (vertexes!). It is defined by the line connecting the x, y, z positions of the two endpoints. While an edge is easier to visualize than a vertex, it is still not as easy to picture as the face.

- A **face** is a filled-in area in 3D space that is bounded by three or more edges. Three surrounding edges means the face is a **triangle**; four edges and it's called a **quad**. There are various other names as we count up the number of edges until we wind up with **n-gon**, which means an arbitrary number of surrounding edges. There are various modeling reasons why you would use one face type over another.

Our focus on low-polygon modeling means we will primarily deal with triangles and quads. It's worth noting that ultimately Unity converts everything to triangles internally, but sometimes it's more convenient to model certain things as quads in Blender. This is okay because it's trivial to convert a quad to triangles by splitting it diagonally (this conversion is done for you automagically in Unity).

What is low-polygon modeling?

It's almost easier to define low-polygon modeling by what it is not: it is *not* high-polygon modeling! While there is no formal technical definition, low-polygon meshes have fewer vertices/edges/faces relative to other 3D meshes according to current industry standards. Low-poly meshes make the trade-off of being very fast to render at the cost of losing detail and fidelity to the thing they are representing. This makes low-poly meshes ideal for real-time applications such as games. Animated films on the other hand, because they are prerendered, can use meshes with huge numbers of polygons and they gain the ability to show minute realistic details. Low-polygon models tend to be chunky in shape and sometimes this modeling style is chosen not just for technical reasons but for its aesthetic value.

Modern hardware is always getting better at rendering. These days a mesh with anywhere from 500 to 10,000 triangles might be considered low-poly. High-poly meshes are limited only by the artist and the processing hardware. Today these models can have hundreds of thousands of triangles if not more.

You have surely seen many low-poly models before. In fact, until just recently mobile devices could only display very low-poly models – if they could display 3D at all!

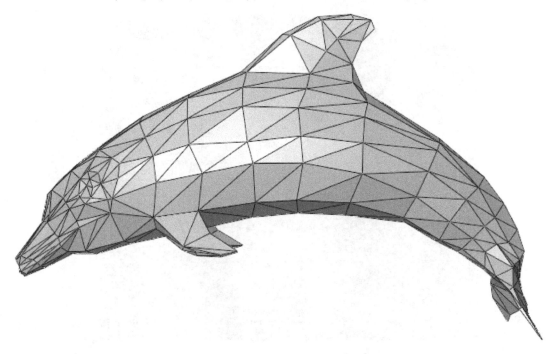

Fig. 3.19 – A low-poly untextured dolphin. "So long and thanks for all the fish!"

The obvious way to switch between vertex, edge, and face selection mode is with the onscreen icons. The pro way is with the hot-keys: *Control + 1, Control + 2,* and *Control + 3.* (Note for Mac users: Be careful! Those combos use the actual *Control* key, not the *Command* key.)

Creating a Monkey-corn

Now we are going to experiment with vertices. Any volunteers? Ah yes, Suzanne! Good!

These are the steps to change her in an interesting way:

1. Create a new Blender file with **File | New | General**.
2. Add Suzanne back in with *Shift +A* then choose **Mesh | Monkey**.
3. Press . on the *Numpad* to zoom in to the Suzanne Front view.

4. Press **Tab** to enter Edit Mode. You should see all of Suzanne's vertices selected by default:

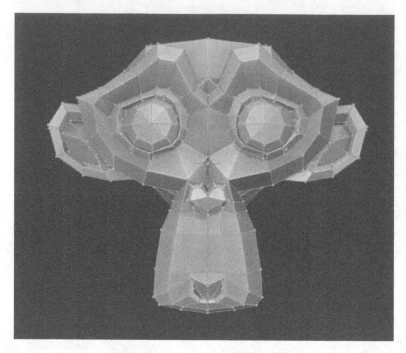

Fig. 3.20 – All of Suzanne's vertices selected. Get the point(s)? (Okay, okay, I'm sorry.)

For our current purpose, we only want one point selected.

5. Press the *A* key twice to deselect everything. You can accomplish the same thing from the drop-down menu by choosing **Select | None**.

6. Now find the single vertex in the middle of her forehead and click it to select it.

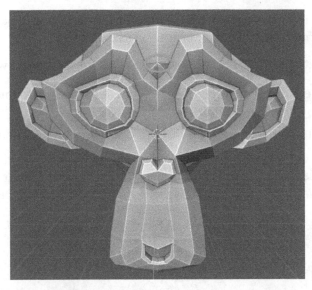

Fig. 3.21 – Select this vertex. (Brace yourself, Suzanne.)

7. Tumble your view a little bit (with the middle mouse button) so you are looking on from a roughly three-quarter view, then press *G* to grab the vertex and pull it straight out. You don't have to be precise here.

8. Left-click to commit your transformation. Congratulations Dr. Moreau, you've created a monkey-corn:

Fig. 3.22 – I can't bear to leave her like this

The important thing to note here is that the same transformations you made to entire objects can be performed on individual vertices, edges, and faces.

Go ahead and **Undo** to get rid of the ugly horn. Let's do something even weirder:

1. Enter **Face Selection** mode by pressing the cube-looking icon to the left of the **View** dropdown or by pressing *Control + 3*.

2. Double-tap *A* to deselect all. (By the way, *Alt + A* is another way to deselect all.)

3. Now click one of the triangles at the center of one of Suzanne's eyes to select it. To add your selection, hold down the *Shift* key. We will learn a faster way to do this, but for now, use *Shift* to select each face in the middle of Suzanne's eyes:

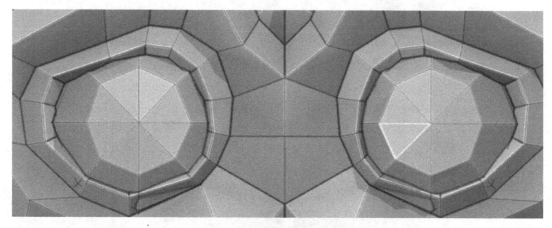

Fig. 3.23 – Selected inner eye triangles. Uh oh. No good can come of this

4. Tumble your view again to get a slight angle.

5. Now we will use our first core modeling command! Press *E* to **extrude** your selected faces. This gives us a cartoon-like effect of a character's eyes popping out of their head. You control the depth of extrusion with your mouse movement. Left-click when you are satisfied.

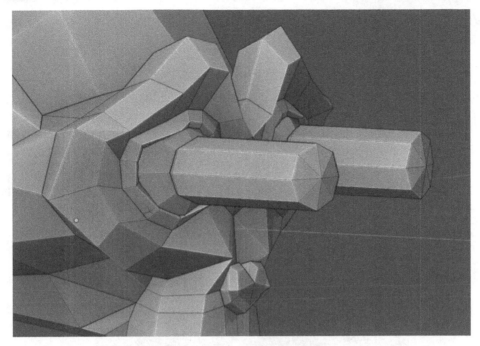

Fig. 3.24 – Extruded faces. Boing!

You may be excited to have gained this level of control over a mesh or you may be horrified at the monstrosities we've created. Regardless, you're now ready to modify the sci-fi turret!

Altering the Turret

Remember that blaster turret that had no way to fire a missile? That's a thing of the past.

Please note: This next section will be intense. I will be throwing a bunch of new commands and ideas at you to get this job done quickly. Do not worry about memorizing everything. Just follow along and get the job done. We are learning what's possible. We will return to Blender in later chapters to explore the tools and options much more in depth.

We'll tackle the turret in phases. First, we'll change the existing geometry so it's easier to work with. Then we'll create our new geometry. Read each step below and be sure you understand it before you do it. It's very easy to wildly mess things up in Blender! Remember, Undo is your friend!

Carving Out a Lid

First, we'll separate a piece of the turret top that will be able to pop up. To do so:

1. Create a new Blender file with **File | New | General**.

2. By default, Blender creates a scene with a camera and a light. We have no need for those. Press *A* to select everything in your scene. (It's okay if you can't see the camera or the light. You can see that they exist in the Outliner window at the upper right of the screen.) Press *X* and confirm you want to delete the objects. The camera and the light should disappear.

3. Now recall the location where you exported the turret asset from Unity. Choose **File | Import | FBX** and locate the exported .fbx file.

4. Leave the other settings alone and click on **Import FBX**. The turret should appear *untextured* in the middle of your view.

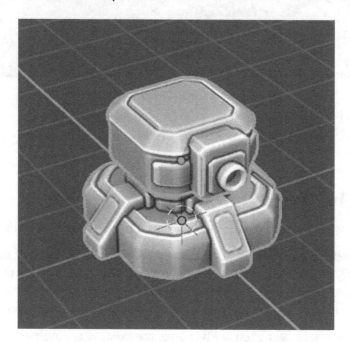

Fig. 3.25 – Your turret made it to Blender!

5. It may be that your turret imported with yet *another* default light and camera. If you see those in the Outliner, highlight each one and delete it with the *X* key. Pesky defaults!

6. Now the turret should be the only object in the Outliner. To the left of its name is a small arrow that you can click to twirl open and see its component parts. Be sure to twirl open the arrows below that to see all the parts. You should see:

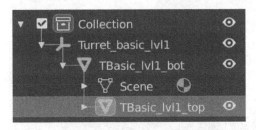

Fig. 3.26 – The parts of the turret

If you look closely, the name of one part of the turret ends in **_bot** and another part ends in **_top**, these are, respectively, the bottom and top parts that can move independently of each other. I prefer more readable names.

7. Double-click the two part names to rename them. I will rename **..._bot** to be **turret_base** and **..._top** to be **turret_top**. If you individually click these new names you should see the appropriate part get an orange highlight in the 3D view.

8. Press *Control / Command + S* to save all your hard work so far. Or choose **File | Save**. Name your file **asdifhuurrelkjnkldfs898dfslksjhdv98ysvvdfassd38t623** or something more pleasing to your human sensibility.

Our goal is to create two new objects. The first of which I will call **turret_lid**. Once in Unity, the lid will be capable of popping up from **turret_top**. We will create the lid from the existing turret geometry. The second object I will call **turret_tube**. As far as geometry goes, this will be a hollow horizontal cylinder attached to the underside of the lid that will act as the missile launch tube. It will also have four thin vertical cylinders I'll call struts that look like they are supporting the lid.

With those goals in mind, let's prepare the patient for the operation...

9. With the **turret_base** selected in the Outliner, press *H* to hide it. Hiding is just a workflow convenience feature allowing you to see only what you want to focus on. Your hidden objects are still there. To prove it, press *Alt-H* to unhide anything hidden. See? No harm done. Go ahead and hide the base again.

Let's switch to a top, isometric view and enter Edit Mode. Do the following:

10. Select Top view with *Numpad 7* or **View | Viewport | Front**.

11. Toggle isometric view with *Numpad 5* or the grid from the Zoopancamper icons.

12. With the object selected, press *Tab* to enter Edit Mode. You should see the following:

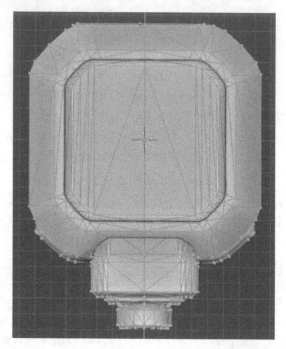

Fig. 3.27 – The turret top with vertices selected.

13. It's okay if all the vertices are not selected. In fact, we don't want them to be, so double-tap *A*.

14. Next, we need to switch into Face Edit Mode in order to select the faces that we want to turn into the lid. Press *Control-3* or click the icon.

    Notice how the center of the turret top has a rounded-square area outlined in blue? We want to select all the faces within this area to turn into the lid. Luckily there is an easy way to do this.

15. With your cursor over one of the faces in the center, press *L* to select all the faces that are linked to this one. (More on linked geometry in upcoming chapters.) The faces within the blue outline should become selected. Be sure you are in Face Edit Mode or nothing will happen!

16. Right-click to pull up the context menu and choose **Separate | Selection**. This creates a new object. In the Outliner, it will get the name **turret_top.001**. Rename this to `turret_lid`.

17. While still in the Outliner, select the old **turret_top** and press *H* to hide it for now. You should be left looking at just the lid. Missile-city here we come!

> **Wonkiness**
>
> Like all Earth software, Blender is not perfect. Sometimes I have experienced trouble with selecting things after I have separated them into new objects. I have found that after separating the object if I return to Object Mode (via *Tab*), reselect the object, and then re-enter Edit Mode I can then select things normally. In case you get into trouble, be aware of this as you follow along.

Okay, phase 1 complete. We've made the mesh easier to work with. Now to customize!

Creating the launch tube

We want to thicken up the lid because it's looking pretty thin. To do so we need to select all the edges around the perimeter of the lid. This is called selecting an **Edge Loop** (more on this later:

1. Press *Control + 2* to enter Edge Edit Mode.

2. Next *Alt + left-click* on a lower edge of the lid to select all the edges around the perimeter. They should highlight in orange like so:

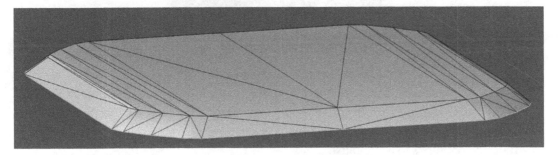

Fig. 3.28 – The perimeter edges selected (if you look closely)

3. Now we will again use the work-horse **Extrude** command. Press *E* and then *Z* to constrain movement to the vertical axis. Move your cursor down to add a little thickness and left-click when you are done:

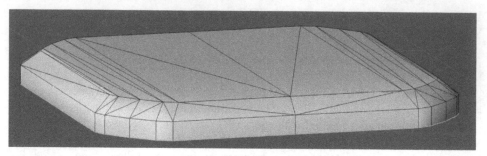

Fig. 3.29 – I made my lid this thick

Be paranoid. Save your work. This is an especially good idea when you are new to Blender and likely—even encouraged—to make mistakes. Resist getting frustrated. We learn a lot from our mistakes. Remember that martial arts masters first teach their students how to fall!

4. Next, tumble your view to look at the bottom or use *Control-Numpad 7*. Our lid is hollow!

5. Ensure the perimeter edges are still selected and press *F*, which will create a new face sharing all the edges.

6. Now to think about the actual launch tube. Press *Shift-A* then click **Cylinder** to add a (huge) cylinder and look closely at the lower left of your screen:

Fig. 3.30 – Where did this popup come from?

This popup is a handy little feature called **Adjust Last Operation**. It is only available *immediately* after performing certain operations and it allows you to make common changes that you might otherwise need to issue multiple commands or open multiple windows to accomplish.

7. If you open it, you will see the adjustments available. I researched some values to transform our cylinder so it becomes a well-placed launch tube below the lid. Enter these values:

- **Radius** = .11
- **Depth** = .9

- **Rotation X** = 90

- **Location Z** = 1.46

The lid and launch tube should now resemble this:

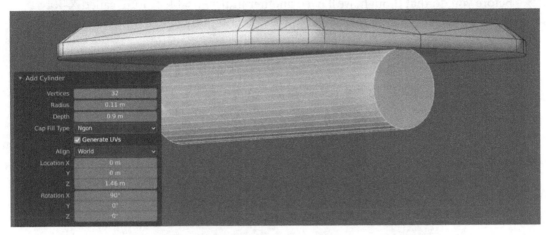

Fig. 3.31 – Adjusting the tube with the Adjust Last Operation popup

8. Once you have a reasonable approximation of the above, be sure you are in Face Edit mode (*Control + 3*) and select the front circular face.

9. You will now use another core command that you will use over and over again: **Inset**. This will create a new face that is nested—inset—on the face you use the command on. We'll use inset to make the launch tube hollow. Press *I* for inset and move your mouse to create a new circular face that is slightly smaller than the parent face. *Left-click* when you have the size you want:

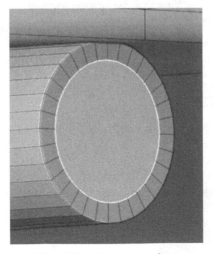

Fig. 3.32 – A new inset face

Next, we will use the Extrude command again to hollow out the tube. We've seen that Extrude can make faces pop out of geometry, but you can also push faces *into* geometry.

Before you do that though, we'll need another indispensable feature called **X-Ray View**, which lets you see through your mesh in a slightly better way than pure wireframe view.

10. To toggle X-Ray View, press *Shift + Z* or click this icon among the view options:

Fig. 3.33 – Toggling X-Ray View

11. Once in X-Ray View, with the circular face still selected, press *E* and move the face back into the tube, almost to the very rear. You can see how far back you are going because of X-Ray View.

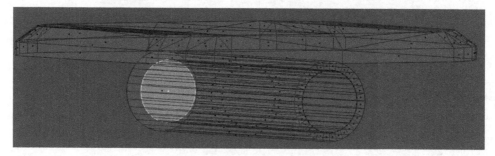

Fig. 3.34 – Use X-Ray View to judge how deep into the tube to extrude

12. When you're happy, left-click to commit and *Shift + Z* to turn off X-Ray View.

Now we have a missile launch tube, but it's just kind of floating there. Let's fix that.

Creating the Struts

The four struts are meant to look like they support the lid. To create them follow these steps:

1. For the first strut, add a cylinder with the *Shift + A* menu. Then open the Adjust Last Operation menu at the lower left and enter these values:

   - **Vertices** = 8
   - **Radius** = .05

- **Depth** = .5
- **Location X** = .4
- **Location Y** = -.3
- **Location Z** = 1.35

This should shrink the strut down to a good size and position it near one corner of the lid.

2. To create the other three struts, switch to Bottom view with *Control- / Command-Numpad 7* or **View | Viewport | Bottom**. The first strut should still be selected. You are going to duplicate this and position it at a different corner of the lid. You'll do this for the last two struts as well. It's okay to just eyeball the positions. Be aware, as soon as we make a duplicate it's going to move along with the mouse. Use the *X* and *Y* keys to restrict axis movement to help position the struts where you want them. Ready?

3. Press *Shift-D* to duplicate. Then place your second strut. Do the same for the third and fourth.

Once you have the four struts created it's time to make a separate object out of the tube and the struts. To do this we'll use the same Link command we used to select the lid in the first place.

4. Hover over the tube and each of the four struts and press *L* to add each linked face to your selection. Finally, right-click for the context menu and choose **Separate | Selection**.

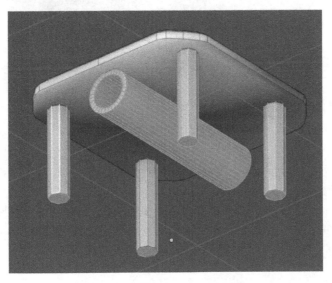

Fig. 3.35 – Use L to select the linked faces and then create a separate object

5.   In the Outliner, rename your new object to **turret_tube**, then save your work!

6.   Go back to Object Mode with *Tab* and unhide all the turret pieces with *Alt-H*.

It looks great! We are very nearly done! But there is one subtle flaw left to be taken care of. Have you spotted it?

Fixing a flaw

In the **turret_top** object, there is some geometry left behind by the lid that obscures the tube structure. If we animated this now it would look as though the tube was coming straight through the surface! What we want to do is push this surface deeper into the turret so that the tube is resting on it, like this:

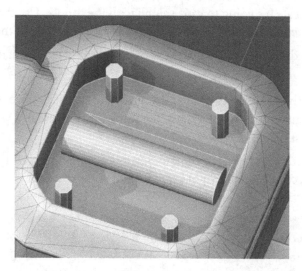

Fig. 3.36 – The surface of turret top after lowering it. (Lid is hidden.)

To do this:

1.   Go into Object Mode. Select **turret_top** and *Shift + H* to hide everything except the top.

2.   Press *Tab* to enter Edit Mode, then press *Numpad 7* to see the Top view. Zoom in a little if you like.

3.   Press *Ctrl + 3* to make sure you are editing faces, then select one of the big fat triangles right in the middle of the surface. We want to grow this selection to include everything within the blue outline.

4. Use the dropdowns to choose **Select | Select Linked | Linked Flat Faces**. The selection is now the right shape, but it is just missing a little around the edges. **Select | Select More/Less | More** to grow the selection a tiny bit. Soooo close now! Repeat the last command and you should now have the surface perfectly selected.

5. Can you guess what to do next? We're going to reverse Extrude this surface *into* the top. Tumble your view to get a good angle then use *E* to make the extrusion to a depth you like.

    Fantastic.

6. Return to Object Mode, unhide everything (*Alt + H*), and save your work. Press *A* to select everything and choose **File | Export | FBX (.fbx).** Leave all the defaults, but give it a name and location you prefer, then click **Export FBX**.

YOU DID IT!!! For a human, you are amazing!

Summary

Somebody break out some trumpets and confetti! We've passed some major milestones in this chapter! You survived examining the default Blender interface without your head exploding, you learned how to transform objects in Object Mode, and you started the long journey of learning how to alter objects in Edit Mode. Armed with that knowledge we went ahead and changed a pre-existing object to our own specifications. (This is a *huge* accomplishment if you don't already know.) Finally, we exported the object for inclusion in our Unity mini-game.

You deserve some fun now! In the next exciting chapter, we return to Unity, lay some groundwork for the mini-game, and bring our turret to life with some motion, visual effects, and sound effects. Woohoo! Pew-pew-pew!

4
Asset Assimilation: Returning to Unity

"The circle is now complete. When I left you I was but the learner. Now, I am the master."— Everybody's favorite dark lord

We made it! Our asset survived the journey to Blender, survived the procedures we performed, and now has the potential for amazing new capabilities. In this chapter, we will achieve the goal we set for ourselves in *Chapter 2, Gathering Our Resources* (getting the turret to fire a missile). Additionally, we will lay some groundwork for our mini-game and start to use some of the awesome free assets we got from the Asset Store.

To add behavior to the turret, we will take our first excursion into C# scripting. Although we will touch upon all the steps involved, you should already understand how to add a new C# script to a Game Object, how to edit it in the code editor of your choice, and how to run your game.

Here is the breakdown of what lies ahead. In this chapter, we will cover the following:

- Import, restructure, and texture the turret
- Animate the turret with a simple tracking and firing script in C#

- Create and shoot a missile (finally!)
- Add some sound effects for turret actions
- Add some visual effects to the turret, including an energy beam and muzzle flash

By the end of this chapter, it will feel like we are starting to make an actual game! Yay, us! And as an added bonus, if you stick all the way through, I will share with you the Ultimate Advanced Unity Tip…

Technical Requirements

We'll spend this whole chapter back in Unity, so Unity is all you need installed. You do have Unity installed, right? OR ARE YOU JUST READING ALONG AND NOT DOING THE WORK? Be honest now. Okay, just checking.

The supporting files for this chapter can be found here: `https://github.com/PacktPublishing/Mind-Melding-Unity-and-Blender-for-3D-Game-Development/tree/main/Chapter04`

The code in action video for this chapter can be found here: `https://bit.ly/3kIs6ju`.

Preparing the Turret for Gameplay

The work we did on the turret in Blender was essential, but that was just the beginning. We can make it better, stronger, faster. Let's get it into Unity, dress it up, and bring it to life.

To get ready for scripting, we will first import the modified turret, alter its hierarchy, and texture it. Then we will grab a useful tweening tool to jazz up the turret motions.

Go ahead and launch Unity and load your SpaceEscape work-in-progress project.

Importing the Turret

Importing the turret is a very simple process. You should have no problem doing the following:

1. From the top menu, select **Assets | Import New Asset** and locate the `.fbx` file you exported from Blender in the last chapter. Your imported turret will appear in your project window. If the model is not already selected, select it and take a look at its properties in the **Inspector** panel. You should see a layout very similar to *Fig 4.1*:

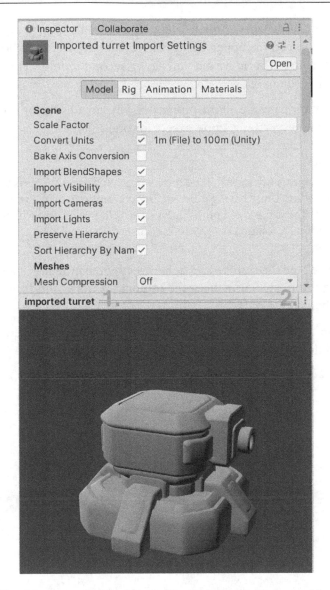

Fig. 4.1 – Inspecting the imported turret. Welcome to the machine

The bottom half of your **Inspector** window is a preview pane of your model. You can click and drag to rotate your model and view it from different angles. Above the pane is a space with the name of your asset, and next to that is a kind of double bar, which is really a handle (labeled *1. In Fig 4.1*). To grow or shrink the preview pane, drag the handle up or down.

Also, conveniently, you can choose to make the pane a floating window if you click the three-dot menu on the upper-right (labeled *2.* in *Fig 4.1*) and choose **Convert to Floating Window**. This is great if you have a second monitor and a number of assets that you want to review in detail.

Above the **Preview** pane are all the properties you can adjust. For now, we are going to leave just about everything alone, except for one small thing.

> **Rotation Issues**
>
> If your turret appears sideways in the Preview pane, don't panic. This is the issue of Blender and Unity having different axes conventions. When you drag your turret into the scene it will probably be right-side-up, but you will notice in the Inspector its X rotation is -89.98. This is okay. See step 5 below.

2. Although we deleted the camera and light object while in Blender, let's get in the habit of being thorough. So, uncheck the **Import Cameras** and **Import Lights** checkboxes then click **Apply**.

   Depending on the size of your monitor and the size of your **Preview** pane, you may need to scroll through the properties list to see the **Apply** button.

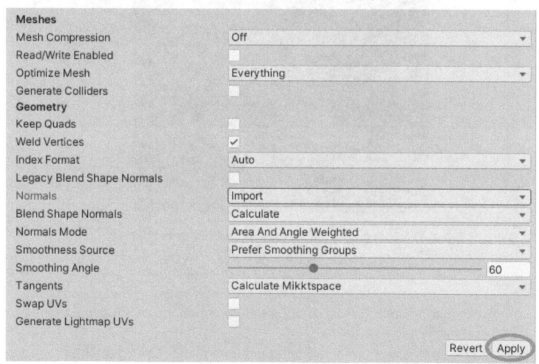

Fig. 4.2 – You may need to scroll down to see the Apply button

> **A note on .blend files**
>
> Blender projects are saved as `.blend` files in a special format. Advanced readers may know that Unity *does* directly support importing `.blend` files (in addition to `.fbx`, `.3ds`, `.obj`, and so on). So why are we exporting as `.fbx` from Blender? Well, when you actually import a `.blend` file, what happens behind the scenes is that Unity winds up silently using Blender's FBX Exporter anyway. In fact, if you don't have Blender installed, Unity will not be able to import `.blend` files. We use Blender's FBX Exporter for full transparency and to be explicitly aware of all the export settings. Also, we side-step the issue of Unity auto-updating whenever you make a change to a `.blend` file. This can often be desirable, depending upon the size of the file, but not always. For our purposes here, we will stick with `.fbx`.

3. Drag the turret model into the **Hierarchy** panel and twirl open the small arrow to the left of the name. Your imported asset will have the following structure:

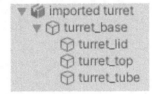

Fig. 4.3 – The turret structure viewed in the Hierarchy Window

4. This is a good opportunity to simplify the asset name. Right-click the top-level turret object and **Rename** it to **turret**.

5. If you have rotation issues with your turret, choose the top **turret** object and set the X rotation to 0. Also, choose the **turret_base** object and set its X rotation to 0.

Now let's alter the parent-child relationships of the parts.

Restructuring the Turret

We'll reparent the turret parts to make them easier to work with and animate. Note that we *could* have done this in Blender, but I wanted to return to the familiar territory of Unity as quickly as possible:

1. We need to turn the model into a prefab before we change its structure. Drag the top-level **turret** object into the `Prefabs` folder you created in *Chapter 2, Gathering Our Resources*. You should be prompted with a popup here so choose to create an **Original Prefab**.

2. You now have a choice of how to enter **Prefab Mode**. In the **Project** window, you can double-click the prefab to edit it in an isolated space where the rest of your scene is hidden. The other option is to enter **Prefab Mode** through the **Hierarchy** window by clicking the arrow to the right of its name:

Fig. 4.4 – Entering Prefab Mode from the Hierarchy window

Entering **Prefab Mode** this way allows you to edit your object in context, meaning you will be able to see it in relation to other objects in the scene, but you will not be able to affect the other objects (they will look like they have been ghosted out). Go ahead, click the arrow.

3. Above the prefab view are several options for this mode. The only option we care about right now is **Auto Save**. Be sure this is checked.

Fig. 4.5 – Prefab Mode options. Check that Auto Save is on

This ensures that any changes you make to the prefab are saved as you make them, and they will automatically get applied to all instances of the prefab in your scenes.

Our goal for reparenting is to create parts of the model that can move independently but have their child objects move along with them. Specifically, we want all parts of the top of the turret to rotate together, independently of the base, and also to have the lid rise up independently of the top but have the launch tube sync with its motions. If we didn't create these parent-child relations the different pieces would not move together.

4. Drag the different parts on top of each other to create the following parent-child relationships:

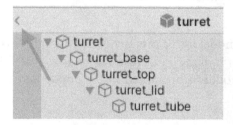

Fig. 4.6 – This is the reparented structure. Exit Prefab Mode with the small arrow

5. To exit **Prefab Mode** and return to your scene, click the arrow to the left of its name.

Okay, with the turret now a nicely structured prefab, it's time to pretty it up again.

Texturing the turret

For most parts of the turret, we are going to use the textures and materials from the original model. So, if your SpaceEscape project doesn't have the original turret imported, go ahead and do so from the **Package Manager**.

Now you should be able to go into the **Robo's turret (free)** / **Materials** folder and see four alternative materials whose names end in **_A, _B, _C,** and **_D**. I'm going to choose the first one (**_A**), which is orange. If you select it, you can see it in the **Inspector** Preview pane. If you want to be a wacky, outrageous rebel, choose something wild like blue instead (**MT_Basic_Turret_D**).

Texturing the turret is actually very easy. It's a matter of drag and drop, like so:

1. Drag your selected material onto **turret_top** in your **Hierarchy**. Since we have not altered the original texture coordinates and Blender preserved them nicely, the turret should start resembling its former awesome self:

Fig. 4.7 – The turret is partially textured. You chose blue, didn't you?

2. Go ahead now and drag the same texture onto the base and lid parts. Notice that the lid part is textured correctly. Even though we separated the geometry in Blender, we did not alter the UV coordinates that are attached to the individual vertices.

But what about the geometry that we created from scratch: the tube and the struts? We didn't pay any attention to UV coordinates. How are we going to texture them? Simple: we will cheat.

We'll learn about UV mapping in Blender later on, starting with *Chapter 5, On the Level: Making Modular Scenery*, but for now, we are going to ignore textures for the tube and struts entirely. We are going to create a simple metallic material—with no texture map—and apply that material to those turret parts.

Creating a material for the missile tube

Our material for the tube could not be simpler. Here's what we need to do to create it:

1. In the **Projects** window, go into your `Materials` folder, right-click, and choose **Create | Material**.

2. Name the material `metal MAT`. (It's always a good idea to have a naming convention. My naming convention for material names is to have them end in `MAT`).

3. With your new material selected, in the **Inspector** window you will see that there are many different properties you can set to create quite impressive materials. We are just going to change two properties. In the **Metallic** input box, set the value to `.7`.

4. Below that, in the input box to the right of **Smoothness,** set the value to `.6`. You can set these two properties to anything you want, we just don't want a flat white material! The Preview Panel shows you what your material looks like. At the top, click the button that looks like a square to see what your material looks like on differently shaped objects. Shiny!

Now that we have our material let's go ahead and apply it. This process is just a bit more complex than we've done previously, but still, it's not bad at all.

Applying the material to the tube

Because the launch tube is hidden by other geometry, it's easiest to apply the new material by going into **Prefab Mode** to make our change. Do you remember the two ways to get there?

1. In the **Hierarchy** window, click the arrow to the right of the turret object.

2. To get a good look at the launch tube, in the **Hierarchy** window select the **turret_top**.

3. In the **Inspector** window uncheck the box next to **Mesh Renderer**. This will turn it off *visually*. Note that this is different than *disabling* the object itself. Doing that would hide all the child objects as well, which is not what we want.

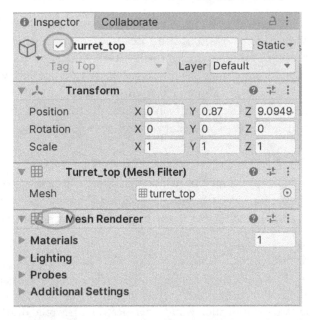

Fig. 4.8 – Leave the object enabled but disable the Mesh Renderer

4. Next, select the **turret_lid** and disable its **Mesh Renderer** as well. You should now be able to easily see the **turret_tube** object.

5. Drag your `metal MAT` material onto the tube in the **Hierarchy** and you should see its appearance change in the view.

6. With that change done, go ahead and re-enable the Mesh Renderers for both the lid and the top. Double-check that prefab **Auto Save** is on.

7. Exit **Prefab Mode**.

Great. Our turret is now all dolled up and ready to roll, but what exactly do we want it to do?

Planning the turret behavior

Before we go any further, let's set some goals by describing how we'd like the turret to behave within the game. I'll describe how I think the turret should act and, no doubt, that will spark your imagination and give you other ideas as well. Once you see how we go about implementing my behavior, you should be well on your way to being able to execute your own ideas.

The turret, as I see it, is going to act like this: before the player is detected it is going to be in a SCANNING mode. This means the turret will point in a direction for a short amount of time, waiting for the player to show up. If no player is detected it will swing a quarter-turn clockwise and continue scanning, doing this indefinitely.

If the player is detected, however, the turret will stop scanning and enter SHOOTING mode. While in this mode, the turret will fire off three blaster bursts with a short cooldown period in between. After three bursts, the turret will enter LAUNCHING mode. 5000 astro-credits if you can guess what happens in this mode. Yes, that's right, we launch a missile. (Talk to my robo-secretary about getting those credits.) BOOM! This is the moment we've been waiting for. After the missile is fired, the turret will go back to scanning and repeat this cycle until either the space marine bites cosmic dust or goes out of range.

Sound good? Engage thrusters!

We're going to finally do some coding, but just before that we are going to take a very brief detour to grab an excellent free tweening tool called **iTween**. This will allow us to add a touch of cool to the behavior of the turret (and other assets later on).

Tip: The secret of life

Perhaps you have never heard of **tweening** and the related concept, **easing**. Tweening has to do with changes that happen to things over time. The term comes from the cartoon animation world where lead artists would draw keyframes of the most dramatic parts of an animation and junior artists would draw "in-between" frames that fluidly linked the keyframes visually. In the digital world, tweening can be applied to any property (not just visual ones) that can change over time.

In code, it is very easy to change a value by a fixed amount over a fixed time step, for example, moving something by 1 meter per 1 second (the fancy name for this is **linear interpolation**). However, this kind of motion can often (not always) look boring! Things in the real world tend to move differently. They speed up and slow down. They "ease in" and "ease out." This is where tweening tools such as iTween help us. They give us different kinds of options for how things should change over time and allow us to inject a little more life into our creations. There are some good examples of tweening/easing here: `https://easings.net/`.

Adding in iTween

Do you remember how to use **Package Manager** from *Chapter 2, Gathering Our Resources*? If you do not already have it docked somewhere in your scene, open it up with **Window | Package Manager**, drag it by its top tab and dock it somewhere convenient. I like to dock Package Manager next to my Game tab.

With **Package Manager** ready and waiting, open up your browser and navigate back to the Asset Store: `https://assetstore.unity.com/`. If you search for `iTween`, it should be the first item in your search list. You'll see that there are additional assets available that can augment working with iTween if you get into it more deeply.

For now, just click **Add to My Assets** and then **Open in Unity**. iTween should show up in your **Package Manager** window and you can go ahead and **Import** it.

That's it for all the turret prep work. We've got it restructured and textured; we created a material for the new parts and we grabbed a tool that will help us animate. Now to put all that to good use.

Scripting the Turret

Here's where the techno-magic really starts to happen. The first thing we are going to do is teach the turret how to scan for the player. We are going to need a new C# script. To do that, follow these steps:

1. In your `Scripts` folder, right-click and choose **Create | C# Script**. Name this script—wait for it—yes, **Turret** seems like a great choice.

2. Select your turret in the **Hierarchy** and drag your new script into the **Inspector** to add it as a component of the turret object.

    Many of you may know that you could have accomplished the same thing by first selecting the turret and then, in the Inspector, choosing **Add Component | New Script**. I prefer my way since it starts the script out in the right folder, and you don't have to move it later, but do as you like. Just remember to try to keep your scripts organized.

3. Launch your code editor. You can either double-click the script in your **Project** view or you can use the dots dropdown for the script component in the **Inspector** and choose **Edit Script**.

Fig. 4.9 – The dots menu is an alternate way to launch your script editor

As mentioned in *Chapter 1, Melding Unity and Blender*, we'll use Visual Studio in this book, but it shouldn't make a difference if you're using Sublime Text or something else. If you are using something else, you probably already know how to edit your code.

With your editor launched you should see your `Turret.cs` script, which is a bare bones descendant of a **MonoBehaviour**. It has two empty, stubbed out methods: `Start()` and `Update()`.

As I've said, I am assuming you have scripted before, but I will give brief explanations, which will either serve as reminders or as points you can further research.

A `MonoBehaviour` is a built-in Unity class that defines a **Component**, which contains some kind of new capability for a Game Object. (For the record, if Earth is conquered, "behaviour" will be spelled without a "u." Consider this a public service announcement.)

Our `Turret` class **inherits** from `MonoBehaviour`, meaning it gains all of its data and behaviors, but it can also extend `MonoBehaviour` with new capabilities. For beginners, the two most common things to change are adding behavior to the `Start()` method, which happens *once* for the Game Object, and the `Update()` method, which happens every time a new game frame is visually displayed.

In our new `Turret.cs` file, the first thing we are going to do is create a data structure that defines all the possible states the turret can be in. The data structure we'll use is an **enum** (short for enumeration). We'll add this definition above (outside of) the class definition for `Turret`:

```
public enum State { IDLE, SCANNING, SHOOTING, LAUNCHING }; //
add this
public class Turret : MonoBehaviour {
    ...
```

Great. That was easy. Now we will add some variables to the `Turret` class itself. Be sure the following code is after the opening curly brace just shown (that is, it's in the class body):

```
AudioSource turretAudio; // for SFX!
State state = State.IDLE;
```

Hopefully, these lines are self-explanatory, but if not: `turretAudio` will reference a built-in Unity component we will add to the turret to manage playing sound effects for the turret's actions: scanning, shooting, and so on. `state` will keep track of the turret's behavior state with one of the values of the `State` enum, starting with an idle state. Remember that C# is case-sensitive, so `state` and `State` are two different things. Confusing, I know!

> **Naming Conventions: Avoiding Disintegration**
>
> At some point, as you encounter other people's C# code (including many Unity tutorials), you will come across variables whose names begin with m_, such as m_myVar. This is an outrage. If you do this with your own variables, I will disintegrate you.
>
> The m_ is meant to indicate a "class member." It is an obsolete, old-school notation from C and C++ that wormed its way into C# and should be stamped out. In C# that notation is useless and reduces code readability, which is a major programming crime. Do *not* do this in your code and when you encounter it in other people's code, please lodge a complaint with a local politician.

Save your file in your code editor (usually *Ctrl / Command + S*) then switch back Unity. **Important**: select your turret and in the **Inspector** add an **Audio Source** component. If you forget this step you will get a frustrating null pointer error later!

The Turret class is going to be a fairly simple controller class that will manage the three actions we encapsulate in the classes we are about to create. Take a deep breath, this is a deep dive…

Setting up turret actions

We've planned for our turret to do three actions so far: scanning, shooting, and missile-launching. These actions have some things in common: they cannot happen simultaneously, they can trigger and then have a cooldown time before triggering again, and they can have sound effects, among other capabilities. Maybe in the future we might get some ideas about new turret actions: new weapons or scanning modes—who knows?—maybe mobile turrets.

We *could* handle all these actions with one long if…else if block within the Turret class, but that is a very rigid, messy way to code it. There is a famous programming principle called **D.R.Y.**, which stands for **Don't Repeat Yourself**. It means avoid duplication of data and logic. If you find yourself cutting and pasting the same code often, that is a strong hint that you should try to write some D.R.Y. code. In our case (using 20/20 hindsight since I've already coded this) we can make the turret use some D.R.Y. code for the three actions we've planned for.

> **Programming Principles: The light side of the force**
>
> D.R.Y. is just one of many excellent and common programming principles. You can find ten of the best ones at https://www.makeuseof.com/tag/basic-programming-principles/, or do a web search. They are all worth memorizing, but if you don't understand some right now, that's okay. Embrace the ones you do understand and revisit the list from time to time as you gain experience. You will make your programming life easier, and that's a good thing!

The way we are going to write D.R.Y. code for our turret is to create an **abstract base class** called CooldownAction, which **encapsulates** shared data and behavior for all turret actions. It's okay if you don't understand some of the advanced terms I just used. The important idea is to have *one place* to define everything that turret actions have in common. Then, if you want to change or add some global behavior to all actions, you know where to go and you don't have to make multiple changes in multiple places, which is a recipe for introducing bugs!

In your Scripts folder, create a new script called CooldownAction and open it up to edit. We are going to make two changes to the default code: we'll add a **using** statement that allows us access to the Unity Event system and we'll make the class **abstract**. An abstract class cannot be directly created, but must have a child class that derives—or **inherits**—from it. Make these changes:

```
using UnityEngine;
using UnityEngine.Events;   // add this line
[RequireComponent(typeof(AudioSource))]    // add this too
public abstract class CooldownAction : MonoBehaviour   // insert
                                                       // this
{
...
```

Below the open curly brace, we will add the variables for the class (note the lack of **m_**!):

```
public AudioClip actionSFX; // 1
public float cooldownTime; // 2
public bool isEnabled = true; // 3
public GameObject target; // 4
[HideInInspector] // 5
public UnityEvent OnReady = new UnityEvent(); // 6
[HideInInspector] // 7
```

```
public UnityEvent OnEnded = new UnityEvent(); // 8
protected bool isTriggered = false; // 9
protected AudioSource audioSource; // 10
private float elapsedTime = 0; //11
```

Let's go through the lines and define what all these variables do:

1. `actionSFX` stores a reference to a clip to play when the action is triggered.

2. `cooldownTime` specifies, in seconds, how much time must pass between triggers.

3. `isEnabled` indicates whether the action is active or not.

4. `target` is an optional generic reference to a Game Object that is affected by the action (for example, the turret top).

5. This is an example of a code **Attribute**, or metadata. It applies to the member that comes after it, in this case, a **UnityEvent** called `OnReady`.

6. The `OnReady` event will fire when the action has cooled down and can be triggered again. Although it is `public`, we hide it in the **Inspector** because it should be affected by the `Turret` class and not the user in Unity.

7. This is the same attribute as before (#5).

8. The `OnEnded` event fires when the action has completely finished its duties. In our case, it is used to tell the turret it's time to change state. We'll see the difference between `OnReady` and `OnEnded` further along.

9. `isTriggered` indicates whether the action is in the middle of performing its function.

10. `audioSource` is a reference to the parent's component for audio playback.

11. `elapsedTime` is used to track the action cooldown.

Does that all make sense so far? Of course, it does!

> **Scope**
>
> As a reminder, `public`, `protected`, and `private` define the **scope** of a variable or a method. `public` means that code outside the class can "see" it. (In a `MonoBehaviour`, `public` variables show up in the Inspector). `protected` means that the member will be visible to child classes. `private` means that the member is only visible within that class. It is not really necessary to write the `private` keyword because that is the default scope, but I am being explicit.

So, those are the variables, or **properties**, we will use. Next, we will define the behaviors, or **methods**, of the class. Add these methods below the properties but be sure they are above the closing curly brace of your class or else you will get an error.

Let's get the easy stuff out of the way first. Add these (empty) methods:

```
protected virtual void DoAwake() { }
protected virtual void DoUpdate() { }
protected virtual void Triggered() { }
protected virtual void Ready() { }
```

These four methods are stubs that child actions can override with meaningful behavior. The **virtual** keyword indicates the method can be **overridden** in a child class.

`Awake()` and `Update()` are standard `MonoBehaviour` methods (`Awake()` happens a single time before `Start()`). `CooldownAction` is going to implement those, so we do not want our child classes to reimplement those, accidentally replacing the behavior in `CooldownAction`. Instead, we provide `DoAwake()` and `DoUpdate()` if the equivalent functions are desired. This bears repeating: child classes of `CooldownAction` should *not* implement `Awake()` or `Update()`. If needed, they should override `DoAwake()` and `DoUpdate()`.

Let's tackle some more real easy stuff. Add this code below the stub for `Ready()`:

```
public void Trigger() {
   if ((!isEnabled) || isTriggered) return;
   isTriggered = true;
   Triggered();
}

protected void Reset() {
   elapsedTime = 0; // restart the cooldown timer
   isTriggered = false; // reset the trigger variable
}

protected void PlaySFX(AudioClip clip) {
   audioSource.clip = clip;  // assign the clip to play
   audioSource.Play();  // play it. badda-bing!
}
```

`Trigger()` is called by outside code (in our case, it will be the `Turret` class) to start the action. The first thing it does is check to see whether the turret is disabled or if it has already been triggered. (Pay close attention to the check for disabled. We are actually checking for *not* enabled, hence the easy-to-miss exclamation-point **not** operator.) In either of those cases, the function returns and does nothing. Otherwise, it stores the fact that the action has been triggered, then calls the virtual `Triggered()` method, which should be overridden in a subclass.

The `Reset()` function is extremely simple and the comments should be self-explanatory. `PlaySFX()` is an example of the D.R.Y. principle in action. Instead of writing the same two lines of code over and over to play a sound effect, we simplify it to one easy method call.

Lastly, `CooldownAction` implements the `MonoBehaviour` class's `Awake()` and `Update()` as follows:

```
void Awake() {
  audioSource = GetComponentInParent<AudioSource>();
  DoAwake();
}
```

When `Awake()` is called after its parent game object is created, it looks in the parent for an `AudioSource` component and caches a reference to it. Then it calls the virtual `DoAwake()` method, which may be overridden in a child class:

```
void Update() {
  if ((!isEnabled) || (!isTriggered)) return; // do nothing
  elapsedTime += Time.deltaTime; // increment cooldown timer
  if (elapsedTime >= cooldownTime) {
    Reset();
    Ready(); // call virtual method
    OnReady.Invoke();   // fire event, alert listeners
  }
  if (isTriggered) DoUpdate(); // call virtual method
}
```

`Update()` is the most complicated method we've tackled yet, but it's not really that complex. Here's what it does: every frame, we first check whether we are disabled or not triggered, if either condition is true, we return and do nothing.

If we haven't returned, we increase the internal counter by the amount of time that has passed since the last call to `Update()` (that is, since the previous frame). If the amount of time equals or exceeds `cooldownTime` we reset everything, call the virtual `Ready()` function for children to deal with, then fire the `OnReady` event to signal other objects (such as the turret).

So that's it for the `CooldownAction` class! The annoying thing about abstract classes is that you can't directly test them by running your game, but they can and will save you a ton of work.

Tag, you're it! Creating a placeholder player hero

Our turret is not going to be very impressive if it has nothing to shoot at! Eventually, we are going to make an awesome space marine in Blender, but for now, we are going to have to make do with a humble capsule primitive as a stand-in.

Go back to Unity and, in the Hierarchy, right-click and choose **3D Object | Capsule**. In the **Inspector** rename this to **Player** and, in the **Tag** dropdown, choose the **Player** object tag:

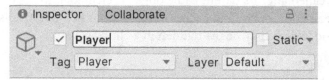

Fig. 4.10 – Choose the predefined Player tag from the dropdown

The first thing we are going to do is get the turret scanning for the player, so we want to start the player off in a place that the turret is not already facing. Also, we want to raise the player up above the ground level. To do all that, change the turret's x, y, z **Position** to 2.6, 1, -4. You can use your own values, but those worked for me.

For now, we'll leave the player as is and dream of greater glories to come. But while we are on the subject of object tags, we are going to create two of our own. Follow these three steps:

1. In the **Tags** dropdown choose **Add Tag…** at the bottom of the list.

2. Use the + button to add two tags to the list: **Top** and **Lid**. Careful! Capitalization matters!

Fig. 4.11 – Custom tags. Watch your capitalization!

3.   Be sure you got *steps 1* and *2* correct, then we move on.

Now to get to some fun stuff that we can actually see happening!

Finally, Scanning!

Our work creating the `CooldownEffect` class will start paying off. In your `Scripts` folder create a new script, `ScanAction`, and drag it onto your turret in the **Inspector**. Open it up for editing.

`ScanAction` is *not* going to inherit from `MonoBehaviour`. Instead, it will inherit from `CooldownAction`. Also, it will have a single new property. So, make these small changes:

```
public class ScanAction : CooldownAction {   // change this
    public float turnTime = 1f; // seconds to make ¼ circle turn
    // add
...
```

The scanning action is going to work like this: the turret top will turn a quarter circle, pause, then continue turning indefinitely. If it detects the player, the action ends, and the shooting starts!

`ScanAction` will have four methods, most of them short. We'll begin with `Start()`:

```
void Start() {
    target = GameObject.FindGameObjectWithTag("Top");
}
```

This is an implementation of the `MonoBehaviour` class's `Start()` method that is called one time after `Awake()`, but before the `Update()` loop begins. It looks for an object with the tag "Top" (we'll get to this shortly) and then stores a reference to that object in the `target` variable. Be careful to capitalize the **G** of **GameObject**. **GameObject** refers to the GameObject *class* itself. **gameObject** refers to the *object* the script is attached to. We will wind up using both.

Next, we will tackle the most complicated method, DoUpdate(), which overrides the parent class's virtual method of the same name. It is called every frame. Conceptually, the method is simple: project an invisible **ray**; if it hits the player object, end this action and inform any listeners. Add this new method below Start():

```
protected override void DoUpdate() {
  RaycastHit hit;  // object to store collision info
  if (Physics.Raycast(target.transform.position,
      target.transform.TransformDirection(Vector3.forward),
      out hit, Mathf.Infinity))
  {
    if (!(hit.collider.gameObject.tag == "Player")) return;
    iTween.StopByName("turning"); // interrupt tween, stop
                                  // turning
    Reset();
    OnEnded.Invoke(); // fire event
  }
}
```

The first thing the method does is declare a variable, hit, to hold info about the ray we will **ray cast** to detect the player. We will not actually use hit, but it's required for what we do next.

The heart of this method is the next convoluted line. What's happening is simple, though: Unity has a built-in Physics.RayCast() method that works out what your ray hits (if anything). So, this line is saying: if we hit something, run the code in this if block, otherwise skip it.

Now that we understand the high-level intention, let's unpack the parameters passed to Physics.Raycast(). The first one is where to start the ray from. In this case, we are going to have target reference the turret_top object. The next parameter is what direction to project the ray in. We use another built-in function to determine which way the turret is facing. The third parameter, out hit, has a slightly strange look. We are passing in our hit variable, but what is that out keyword? Unfortunately, you need Top Secret Clearance to get that answer. I could tell you, but then I'd have to disintegrate you. Suffice to say, just type it in and be happy it will make the whole thing work. You will almost never ever encounter out again as long as you live. The final parameter is how far to project the ray. In this case, we are saying "To infinity and beyond!"

Having performed that hit test, if we hit something, we run this code within the `if` block:

```
if (!(hit.collider.gameObject.tag == "Player")) return;
    iTween.StopByName("turning"); // interrupt tween, stop
                                  // turning
    Reset();
    OnEnded.Invoke(); // fire event
```

This code is saying if the thing we hit is not tagged as the player, we're done. Otherwise, stop any iTween motion going on. What's that? We haven't started any iTween motion? Well, we will, coming up next! Finally, to close things out, we `Reset()` the action and fire `OnEnded()` to inform any listeners.

The next method also looks complex but is conceptually even simpler than the last one: play a sound effect and start a turning animation to go along with it:

```
protected override void Triggered() {
  PlaySFX(actionSFX); // method in parent class
  iTween.RotateBy(target, iTween.Hash(
    "name", "turning",
    "y", .25, // quarter turn, 25% of circle
    "time", turnTime,
    "easeType", "easeOutBack"   // this motion looked good to
                                // me
  ));
}
```

There are actually only two commands here, but the second one, a call to an iTween method, is split across lines for readability. Here's what's going on: we start by playing the sound effect. Then we call iTween's `RotateBy()` method, which will turn an object by a certain amount. (All of iTween's methods are listed here: `http://www.pixelplacement.com/itween/documentation.php`.)

The parameters we pass to `RotateBy()` are a name (`turning`), an axis to rotate (`y`) and by how much (`.25`), a length of time to complete the turn (`turnTime`), and the type of motion (`easeOutBack`). I chose a motion that looked a little interesting and jerky.

One more method to go, but it's super easy! Here goes...

```
protected override void Ready() {
    // when cooled down, re-trigger (so, continuously scan)
    Trigger();
}
```

This method overrides the virtual `Ready()` method from `CooldownAction`. It basically says as soon as we've cooled down, keep scanning in a circle indefinitely.

Save your file. Ready to start scanning? Let's test this!

Testing the ScanAction

If you return to Unity, it may take a moment to compile your new script. When that's done, if you select the turret you should now see the **ScanAction** component with properties we can fill in.

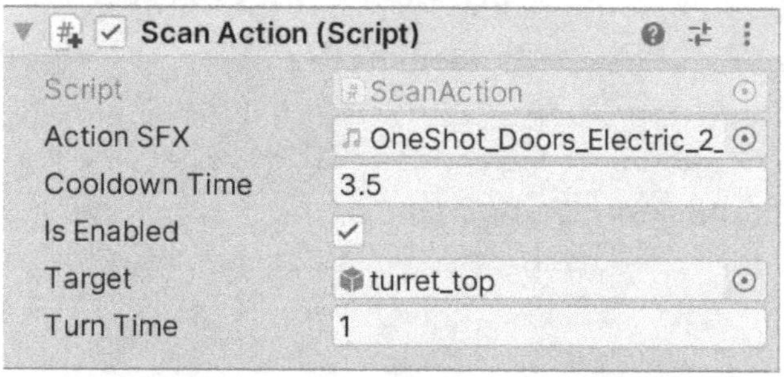

Fig. 4.12 – ScanAction's properties filled in

The first one, **Action SFX**, is the clip to play while the turret is turning. I chose one from the Sci-Fi SFX package we got in *Chapter 2, Gathering Our Resources*. Click the circle-select on the left and use the search box to find **OneShot_Doors_Electric_2_Open** in the dropdown.

The next property, **Cooldown Time**, I set to 3.5 seconds. Peeking ahead, you'll see the **Turn Time** is only 1 second. This has the effect of the **turret_top** turning for 1 second, pausing for 2.5 more, then continuing to turn, pause, turn, pause, and so on.

We'll leave **Is Enabled** enabled so we can test.

To fill in **Target**, we need to do a tiny bit of work:

1. In your **Hierarchy**, drill down in the turret and select **turret_top**. In the **Inspector** assign it the tag **Top** that we created earlier.

2. Next, reselect the parent turret object so you can see Scan Action again and drag the **turret_top** from the Hierarchy into the **Target** slot in the Inspector.

   Just a tiny bit further and we can run our game for the first time!

3. Open up your Turret script for editing. Add the following declaration below the earlier code:

```
State state = State.IDLE;
CooldownAction scanAction; // add this line
```

4. Next, we are going to populate two references in a `Start()` method:

```
void Start() {
    turretAudio = GetComponent<AudioSource>();
    scanAction = GetComponent<ScanAction>();
}
```

   We'll add more to Turret's `Start()` method later when we have more actions, but that's it for now.

5. Next, add a short, simple function to begin the scan:

```
void StartScan() {
    state = State.SCANNING;
    scanAction.Trigger();
}
```

6. And finally, we need something that actually calls `StartScan()`. For now, we will create a keyboard input (the *S* key) for testing. We'll change this later, but for now, add this:

```
void Update() {
    // code for testing
    if (Input.GetKeyDown(KeyCode.S)) StartScan();
}
```

7. Be sure to save your script then return to Unity. Double-check that you have tagged **turret_top** and that you have filled in the properties of **ScanAction**.

Ready? Then WHAT ARE YOU WAITING FOR? Press the **Play** arrow and run your game!

Press the *S* key to start scanning. The turret top should turn, and you should hear a sound effect. The turret should keep turning until it faces the player, then it should stop. Did you get it to work? I know you did because you are awesome, and this code is excellent!

> **Tip: If you encounter problems**
>
> Bugs are a fact of life even for professional programmers. Someone once estimated that 70% of your coding time is spent debugging. One critical piece of advice is to read all error messages very closely. Never ever *assume* you know what the problem is; see what Unity *actually* reports. Having said that, if you got past the script compilation stage with no errors, any runtime errors you get at this point are likely due to something not being assigned a value correctly.
>
> For both compilation and runtime, errors reported in Unity's Console can often be double-clicked to jump to the line of code causing trouble. Books have been written on debugging alone and we can't do that here, so if you hit trouble, take a deep breath, breathe out your frustration, then go back and methodically go through the chapter code looking for something you missed.

To test one more thing about the **ScanAction**, disable the **Player** capsule in the **Inspector** and re-run the game. This time the turret should keep turning forever since it can't find the player.

Now it's time to start shooting!

Preparing for the ShootAction

The **ShootAction** is much, much cooler than the **ScanAction**, but it also requires a little more infrastructure to work correctly. The two pieces we need are a **light** to act as the muzzle flash and a **LineRenderer** to represent the blaster beam. Here goes:

1. In the Unity Editor, select your turret and enter **Prefab Mode**.
2. In the **Hierarchy**, right-click and create **Light | Point Light**. Rename this to **blaster**.
3. Drag blaster so it is a child of **turret_top**.
4. Begin changing the properties of the light in the **Inspector**. We want to position it directly in front of the **turret_top**'s red-eye thingy. Make the **Position** of the light `0, 0.37, 1.25`.

5. Set the **Range** to `.24`.

6. Use the **Color** selector and set the light's color to bright red to match the eye thingy.

7. Be sure to check **Draw Halo**; this will be the glow of our muzzle flash.

Next, we will create the actual blaster beam. We'll start by creating a material for it:

1. In your `Materials` folder, create a new material and rename it **blaster MAT**.

2. In the **Inspector**, drop the **Metallic** and **Smoothness** properties all the way down. Enable **Emission** and choose a red color from the selector below that.

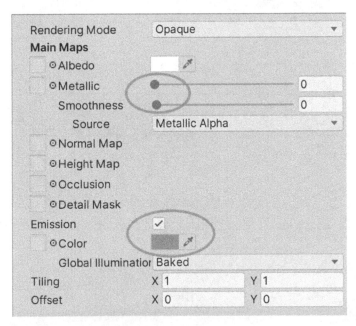

Fig. 4.13 – Set these properties on your blaster material

3. Now select your blaster object again in the **Hierarchy**. Click **Add Component** and choose **Line Renderer**. This should appear right below your **Light** component.

We want our blaster beam to emerge from *inside* the turret (hence a negative z value) and for now, it will extend 5 units. We also want it to be really thin.

4. So, to do that, set the position of the first point on the line (index 0) to 0, 0, -0.5. Set the position of the second point (index 1) to 0, 0, 5. Set the line's **Width** to 0.04.

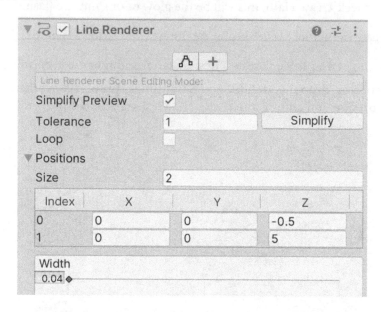

Fig. 4.14 – Set these properties on the blaster beam

5. Twirl open the **Materials** section and drag your **blaster MAT** into the slot to reference it.

Fig. 4.15 – Apply your new material. Are you seeing red yet?

6. Exit **Prefab Mode** and save your Unity project just in case of a meteor strike.

Now we have the all the Game Objects we need to make shooting work.

Creating the ShootAction

We are going to go through a process very similar to creating the **ScanAction** and, trust me, we're saving a lot of effort by having created the abstract `CooldownAction` first.

ShootAction will be called when we want the turret's blaster to shoot. The script will track some data and also have references to objects responsible for the visual effects. To do this:

1. In your `Scripts` folder, create a new script and rename it `ShootAction`. Drag this onto your turret right below **ScanAction**. Open it up for editing.

2. Just like with `ScanAction` we'll change this class to inherit from `CooldownAction`. `ShootAction` also defines three private variables:

```
public class ShootAction : CooldownAction {   // change
this
    private int shotsFired;
    private Light glow;
    private LineRenderer beam; // the blaster beam
...
```

The turret will fire three times before launching a missile, so `shotsFired` keeps track of that. We cache references to the `Light` and `LineRenderer` so we can turn them on and off.

3. Before we add methods, save your file and jump to Unity to fill in these properties.

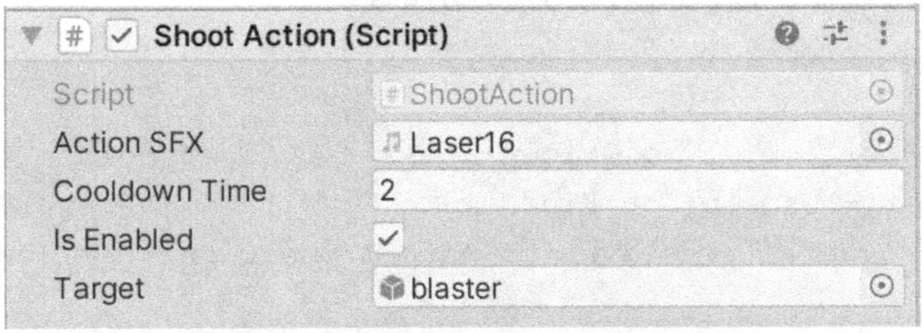

Fig. 4.16 – Set these ShootAction properties

Laser16 comes from the Futuristic Gun SFX library we got in *Chapter 2, Gathering Our Resources*. A two-second cooldown for the blaster seemed right to me.

4. Finally, in the **Hierarchy**, expand the turret until you see the **blaster** object, which has the `Light` and `LineRenderer`. Drag that into the slot on **ShootAction**.

Now you can go back to editing the script. `ShootAction` has four methods. One is trivial and one is more involved. Let's start by adding the trivial one below the `beam` declaration:

```
protected override void DoAwake() {
  target.SetActive(false); // turn off light and line renderer
```

```
    glow = target.GetComponent<Light>();
    beam = target.GetComponent<LineRenderer>();
}
```

DoAwake() begins by disabling the blaster object until it's time to shoot. Then it fetches and stores a reference to the Light and LineRenderer objects.

To understand the rest of the code, we need to understand the plan behind the muzzle flash. What we want to happen is that when we shoot, we play a sound and make the **Range** of the light very large. Very quickly, we shrink the range of the light back down. Since the light has a halo, this change will be visible. We make most of this happen in this method:

```
protected override void Triggered() {
  shotsFired++; // increment how many times we've shot
  PlaySFX( actionSFX );
  target.SetActive(true); // turn light on
  beam.enabled = true; // turn beam on

  var origin = transform.TransformPoint(Vector3.zero);   // 1
  var adjOrigin = new Vector3(origin.x,
      target.transform.position.y, origin.z);   // 2

  beam.SetPosition(0, adjOrigin);   // set first point
  var player = GameObject.FindGameObjectWithTag("Player");
  beam.SetPosition(1, player.transform.position);   // set 2nd
                                                    // point

  iTween.ValueTo(target, iTween.Hash(
    "from", 5f,
    "to", .5f,
    "time", .4,
    "onupdate", "OnTweenUpdate",
    "onupdatetarget", gameObject,
    "oncomplete", "OnTweenComplete",
    "oncompletetarget", gameObject
  ));
}
```

Let's break this down. First, we increase the count of how many shots are fired. Then, we play a shooting sound effect. Next, we turn the light and beam on.

After that, we want to set where the blaster beam begins and ends. To do so, we first convert the position of the blaster from its *local coordinate space* to *world space* with the built-in `TransformPoint()` method at `//1`.

Next, we adjust that coordinate to lift it up on the y axis to where the blaster is at `//2`.

Following that, we set the beam origin and get where the player is. We set the end of the beam to that point. Right now, that is at the player's feet, since that is its origin. Later on, we will adjust it so it looks better.

The rest of the method is just a call to a new iTween method, `ValueTo()`. This changes the range of the light from 5 units to `.5` units in `.4` of a second, so it will be very fast.

The last four parameters we pass to `ValueTo()` translate to the following: on every update, look for a method on `gameObject` called `OnTweenUpdate`. This method will be passed the current tweened value. When the whole tween is finished, look for a method on `gameObject` called `OnTweenComplete`. We are going to write those two missing methods right now:

```
void OnTweenUpdate(float value) {
   glow.range = value; // set to current tweened value
   if( value < 2f) beam.enabled = false;  // a small visual
                                           // touch
}
```

`OnTweenUpdate()` is simple. Every frame, it shrinks the light range. If the range is below a threshold it turns the beam off before the glow has shrunk completely. Though not necessary, this simply looked good to me during experimentation:

```
void OnTweenComplete() {
   target.SetActive(false); // turn off blaster object
   if (shotsFired < 3) Triggered();   // shoot again
   else {
     Reset();   // reset the action
     OnEnded.Invoke(); // fire event to alert listeners
   }
}
```

`OnTweenComplete()` is also simple. It is called when the value reaches the minimum we specified. First, it turns off the glow (the beam is already off). Then, it counts the number of shots fired; if it's not three yet, we re-trigger the action. If it is three, we reset and fire the ended event.

Save your script and open the `Turret` script.

Testing the ShootAction: Pew! Pew! Pew!

We're close to seeing something fun again. We just need a few changes to the `Turret` script. First, add a property to reference the action:

```
CooldownAction scanAction;
CooldownAction shootAction; // add this line
```

Then we will add two lines in the `Start()` method:

```
scanAction = GetComponent<ScanAction>();
scanAction.OnEnded.AddListener(ScanEnded);  // add this line
shootAction = GetComponent<ShootAction>();  // add this line
```

The first line says listen for the `OnEnded` event and call `ScanEnded` when you hear it. The second line merely stores a reference to the shoot action.

To test shooting, we only need two very simple methods:

```
void ScanEnded() {
  StartShoot(); // we have found player, start shooting
}
```

`ScanEnded()` will only be called when the player is located. All it does is call the following:

```
void StartShoot() {
  state = State.SHOOTING;
  shootAction.Trigger();  // pew! pew! pew!
}
```

Yes, we could have combined both methods into one, but do you remember what I said is hugely important? Program readability!

Time to test! Be sure your player capsule is enabled then run your game. Press *S* to start scanning. This time, when the turret stops turning it should unleash three mighty blasts with sound effects and visual effects (we'll worry about damaging the player later).

Amazing! Great job!! Now let's tackle the coolest thing the turret can do: fire missiles!

Preparing for the LaunchAction

Before we get to Missile City, we're going to need a missile. We are going to create a very, very simple missile out of Unity primitives. Once it's working well, you may be inspired to go and create something fancier in Unity or in Blender.

Creating a Missile

We'll create the missile in the **Scene** and then turn it into a spawnable prefab. Follow these steps:

1. In the **Hierarchy**, right-click then **Create Empty**. Rename this parent object **missile**.

2. Also in the **Hierarchy**, right-click and choose **3D Object | Cylinder**. Drag this object to be a child of missile.

3. Similarly, choose **3D Object | Capsule** and also make this a child of missile.

4. Select the cylinder. In the Inspector, set the **Position** to 0, 0, 0. Set the **Rotation** to 0, 90, 90. Then set the **Scale** to .15, .25, .15.

5. Now select the capsule. In the Inspector, set the **Position** to 0, 0, 0.17. Set the **Rotation** to 0, 90, 90. Then set the **Scale** to .15, .25, .15.

6. Drag the missile object into your Prefabs folder and delete the object from the **Hierarchy**.

That's all there is to it. Here is the result:

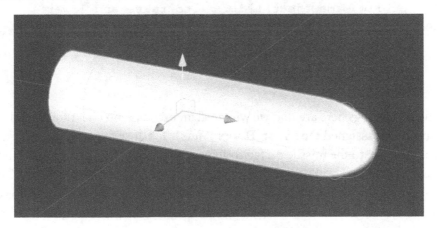

Fig. 4.17 – Our sleek and deadly missile

Now, my friends, where does that missile launch from?

Creating a launch spawn point on the turret

This is the last bit of preparation before we get to the code. We need to define where on the **turret_tube** the missile gets created and launched from:

1. Open up your turret prefab in **Prefab Mode** and expand it so you can see **turret_tube**.

2. Create a new empty Game Object, name it **missile_spawn**, and drag it to be a child of the **turret_tube**.

3. Set the **Position** of **missile_spawn** to 0, 0.59, 0. This puts the spawn point in the middle of the tube, but lifted up a bit so the missile can sit comfortably in the tube.

We're now ready to make use of all this.

Creating the LaunchAction

You've already created two actions; can you guess how this one is going to go?

In your Scripts folder create, and name LaunchAction then inspect the turret and drag the new script below the other actions. Then open the script for editing and follow these steps:

1. Change the inheritance of the class and declare its variables:

```
public class LaunchAction : CooldownAction {
    public GameObject missilePrefab;
    public GameObject lid;  // to raise and lower
    public AudioClip lidSFX;
    private float lidLiftTime = 1.5f;
    private GameObject missile;
    ...
```

The notable things here are that we will need an extra sound effect for the lid motion (to be assigned **One Shot_Doors_Metal_1_Close** from Sci-Fi SFX) and also a reference to the missile prefab to spawn. The inherited actionSFX from CooldownAction will be the launch sound effect (assigned **Plasma_Gas_Tube_Burst_2** from Epic Arsenal – Essential Elements Demo Packs by Epic Sounds and FX on the Asset Store) and the target will be assigned the **missile_spawn** point.

2. Detour back to Unity and assign all these properties. You will need to drag the **turret_lid** and **missile_spawn** point from the Hierarchy and the missile prefab from your Prefabs folder.

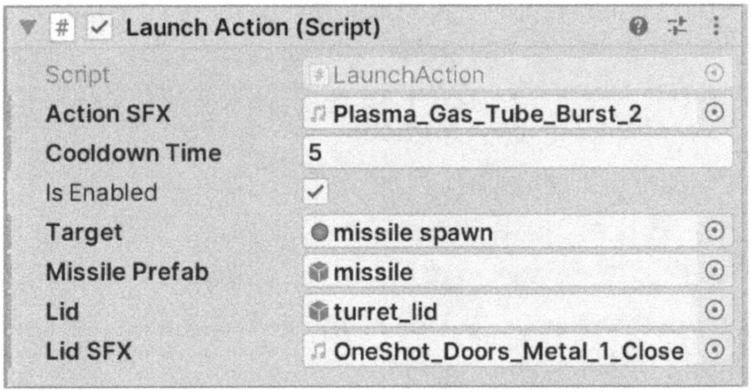

Fig. 4.18 – Assign these properties to the action

3. Jump back to your code and we'll add methods for LaunchAction. There are hardly any surprises at this point. Let's start with the code that happens when the action is triggered:

```
protected override void Triggered() {
  // create the missile at spawn point...
  missile = Instantiate(missilePrefab, target.transform);
  RaiseLid();  // can you guess what this does?
}
```

4. Only two things to do here: create a missile object inside the launch tube, then raise the lid. You have probably created new Game Objects with Instantiate() and prefabs before, but if you haven't, this is the way to create new game elements at runtime (which is to say, objects that don't start out in the scene hierarchy):

```
void RaiseLid() {
  PlaySFX( lidSFX );
  iTween.MoveBy(lid, iTween.Hash(
    "y", .25,  // raise up .25 units
    "time", lidLiftTime,
    "oncomplete", "OnRaiseComplete",
    "oncompletetarget", gameObject
  ));
}
```

You should be able to figure out `RaiseLid()` even though we are using a new iTween method called `MoveBy()`. Can you do it?

First, we play a sound effect. Then we start a tween via iTween. It says to move the lid object by .25 units on the y axis over the number of seconds specified by `lidLiftTime`. This movement is *relative* to the current position. When that is done, it tries to call the `OnRaiseComplete` method in gameObject. Did you figure all that out? Here's the next method:

```
void OnRaiseComplete() {
  LaunchMissile();
}
```

Here comes `LaunchMissile()`. Do I really need to explain this one? When the lid finishes lifting, we launch the missile...

```
void LaunchMissile() {
  PlaySFX( actionSFX );
  // locate the player to have a target for the missile
  var player = GameObject.FindGameObjectWithTag("Player");
  iTween.MoveTo(missile, iTween.Hash(
    "position", player.transform,
    "time", 1f,
    "oncomplete", "OnLaunchComplete",
    "oncompletetarget", gameObject
    ));
}
```

Almost nothing new here in `LaunchMissile()`. First, we play the launch sound effect then we find the object tagged Player to aim at. Then it's good old iTween to the rescue. Note that we are now calling `MoveTo()`, which uses absolute coordinates, and not `MoveBy()`, which we used for the relative lid motion. We give iTween the **missile** object, the position to move it to, the duration of movement, and the method to call when everything is done, which is as follows:

```
void OnLaunchComplete() {
  // Hmm, any ideas about this? Readability rules!!!
  LowerLid();
}
```

That was pretty simple. Here's what happens when we call `LowerLid()`:

```
void LowerLid() {
  PlaySFX( lidSFX );
  iTween.MoveBy(lid, iTween.Hash(
    "y", -.25, // notice the minus sign!
    "time", lidLiftTime,
    "oncomplete", "OnLowerComplete",
    "oncompletetarget", gameObject
  ));
}
```

This is the same code as `RaiseLid()` except for a minus sign and a different **oncomplete** method:

```
void OnLowerComplete() {
  Reset(); // reset the action
  OnEnded.Invoke(); // fire event to inform listeners
}
```

We have seen this code in the other actions we've made.

5. Save your file and edit the `Turret` script. Declare a property to cache the new action:

```
CooldownAction shootAction;
CooldownAction launchAction; // add this line
```

6. In the `Start()` method listen for shooting to end and populate the cache property.

```
shootAction = GetComponent<ShootAction>();
shootAction.OnEnded.AddListener(ShootEnded); // add this
                                             // line
launchAction = GetComponent<LaunchAction>();  // add this
                                             // line
```

7. We finish things off by supplying the missing method and defining one new one:

```
void ShootEnded() {
  StartLaunch();
}
```

```
void StartLaunch() {
  state = State.LAUNCHING;
  launchAction.Trigger();
}
```

8.   Save and return to Unity.

We have been making all our script changes to the turret object in the **Hierarchy**. We need to be sure all our changes get saved into the turret prefab. To do this, select the turret and, in the **Inspector**, click the **Overrides** dropdown, then **Apply All**.

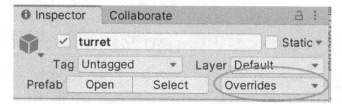

Fig. 4.19 – Apply your changes back to the prefab

Now we come to the final moment.

Testing the LaunchAction

Fix any code compilation errors you might have and then run your game. Remember to press *S*. Drumroll please. The turret should scan, then stop and shoot three times, then the lid pops up, a missile flies out at the player, and the lid closes.

WE DID IT!!!

(Well, except for having the missile explode, but that is a task for another chapter…)

Use your appendages to give yourself a big pat on the back. We created an abstract base class (CooldownAction) that captured shared functionality and data across turret actions. Then we created three child classes (ScanAction, ShootAction, and LaunchAction) that inherited from CooldownAction. Lastly, we modified the Turret class to use all three actions. You've come a long way, baby!

Code Checklist for the Chapter

The code in this chapter was presented in easy-to-analyze bite-sized chunks, but when following along with a book it can be easy to miss a bit and get frustrated (this has happened to me plenty). Here is a checklist of the classes we created in this chapter and their methods. Be sure you got everything!

Turret	CooldownAction	ScanAction	ShootAction	LaunchAction
ScanEnded()	Awake()	DoUpdate()	DoAwake()	LaunchMissile()
ShootEnded()	DoAwake()	Ready()	OnTweenComplete()	LowerLid()
Start()	DoUpdate()	Start()	OnTweenUpdate()	OnLaunchComplete()
StartLaunch()	PlaySFX()	Triggered()	Triggered()	OnLowerComplete()
StartShoot()	Ready()			OnRaiseComplete()
Update()	Reset()			RaiseLid()
	Trigger()			Triggered()
	Triggered()			
	Update()			

Fig. 4.20 – Chapter code checklist

The Ultimate Advanced Unity Tip

Start is called before the first frame update. Update is called once per frame. Re-read those last two sentences 42 more times. Got it yet? Unity inserts these reminder comments into *every single* script you create, but it gets kind of annoying after a few years of seeing them. You would think there would be a simple preferences checkbox to turn this off, but there isn't. Many people would trade their last warp-core for knowing how to be rid of these comments, but I will share the secret with you for free.

The secret is to edit the **Script Template** for new MonoBehaviours. The very slight downside is that you must do this for each version of Unity you have installed (you probably don't have many). The choice is yours. If the repetitive comments don't bother you, skip the rest of this tip.

The location of the Script Templates depends on your operating system:

- **Windows**: C:\Program Files\Unity\Editor\Data\Resources\ScriptTemplates.
- **Mac**: /Applications/Unity/Hub/Editor/ <Unity version> / Unity.app/Contents/Resources/ScriptTemplates (Note: you will need to right-click on **Unity.app** and choose **Show Package Contents**).

You should see a file named **81-C# Script-NewBehaviourScript.cs.txt**. Open this up in a text editor and you should see two lines beginning with // and then the agonizing comments. Very carefully delete just those two lines and leave all other lines alone. Save the file. To enjoy your new comment-free existence you must quit and restart Unity. Once you do, create a new junk script in your project. Open it up and—amazing!—no more auto-comments. Too good to be true! If you would like to be insane and create other kinds of custom script templates, you can find more information here: `https://4experience.co/how-to-create-useful-unity-script-templates/`.

So that's the Ultimate Advanced Unity Tip. You're welcome. And you can keep your warp-cores!

Summary

Wow. Just wow.

We finished a round-trip excursion that took us three chapters to complete. In this chapter, we took the turret we altered in Blender and truly brought it to life with motion and sound. We started C# scripting for the first time. Along the way, you learned some excellent programming best practices and we touched on a few other "missile-laneous" topics. (Yes, I went there).

Unbelievable. Our turret now kicks asteroids! That Space Marine doesn't stand a chance. In the next chapter, we return triumphantly to Blender, now confident that the two tools work great together and you are becoming a master. We'll start a new expedition learning many new Blender secrets and creating cool modular interactive sci-fi scenery pieces to dress our game up.

I can't wait.

Section 2: The Right Stuff: Scenery, Props, and Characters

Now that we understand and have applied the fundamentals, it's time to really start exercising our skills with a number of interesting challenges.

This section comprises the following chapters:

- *Chapter 5, On the Level: Making Modular Scenery*

- *Chapter 6, Living It Up: Adding Fun with Animations*

- *Chapter 7, Prep Work: Materials, Grids, and Snapping*

- *Chapter 8, Laying Out the Level*

- *Chapter 9, Secret Weapon #1: Deploying ProBuilder*

- *Chapter 10, Secret Weapon #2: Animating with Timeline*

- *Chapter 11, We Could Be Heroes: Blender Character Modeling*

- *Chapter 12, It was Rigged!: Character Rigging*

5
On the Level: Making Modular Scenery

"The end of all our exploring will be to arrive where we started."

— *T.S. Eliot*

That's it, we're done. You now know everything and you're on your own. Good luck.

…

Hmm.

Okay, perhaps there are a few more topics we can cover, just to pass the time before the inva—before the good weather gets here. First, we'll start by thinking about how we can create our mini-game level in a smart, modular way, and then we'll block out the level. After that, we'll quickly review what we've learned in Blender in *Chapter 3, Entering the Blender Zone for the First Time*. Before we actually create some reusable meshes, we'll have a first look at textures and materials.

Finally, we'll spend time learning new tools and creating some simple, non-interactive scenery pieces, and then we'll proceed to UV-unwrap/map and texture them. If you're addicted to bullet points, here's what I just said we'll cover:

- Basics of modular design, including blocking out the level
- Blender recap – functionality and hot-keys
- Fundamentals of UV mapping and unwrapping
- Creating meshes for floors, walls, and corners

By the end of the chapter, we will be well on our way to having a cool environment to house our sci-fi turret and you will know enough to create a huge variety of your own pieces of scenery!

Technical Requirements

We're back in good old Blender in this chapter so you shouldn't have any troubles there.

Be advised we are going to use some free textures from the Asset Store, so you can go ahead and download and import **eU Sci-Fi textures set Volume 1**.

If you want to customize your own textures, you will want to have an image-editing program handy. Photoshop is the tool of choice and GIMP is an open source alternative, but really any image editor that supports layers is fine.

Also, if you are going the custom textures route, there are many, many sites with free resources besides the Asset Store. One excellent one is `https://www.textures.com`.

The supporting files for this chapter can be found here: `https://github.com/PacktPublishing/Mind-Melding-Unity-and-Blender-for-3D-Game-Development/tree/main/Chapter05`

The code in action video for this chapter can be found here: `https://bit.ly/3kOIvmt`

Understanding Modular Level Design

Okay, in this chapter, I've used the word "modular" four times so far (five including this sentence) and we've only just started, so what the heck am I going on about? Designing in a modular fashion means you put in thought beforehand about how all your parts will work together and you create them to be simple to use, compatible with each other, and highly reusable in different contexts. A great analogy is the world of Lego bricks. Each brick is compatible with all the others and can be used in a myriad of ways. The main difference between Legos and the digital assets we'll create is that ours won't hurt as much when you step on them!

One of the first things to consider in modular design is your **unit basis**. This is another way of saying that you make a conscious decision as to how big one of your 3D units is. Conveniently, this decision has already been made for us. In both Unity and Blender, the default measurement is 1 3D unit = 1 meter. It's worth noting that the Unity physics system is set up to expect this. Unless you are modeling galaxies or nanomachines, this default unit basis should work for a majority of your projects.

> **Tip: Model at scale**
>
> This means that you should create your assets at the "true" size they are meant to be and not create them at, for instance, a larger size and then shrink them down later. (Note: this is entirely *unrelated* to Level of Detail, or LOD, where you model something at a high level of *detail* and then create versions with lower detail to help performance.)
>
> What you want to avoid is trying to put together a level and finding out your doors are too big/small, props won't work with characters, and so on, and then having to do a bunch of last-minute eyeballing and guesswork to get things to work right.

If you are mixing your own assets with those from a third party, or "kit-bashing" multiple assets from other parties, check the scales! Take care of scaling issues sooner rather than later. If you are working in Blender, scale the asset to the correct size and then **Apply** your transformation, so the new correct scale becomes the default. If you are working in Unity, it is much better to make any scale adjustments in a model's **Import Settings** than it is to make adjustments to prefabs or instances.

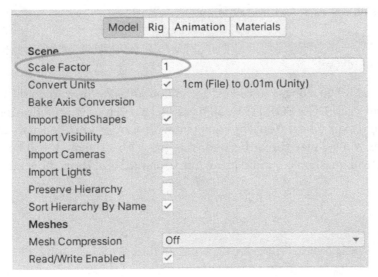

Fig. 5.1 – Make any scaling adjustments in the mesh's Import Settings

Scale is just one of the considerations you need to make when designing for modularity. To a greater or lesser degree, you will also need to think about tiling, connections, origin points, symmetry, occlusion, and lighting. You'll need to ask yourself questions such as "Will there be a lot of these pieces appearing together?", "Do some features (such as exits) need to line up across pieces?", and "Will some features be visible from my game camera point of view?" Here is where the type of game you are creating makes a big difference. For instance, the top-down shooter-style game we're making has different needs than a **first-person-style** (FPS) game, which might have different needs from a strategy game, and so on. One thing that sets our game style apart from an FPS is that we won't have any ceilings and we have to make sure our geometry isn't so big that it obscures the player.

As we shall see, modeling and laying things out in orthographic (non-perspective) view is a great help with modular design and being comfortable with Snap settings is essential. This applies to working in both Blender *and* Unity.

Setting our Goals

So, what are we going to build? Well, you have to learn to walk before you can fly, right? (At least, for humans.) So, we will start out by building some basic, non-animating structural elements: floors, walls, and corners. Along the way, we will also learn the very basics of UV-unwrapping and how to texture and create materials for our objects. In later chapters, we will up the complexity of the objects we are working with; simultaneously, we will learn more advanced unwrapping techniques and we'll add in animation!

For now, our chapter creation checklist is going to be as follows:

- Two floor pieces, each textured differently
- One wall piece
- One corner piece

I guarantee that as we go along, you will get 11 million ideas for how to do things *your* way and use *your* vision. GO FOR IT! By all means take a detour from following along with the book and experiment. You'll be equipped with enough knowledge to accomplish a lot. Some ideas you get may still be beyond your grasp. That's okay! It will be good to keep these practical questions in mind as we move forward and learn more advanced techniques.

The Humble Floor

Here's a topic that's beneath me. (Sorry. In space, no one can hear you groan.) It's hard to get any more basic than a simple floor, but to make it modular, we need to set some ground rules. Yuk yuk yuk. (Okay, I'll stop.)

Each of our floor pieces has to respect our unit basis, so in our case, we want to create pieces that have their boundaries on whole unit increments. Since our future space marine (currently a placeholder capsule) is about 2 meters (6 feet) tall, I think he needs a minimum floor area of 2 meters x 2 meters to maneuver in. That's not to say that we can't make tiles that are 1 x 1 unit, but when we place them, there should be a minimum of two tiles together. Larger tiles need to scale by whole units, so we'll avoid making tiles that are 3.5 units by 4.1 units, although a 4 x 6 tile is perfectly fine.

Walls and corners

Walls are a bit more interesting than floors; they can have more geometry and you are free to add greebles and nurnies (see the following tip box) without worrying about messing up player navigation. We'll need to create at least one corner piece to allow smooth visual transitions around corners.

Glossary: Greebles and nurnies

Yes, you are forgiven if you are confusing these terms with the voracious amphibians from the oily swamps of Gliese 667Cc—an easy mistake to make! But on Earth, greebles and nurnies refer to 3D detailing you can add to the surface of an object that makes it look more complex, and thus more visually interesting. Often, they are used to give a viewer an impression of increased scale. Picture the surface of the Death Star or the Battlestar Galactica; they are both lousy with greebles and nurnies!

So now you know a number of issues to keep in mind when you make models for a level. Next, let's do a brainstorm of how we would like to use our models once they are built.

Blocking Out our Level

Before we get to creating new geometry, let's create a rough layout that will structure our level and help guide us with placement as we create each new piece. To do so, launch Blender and create a new file. Call it anything you like so long as it's `SpaceEscapeObjects`. Here is the plan that I have in mind:

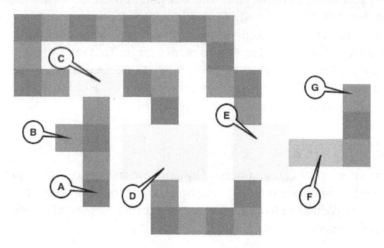

Fig. 5.2 – A rough level layout for our mini-game

Let's examine *Fig 5.2*. It should be noted that each grid square is meant to be about 8 x 8 units (1 meter). The alternating blue and pink areas are indicating corridors. Yellow areas are rooms.

Note: before I present my ideas, I want to say that for this section, do anything you want. This book is not focused on level design and you can still have a lot of success and fun by following your own ideas.

Here's the big idea behind the layout: the player will start out in the area marked **A**. You might put a turret in area **B** that the player can hear before they see.

There will be a single turret in area **C**. You might create a longer, more "puzzle-y" route to the left, or a more combat-intense route to the right. Area **D** should be tough. Maybe have four different turrets turning at different speeds, one turret in each corner of the room. And maybe we'll put an obstacle in the center of the room so the player can't just charge across.

Area **E** will be a junction you are at regardless of whether you chose the left or right path. This is a chokepoint where you might have two turrets that you have to deal with while activating the extending bridge that we'll build later.

Area **F** will be the space that the bridge extends across and **G** will be the victory zone. Sounds exciting, right?

Just before we begin the actual layout, let's glance back at some of the most useful stuff we've learned about Blender so far. Throughout the book, I am assuming you are very new to Blender and I try to hammer home the basics. If you are a bit more comfortable, you can skim or skip ahead.

A Quick Recap of our Blender Know-How

Just to refresh your memory (or to "fresh" it, if you skipped the previous Blender chapter!), let's quickly go over what we've already learned about Blender. If anything seems unfamiliar, I suggest you review *Chapter 3, Entering the Blender Zone for the First Time*.

Navigation and hot-keys

Okay, so then, Blender defaults to opening in the 3D Layout workspace in Object mode. Using your mouse and keyboard, you should understand how to pan, zoom, and orbit your viewpoint.

You should remember you can add meshes to your scene with the *Shift + A* menu and you can delete objects with the *X* key.

With an object selected, you should understand how to do the three basic transformations of translating, rotating, and scaling. You have many ways to accomplish these. The preferred way, of course, is with the hot-keys that let you (*G*)rab, (*R*)otate, and (*S*)cale, but you can also select the tools from the tool bar (*T* to toggle), and additionally, you can set the position, rotation, and scale from the **Adjust Last Operation** popup, from the sidebar (*N* to toggle), or from the Object properties tab in the **Properties** pane. Whew! Talk about options!

Recall that using *Tab*, you can toggle Edit mode where you can perform all your transformations on vertices, edges, and faces.

Lastly, we were introduced to two of the most used modeling tools: (*E*)xtrude and (*I*)nset.

Knowing Your Numpad

Blender allows you to do some highly efficient maneuvers entirely from the numpad. You're not a Blender pro until you can let your fingers do the walking. Just listing the numpad shortcuts doesn't make as much sense as seeing the layout, because the layout is somewhat intuitive. See *Fig 5.3*.

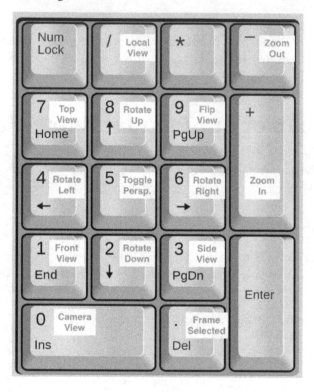

Fig. 5.3 – A handy cheatsheet for the numpad. Download this into your brain

The *Numpad 9* "flip" command is especially worth paying attention to. It gives you the opposite view of whatever you have selected. So, for example, if you pressed *Numpad 1* for **Front** view, pressing *Numpad 9* will show you the **Back**. Likewise, if you chose *Numpad 7* for **Top** view, *Numpad 9* will get you the **Bottom**. If you selected **Side** with *Numpad 3*, *Numpad 9* will switch from **Left** to **Right**.

You might not suspect it, but you can do a surprising amount with what you know so far. Of course, this is just the beginning, and Blender has so many more capabilities in store, but let's start applying our basic knowledge to our level design.

Creating Floors

So, let's start flooring it. First, we'll set up the 3D view in a configuration well suited to the type of modeling we'll be doing. I'm going to add a Suzanne head just so you'll be able to see the result of our changes, but there's no need for you to do it if you just want to follow the steps:

1. Create a `SpaceEscapeObjects` Blender file.

2. Let's get into **Front** view. Do you remember two ways to do it? You can choose **View | Viewport | Front**, but the pro way is to jump straight there with *Numpad 1*.

3. You're going to want to use the numpad anyway because we're going to raise up our view a bit by pressing *Numpad 8 two* times.

4. Then, we're going to swing around the vertical axis a bit by pressing *Numpad 4 three* times.

5. Finally, we'll switch from perspective to orthographic view either by clicking the icon in the "zoopancamper" controls area or pressing *Numpad 5*.

Fig. 5.4 – Click the grid to switch to an orthogonal view or press Numpad 5

Tip: Saving Your Default Settings

You already know that one of the best things about Blender is how customizable it is—you can tweak it until you come up with a configuration that best suits your work style. But if you start a new .blend file, you need to re-configure everything. That's obviously no good and also completely avoidable. What you can do is save the entire state of Blender to be your startup state when you create a new .blend file. You can easily do this from the top menu by choosing **File | Defaults | Save Startup File**. Be aware though that this saves *everything*, including invisible geometry. So, if you wanted to save the isometric view we just created as the startup view, be sure to first delete Suzanne or any other objects.

Use **File | Defaults | Load Factory Settings** to restore the configuration to Blender's original state, but be aware that this restores *all* settings, so you may need to spend some time adding your favorites back in.

With all those adjustments we made, you should now have a view that is similar to this:

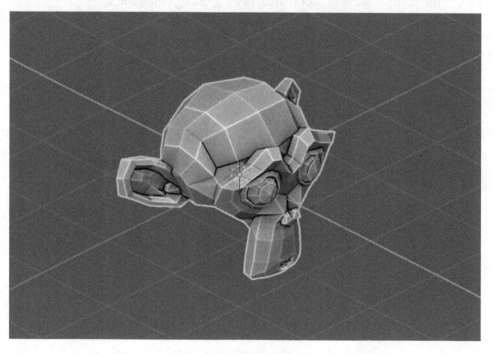

Fig. 5.5 – This is like the view in 2.5D games, such as Diablo

Remove your monkey head if you have one. (Err, I mean to say "monkey object." If you personally have a monkey head, there is nothing wrong with that, and certainly don't try to remove it!)

The first couple of floors we make will be placeholders that allow us to quickly recreate the level layout we made earlier. Here's what to do:

1. Create a flat plane by pressing *Shift + A* and choosing **Mesh | Plane**. By default, this will create a 2 m x 2 m mesh centered on the 3D cursor, which is at the view origin at 0, 0, 0.

2. In the **Adjust Last Operation** pane, set the size to 8.

3. For our purposes, we don't want the pivot of the plane in its center; we want it on a corner, so it is easier to snap and rotate. To move the pivot, first use *Tab* to enter **Edit** mode, then make sure you are in **Vertex Selection** mode (*Ctrl / Command + 1*).

Fig. 5.6 – Edit mode with Vertex Selection chosen

4. Click the vertex in the lower left of the plane (which is where we want to set the origin).

5. Choose **Mesh | Snap | Cursor to Selected** to set the 3D cursor to the vertex position.

6. Switch back to Object mode (*Tab)*, then choose **Object | Set Origin | Origin to 3D Cursor**.

7. Send the 3D Cursor back to 0, 0, 0 with *Shift + C*. This will avoid future transform surprises.

8. Lastly, right-click and choose **Snap | Selection to Cursor**. Your plane will now align its lower-left vertex to 0, 0, 0.

9.   Rename the Plane to `Floor` in the Outliner. Okay, we're all set!

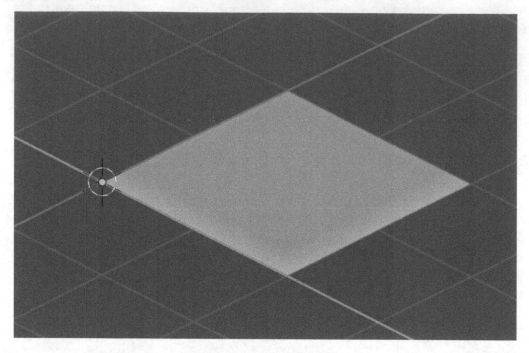

Fig. 5.7 – Origin of plane aligned with 3D Cursor at 0, 0, 0

Please note that this is the simplest piece of geometry ever, and we *could* have created it in Unity, but we're supposed to be getting Blender practice right now. Let's try something more sophisticated.

Hide the floor in the Outliner and move on.

Creating a Wall

When trying to model something in Blender, you will find that it is often convenient to start with a simple cube and build it out from there. So that is where we will start. Follow these steps:

1.   Right-click in the **Outliner** pane in the upper right. Choose **New Collection** and name it `Walls`.

2.   In the 3D View, create a new cube (*Shift + A*) then rename it `Wall01` in the Outliner.

Our wall is going to be 2 m high and 2 m long, but only .5 m thick.

3.   Open the Sidebar with *N* and set the X, Y, Z **Dimensions** to .5m, 2m, 2m.

4.   We want the wall to rest on top of the floor and to extend from the origin. So, also in the Sidebar, set the **Location** to 0, 1, 1.

5.   Choose **Object | Set Origin | Origin to 3D Cursor**. Note that we are setting the origin in the middle of the wall. Thus, when we snap it with a floor, it will overhang it by 50%.

6.   Make all your transformations the default for the wall by choosing **Object | Apply | All Transforms**.

You should now have this. Note the X and Y axes alignment:

Fig. 5.8 – Our wall in progress. So far, so good?

Now, we will create a more sci-fi profile for the wall, and we'll learn some new super-useful tools along the way. The following figure will help:

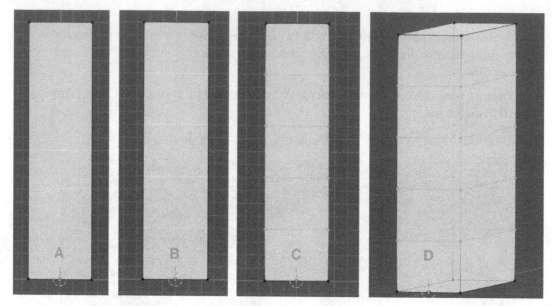

Fig. 5.9 – The loop cut process

7. Switch to Edit Mode with *Tab*.

8. Switch to Front view with *Numpad 1*.

    Read and understand the entire next step before you do it. We are going to add four **loop cuts** to the wall—basically slicing it to create some new geometry to manipulate.

9. Refer to *Fig 5.9* for this step. Switch back into Editor mode. Move your cursor near the left or right edge of the wall and press *Ctrl / Command + R* to add a yellow horizontal cut (**A**). (If you had placed your cursor near the top/bottom, you would have created a vertical cut.) Roll your mouse wheel to increase the number of cuts to four (**B**). Commit the cuts with a left-click. But wait! You are immediately placed into a slide mode in case you want to position the cuts. We don't, so immediately right-click to leave the slide mode (**C**). Notice how your cuts have gone all the way through (**D**).

10. In order to see through the mesh, you need to turn on **X-ray view** with *Alt + Z* or the icon:

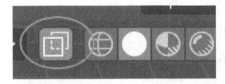

Fig. 5.10 – Toggle X-ray view with this icon or Alt + Z

We're going to use the following figure as a guide for the next few steps:

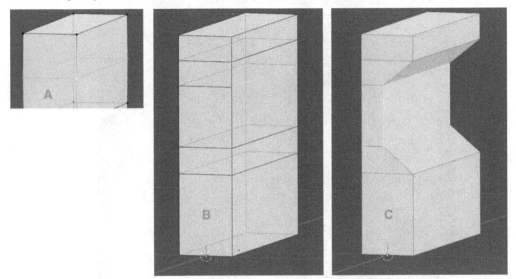

Fig. 5.11 – We'll use this figure as a guide for the edge loops

11. Enable Edge selection with *Ctrl / Command 2*. *Alt + left-click* the top-most loop cut to select the whole edge loop (**A**).

12. We are going to **edge slide** it up, about halfway closer to the top edge. *G* to grab the loop, *Z* to limit axis movement, then mouse move it up into position and left-click to commit. There's no need to be precise.

13. Position the other three loop cuts the same way, using *Fig 5.11* as a guide (**B**).

14. Enter Face selection mode with *Ctrl / Command 3*. Select the middle-front face of the wall and *G* then *X* to move it inward to produce the result in **C**. Looks like a sci-fi wall!

Still with me? Fantastic!

While we are here, it is a convenient time to create a corner piece.

Creating a wall corner

Here is the plan: we are going to copy the edge faces of the wall and use the **Spin** tool to create a rounded corner that has the same profile as the wall and turns a 90-degree angle. Follow these steps and may the Force be with you:

1. To start, deselect the front face you extruded if it is still selected.

    Refer to *Fig 5.12* for the next few steps:

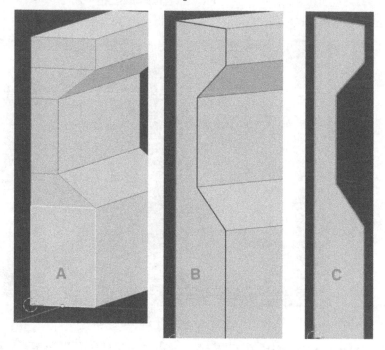

Fig. 5.12 – We are copying one side of the wall

2. Now select all the faces on the near side by *Shift* and left-clicking (**A**).

3. We are going to do something unusual with the Extrude command. Press *E* to extrude, but immediately right-click to "cancel" it (**B**). The reason that is in quotes is that it didn't really cancel the command—it actually *did* an extrude but with an offset of 0, meaning it just duplicated the selection! Most of the time, this is a hidden gotcha because it creates unseen duplicate vertices, but in this case, it is what we wanted.

4. Choose **Mesh > Separate > Selection** and these new faces will become their own object, separate from the wall. Name this new object `WallCorner01`.

5. In the Outliner, click the eyeball next to `Wall01` to hide it. We are left looking at the wall corner face (**C**). If you have been switched back to Object mode, re-enter Edit mode with *Tab*.

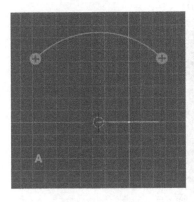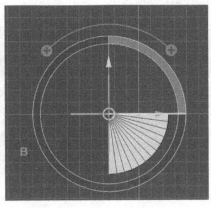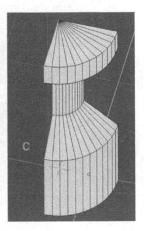

Fig. 5.13 – Steps 6, 7, and 8 refer to this figure

6. Go into Vertex Edit mode and select the vertex on the lower left.

7. Choose **Mesh | Snap | Cursor to Selected**. We will use this as a pivot point to rotate around.

8. Select all with *A* and switch to Top view with *Numpad 7*. Choose the **Spin** tool from the Toolbar on the left and the spin gizmo will appear over your selection (**A**).

9. Drag the right handle of the gizmo to spin out the faces. As you are dragging, press *Ctrl* to snap in precise increments. Spin around 90 degrees (**B**).

10. Your corner is complete. It should now resemble **C**.

Okay, we've created two pieces of scenery and you've got enough knowledge that you could create lots more, but they are looking pretty bare. Let's fix that!

Hide your wall corner, save your file, and move on.

Texture Mapping, UV Mapping/Unwrapping, and Materials

So, what the heck is this stuff and why is it so important? Well, you want your models to look great, right? Let's begin our discussion with something we are familiar with: blaster turrets. To simplify things, we are just going to focus on the turret base.

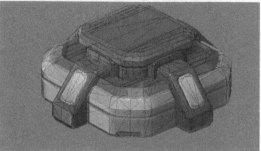

Fig. 5.14 – The textured turret base and its geometry overlaid in wireframe

Texture mapping is the process of adding visual detail to a mesh with one or more 2D images (textures). You are well aware that our lovely turret is actually composed of many vertices, edges, and faces. Texture mapping describes how different parts of a mesh are visually affected by different images. Because we were working with a premade model, all the texturing work had already been done for us, but when we create our own models, that task falls to us.

> **Procedural textures**
>
> Okay, yes, all you know-it-alls out there, there is a thing called a procedural texture that doesn't rely on images. Instead, it uses mathematical formulas to calculate visual details. A common procedural texture might be used to create a marble rock surface. We will not be using procedural textures, so there.

Now, prepare yourself. This is the beginning of a *very* big topic. So big that we couldn't possibly cover everything in this whole book. We'll start with basic concepts, build them up, and then start applying them to our work. With these new skills, I will officially allow you to level up.

UV Mapping 101

UV mapping is the process of projecting a 2D image onto a 3D surface. To do this, vertices on the 3D mesh are assigned *UV* coordinates, which correspond to points in a 2D space. The U coordinate corresponds to an X-axis value and the V corresponds to a Y-axis value.

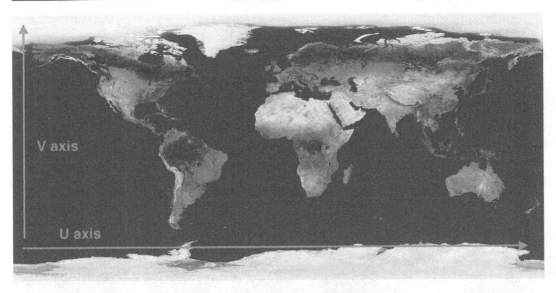

Fig. 5.15 – This could be a texture for a model of the Earth

Why U and V, you may ask? The idea was to avoid confusion with the X, Y, Z axes from 3D space. (As an aside, the letter W is reserved for operations having to do with quaternion rotations.) UV space is normalized, which is to say that no matter the actual dimensions of the texture, both the U and the V values will be between 0 and 1, inclusive, with the 0, 0 origin always on the lower left. If 0 to 1 seems a little strange to think about, instead imagine that all coordinates are expressed as being a percentage of the width or height, ranging from 0 to 100%.

Very often, but not always, a texture image will be square, and its dimensions will be a power of two; for instance, 1,024 x 1,024 pixels and 2,048 x 2,048 pixels are two of the most common formats. The reason for this is technical and has to do with how efficiently the computer can process the texture.

In order to generate UV coordinates for our meshes, we need to **unwrap** them.

UV Unwrapping 101

One of the easiest ways to start to understand UV unwrapping is to imagine that you wanted to create a six-sided die out of a piece of paper. After some experimentation, you would find that you could create a "cross" shape of squares that, when cut out, could be folded together to make the cube shape of the die.

The equivalent in Blender looks like this:

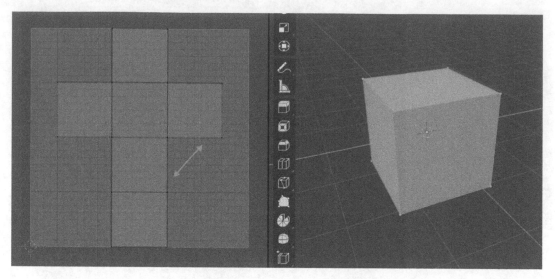

Fig. 5.16 – A UV-unwrapped cube in Blender

Fig 5.16 shows a cube in the **UV Editing** workspace in Blender. On the right is our familiar object-editing space and on the left is the UV editor. The six faces of the cube have been neatly unwrapped. Blender conveniently generates default UV coordinates for its mesh primitives, but 99% of the time, you will want to adjust these.

One important and interesting thing to note is that the red arrows point to two different edges in the UV map but there is actually only *one* edge on the mesh. What has happened here is that Blender has performed a *visual* separation along a **seam**, which has been marked on the mesh. The geometry of the mesh has *not* been changed at all. Try to imagine what the UV map would look like if the edge seam wasn't separated—the cube faces would still touch but they would be grossly distorted and no longer resemble squares. The more distorted a face is on a UV map, the harder it is to texture well and the more likely you are to introduce unwanted visual artifacts in your final display.

UV unwrapping is always a compromise of causing as little distortion as possible, while also keeping seams to a minimum.

Now a cube is an extremely simple example for UV unwrapping. But meshes get much, much more complex and UV unwrapping gets much, much trickier. You will see that there is a fine art to UV unwrapping as we move forward.

To illustrate this, let's return to our turret base:

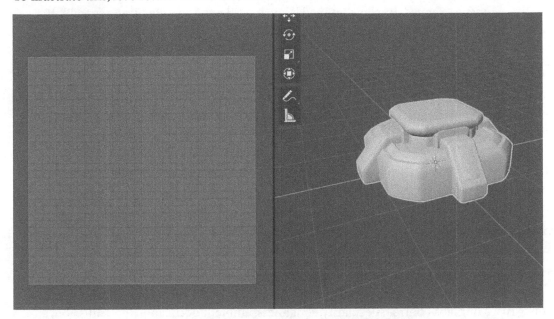

Fig. 5.17 – The turret base seen in the UV Editing workplace

In order to see the turret base unwrapped, we need to be in Edit mode on the right side, and we *need to have something selected*. That last point is important because it can be confusing and frustrating if nothing is showing up on your UV map.

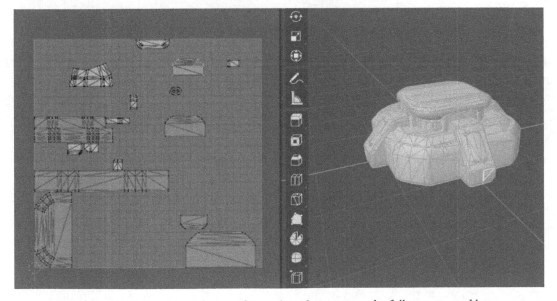

Fig. 5.18 – In Edit mode with everything selected, we can see the fully unwrapped base

What we can see in *Fig 5.18* is that not only has the mesh been divided along the seams, but the geometry was so complex that the UV map has been separated into several **UV islands** (one of which is highlighted in orange). We will deal with these more later.

Materials 101

Textures and materials are often referred to interchangeably (I can be guilty of this), but they are actually two different things. A texture, as mentioned, is a 2D image. It's a grid of pixels that have RGB values defining the intensity of their red, green, and blue channels. Very often a texture will have an **alpha** value for each pixel as well. This controls the transparency, or opacity, of the pixel. Textures with an alpha channel are referred to as being in an **RGBA** pixel format.

A material, on the other hand, is a collection of all the things that go into defining the visual surface qualities of an object. These can include several different types of textures as well as values that define things such as the metallic shininess of a surface.

The most common types of textures used in a material are the diffuse map (also known as the albedo or color map) and the normal map, which affects how light strikes the surface. Other types of maps control specularity, roughness, ambient occlusion, light emission, and others. We'll explore some of these later.

So, we've covered the high-level concepts of how you can unwrap and map a mesh in order to apply materials, but the specifics are different in every program. Let's start to apply what we've learned.

Unwrapping and texturing the Wall

The texture we will use for the wall is from the same free library as the one we used for the floors. It is called `eU_wallpanel4_BaseColor.png`. Find it on your disk and note the location because we will need it shortly.

Just before we unwrap the wall, we are going to clean up and simplify the geometry. Simple is always better. Let's focus on getting rid of faces that won't be seen: the sides and bottom of the wall. I am going to stop being explicit about changing selection modes. You can assume that if I'm talking about manipulating a vertex, edge, or face, then you should be in the correct mode. Double-check your mode if nothing seems to be happening.

Let's start the cleanup this way:

1. Starting in Object mode, select your wall and *Shift + H* to hide everything else. *Tab* into Edit mode.

2. Swing around to the Back view by pressing *Numpad 1* then *Numpad 9* to 'flip' the view.

3. Enter Edit Mode.

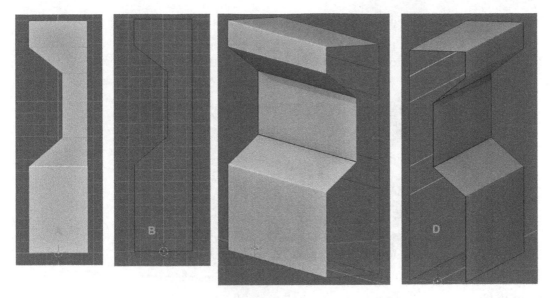

Fig. 5.19 – Dissolving and deleting faces and edges

4. Shift-select the front faces (**A**) and then right-click and choose **Dissolve Faces**. This will leave you with one big face.

5. Right-click again and choose **Delete Faces** (**B**).

6. Also, be sure to delete the bottom face (**C**). Delete the edge at the bottom connecting the front and the back.

7. Switch to the Front and get rid of the bottom edge connecting the front and the back (**D**).

8. Select the four inner edges on the back and right-click to **Dissolve Edges**. You now basically have a single surface that is folded, and it has no sides or bottom.

Cleanup complete. Doctor, the patient is now ready for the operation.

Working in the UV Editing Workspace

Now we're really getting somewhere. UV Editing can be very confusing at first, but it can get to be fun. One important point to drive home is that the exact same transformations (rotate, and so on) you use in modeling, you can also use on the vertices, edges, and faces in the UV Editor.

Let's begin the unwrapping process:

1. Switch into the UV Editing workspace by choosing its tab from the top of the screen.

2. Select the **Image** button and choose **Open**. Locate eU_wallpanel4_ BaseColor.png.

Fig. 5.20 – Select the workspace then open the wall image

3. If the image view is too large, shrink it down with your scroll wheel.

    The workspace has two panes: the UV Editor on the left and the 3D space on the right. You should see your wall on the right.

4. Select all with *A* and then choose **UV | Smart UV Project**.

Fig. 5.21 – Smart UV Project is a helper tool for unwrapping

To see what this mapping looks like, we will give the wall a material.

5. In the **Materials** tab of the **Properties** pane, create a **New** material named Wall01 MAT.

6. Click the dot next to **Base Color**, choose **Image Texture**, then open the dropdown to select eU_wallpanel4_BaseColor.png:

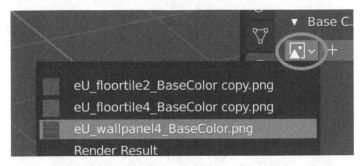

Fig. 5.22 – Find your image in the drop-down list

7. You need to turn on **Material Preview**. Depending on your monitor size, you may need to temporarily expand your 3D view to access the icon. If so, drag the screen divider until you can see the icon to click it. You can also use the mouse wheel to scroll the visible icons.

Fig. 5.23 – Resize the panes with the screen divider then click Material Preview

8. If you expanded your view, restore it now.

9. The UVs got unwrapped sideways. Let's fix that. In the Editor Pane, select everything (*A*).

10. In the UV editor window, use *A* to select all then *R* to rotate everything 90-degrees clockwise.

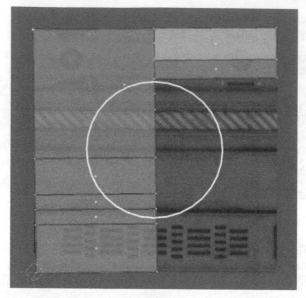

Fig. 5.24 – Use the rotate tools to align the UVs horizontally

This is a step in the right direction, but the actual mapping is still all over the place. What you can do is select a face in the 3D pane and see the corresponding shape in the UV map. Then you can use the transformation tools to alter and place the shape.

In this example, I've selected the lower wall panel on the right side and the corresponding shape on the left is too small:

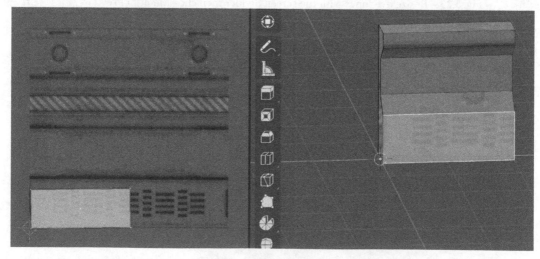

Fig. 5.25 – The UV unwrap for the panel is too small

To fix this, you can select the top and right edges of the UV shape and move them (with the good old *G* key) so that it covers the whole lower rectangular shape of the texture image.

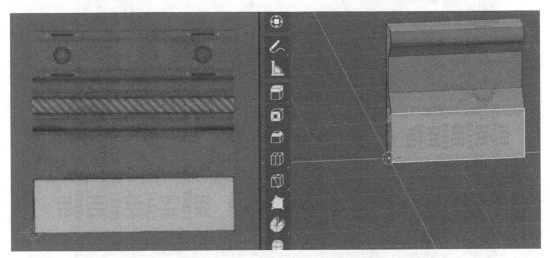

Fig. 5.26 – The problem is fixed by resizing the UV rectangle

You can do this same process for each face of the wall. I chose a non-descript blank metal for the top and back of the wall. Here is what my UV map wound up looking like:

Fig. 5.27 – Map it according to your taste. Try using a different image even!

My wall wound up looking like this:

Fig. 5.28 – My final mapping. Remember that the texture will improve in Unity

And now for the final trick of this chapter.

Unwrapping and texturing the wall corner

The process we will go through to unwrap the corner is *exactly* the same as for the wall. It's just that the corner shape is more complex. So, I will abbreviate a lot of the instructions and if you get confused, you can refer back to the last section.

We're in the home stretch. Here's what to do:

1. To start, go back to the Layout workspace and in Object mode, unhide everything with *Alt + H*. Select the corner piece and hide everything else with *Shift + H*.

2. Switch to the UV Editing workspace. We'll refer to this figure:

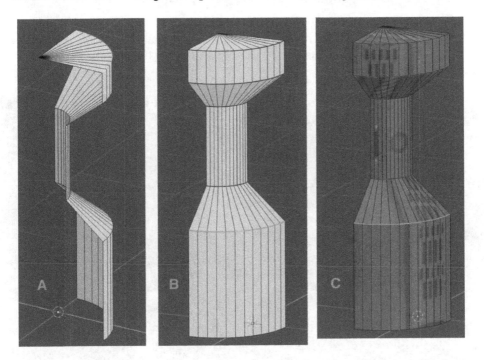

Fig. 5.29 – Cleaning and mapping the wall corner. Steps 4, 5, and 6 will reference this figure

3. Use the drop-down menu in the Properties pane to assign the **Wall01 MAT** material.

4. Delete all faces, edges, and vertices that will not be visible. This includes the bottom (**A**). You may encounter situations where there are multiple vertices in the same spot that you want to delete. You can toggle X-Ray mode to be able to box-select everything in a spot.

5. Mark five seams on the corner (**B**). A great shortcut is to press *Alt + click* an edge to select the whole row of edges. Once selected, right-click and choose **Mark Seam**. Do this for all five.

6. Select all with *A*, then from the top menu on the right side, choose **UV | Smart UV Project**. The corner is now unwrapped but poorly mapped (**C**).

7. On the left side, use your move, rotate, and scale tools to create a pleasing UV mapping. Remember that in addition to being able to manipulate vertices, edges, and faces, the UV editor also allows you to manipulate **UV islands**. I wound up being happy with this:

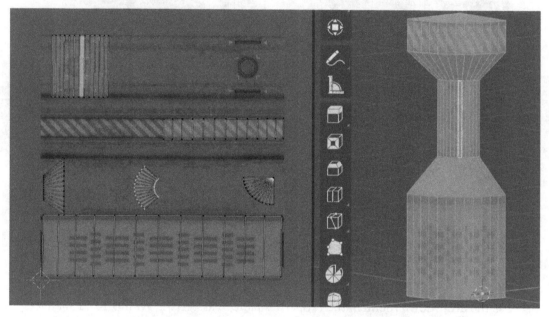

Fig. 5.30 – Create a mapping you like with your transform tools

8. When you have something you like, switch back to the Layout workspace and unhide everything with *Alt + H*.

9. Admire your handiwork!

Fig. 5.31 – You've really "turned a corner" with what you are capable of!

That's all for this chapter. I can't wait to get our structures into Unity and start playing around, but there's more to do first in Blender. Stay tuned!

Summary

Another amazing chapter full of discovery. I hope you don't feel overwhelmed by all you are learning. Go at a pace you are comfortable with. Everyone learns differently and remember that the real learning happens off the page.

In this chapter, we started off by very abstractly talking about modular design and the fundamentals of texturing. We created a plan for our mini-game level layout and then we spent a good deal of time dealing with UV unwrapping as we created a floor, wall, and corner piece.

Be sure you are comfortable with what we covered in this chapter because everything that follows builds on what we've done so far. By all means create other floors, walls, and corners! Use different textures or make your own.

Next up: we'll create more sophisticated scenery and start to learn Blender animation with sci-fi blastdoors!

6
Living It Up: Adding Fun with Animation

"Life. Don't talk to me about life."

— Marvin the paranoid android

When it comes to animation for games, you have a lot of options. In *Chapter 4, Asset Assimilation: Returning to Unity*, we learned how to do very simple tweening animation using iTween, but that is just the very beginning of what you can do. The animation systems in Blender and Unity have different tools and different strengths and weaknesses. Basic object animation in Blender is straightforward although you can go deeper and deeper and get more sophisticated. Unity's Mecanim animation system offers great special features for dealing specifically with humanoid characters and its Timeline (not to be confused with the Blender Timeline!) feature makes cutscenes and other sequences easy to work with. Going forward, we will learn how to animate in both Blender and Unity.

In this chapter, we will do the following:

- Learn some general animation concepts
- Explore Blender's animation capabilities with the Timeline
- Create and animate two versions of a sci-fi blast door
- Texture the doors and export them for use in Unity

By the end of the chapter, not only will we have some great new pieces to add to our Unity minigame but you will have the skills and knowledge to create your own unique ones whenever you want!

Technical Requirements

We're back in Blender for this chapter, so you'll need that handy. And we'll make use of some of the free textures you downloaded from the Asset Store, so you should know their folder location. Also, if you happen to know the deactivation codes for Earth's orbital defenses, why don't you go ahead and post those on the Packt website? You know, just for fun.

The supporting files for this chapter can be found here: `https://github.com/ PacktPublishing/Mind-Melding-Unity-and-Blender-for-3D-Game- Development/tree/main/Chapter06`

The code in action video for this chapter can be found here: `https://bit.ly/3npGBKF`

Understanding Basic Animation Concepts

Animation always involves some kind of changes over time. Your 3D objects can be animated in several ways:

- You can *directly* move the object as a whole, changing its position, orientation, or size over time.

- You can *indirectly* animate the object through inherited animation, causing the object to move based on the movement of another object (for example, its parent, an armature/bone, and so on).

- You can deform the object, animating its vertices.

Other things can be animated as well, including audio properties, material properties, and more.

Keyframes

When we introduced iTween to animate our turret in Unity, we introduced the notion of **tweening**. Tweening--or "interpolation," if you want to sound smart—is the process of transitioning between two values or states. With our turret, we interpolated the rotation (see how smart I sound?), but we could just as easily have tweened any other transformation, such as position or scaling. It doesn't stop there, however. Any time you have two different values, you can potentially interpolate between them, such as loud to soft audio or opaque to transparent colors.

A **keyframe** represents the value(s) of one or more animated properties at a moment in time. One keyframe by itself is not much use, but at soon as you have at least two of them you can start animating. For example, a keyframe might capture the values of an object's position and rotation. Two of these keyframes could represent the start and end states of the object. Three of them would allow for an intermediate state between the start and end, and so on.

In Blender you can set keyframes on almost anything: this includes the three basic transformations we have encountered before (translation, rotation, and scaling) as well as materials, custom properties, and advanced features such as constraints and drivers.

> **Constraints and Drivers**
>
> **Constraints** and **drivers** are advanced animation-control features that we will not get to use, but they are good to know about. A constraint is a kind of limit or control on animation properties. A simple example would be a joint that can only bend so far. A constraint might be a numeric value or it could even be another object. A driver is a similar idea except that the animation limits are dictated by a mathematical function or expression.

There are, of course, many other animation concepts besides keyframes and interpolation/tweening, but if you have a handle on those, you're ready to move ahead.

Animating in Blender

Due to Blender's customizable nature, you *could* animate in any of the default workspaces, but why re-invent the wheel? Blender gives us an Animation workspace for free, so let's have a look at that. Open a new Blender project, add a Suzanne mesh (**Add > Mesh > Monkey**), and now select the **Animation** workspace from the default workspaces at the top of the screen.

Fig. 6.1 – Choose this preset, but remember you can customize or create your own workspaces

A lot of the Animation workspace should look familiar by now. Let's break down what you see:

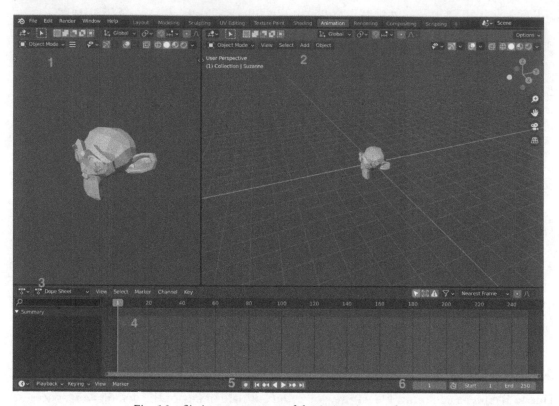

Fig. 6.2 – Six important areas of the Animation workspace

In *Fig 6.2*, area **1** is a camera view. If you deleted the default startup camera as we did previously, the view will really just look suspiciously like the 3D view without the grid lines and X, Y axes, otherwise, you will see your scene framed the way the camera sees it. This would be useful if we were using Blender to create an animation rendered to video (we are not).

Area **2** is the good old 3D view we know and love. If you've had a mindwipe and it looks unfamiliar, refer back to *Chapter 3, Entering the Blender Zone for the First Time*.

Area **3** is where things start to get interesting. In the Animation workspace, at the bottom left of your screen is the **Dope Sheet** panel. This is based on a tool of classical 2D hand-drawn animation, where animators make a chart showing exactly where each drawing, sound, and camera move will occur and for how long. In the hand-drawn world, this can also be called an **exposure sheet**. The dope sheet can give you an overview of all keyframes in your project, but this can get confusing so we will start more simply.

Area **4** is a **timeline** where you can place and manipulate keyframes. Note that this is distinct from the **Timeline** editor, which you can also use for animation for a single object at a time. Yes, confusing, I know. We are, in fact, going to first focus on the Timeline editor, which is sneakily hidden along the bottom of your screen and gives you access to playback controls and frame information (see that little clockface icon at the lower left?).

We are going to shrink the Dope Sheet panel and expand the Timeline panel. To do this, hover your mouse over the separator between the Timeline and the Dope Sheet. Your cursor should turn into a little bar with arrows pointing up and down. Drag the bar upward to reveal the Timeline and shrink the Dope Sheet. This is hard to get a screen capture of, but you should position your mouse here:

Fig. 6.3 – Hover over the separator until you see the drag bar cursor. Then drag upward

We could remove the Dope Sheet entirely, but we'll leave it for now and keep moving. You should now have easy access to the Timeline editor at the bottom of your screen, like so:

Fig. 6.4 – The Timeline panel with the Dope Sheet editor resting on top

The Timeline packs a lot of punch. It has many capabilities, but basically, it allows you to view all your keyframes, add or remove them, move them around, and scrub your animation forward and backward to test it. The Timeline works with both 3D scene objects as well as armatures (bones), which we will get into when we learn about character rigging.

Fig. 6.5 – Familiarize yourself with the most important Timeline features

In *Fig 6.5*, on the left, you can see Timeline's most important feature, the **playhead**, which shows you the current moment in your animation that you are viewing. The simplest way to move the playhead is just to drag the keyframe number in the highlighted box.

In the middle of *Fig 6.5* you see the sophisticated **transport controls**. These are a handy way to navigate and view your timeline and there are a lot more options available here than just Play and Pause! We will have a closer look when we actually have some keyframes to work with.

On the right side of *Fig 6.5* there is more frame information, starting with the current frame number. (If you're *still* unsure about the current keyframe after having it displayed in two places, it's shown a *third* time by default in the upper left of the 3D view). After the keyframe number is information relating to the starting and ending frames of your sequence. Blender has a preview mode that allows you to focus in on just a certain section of your keyframes while you are working on them. You can use the mouse wheel to zoom in and out of your keyframe view.

The left and right arrow keys will move you to the previous or next frames respectively, and the up/down arrows will jump you forwards and back between the next and previous keyframes.

If you don't want to use key controls, you can use the transport controls, which I'll quickly break down.

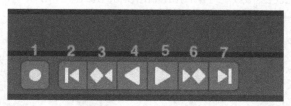

Fig. 6.6 – A reference for the Timeline transport controls

Use *Fig 6.6* for the following explanations:

- Button **1** is a toggle for **Auto-Keying**, which we will come back to once we cover the basics of adding keyframes.

- Button **2** jumps to the start of the animation.

- Button **3** moves to the previous keyframe, if any.

- Button **4** plays the whole animation *in reverse*, which I've never needed to do, but—who knows?—it could come in handy.

- Button **5** plays your animation forwards. The button turns into a pause key when you are playing.

- Button **6** jumps to the next keyframe.

- Button **7** jumps to the end of the animation.

Okay, just before we set some keyframes, let's talk about the frame rate.

Frame rate

By default, Blender will play back at 24 frames per second, which is the common FPS (frames per second) of the cinema/animation world. Games, however, commonly chug along at 60 FPS, sometimes more. So, does that mean you should always use 60 FPS for games? Not necessarily.

The higher the frame rate, the smoother the perceived motion, but the more there is to animate and the more overall animation data there is to store. Games running at 60+ FPS can actually take **sub-samples** of animation data recorded at a lower FPS to then **up-sample** and play back at the higher rate. Most games that run at 60 FPS are actually modeled at 30 FPS. Why 30 FPS? 30 FPS makes the up-sampling very efficient since it just needs to be doubled.

You can change the rate of animation in the **Properties** panel at the lower right of the screen. Look for the Output tab, which has an icon that looks like a printer. See *Fig 6.7*. Go ahead and change your frame rate to 3 0 FPS:

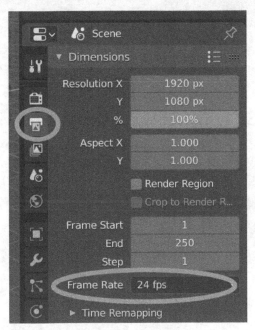

Fig. 6.7 – Adjust your frame rate under the Output properties tab

Once you have the proper frame rate set, you are ready to get busy with keyframes.

Working with Keyframes

We've talked a lot about how to view keyframes. How about we learn how to create some? Good thinking!

You should still have Suzanne waiting patiently in your Blender scene. Now do the following:

1. Be sure the Timeline playhead is at frame **1**.

2. With Suzanne selected, go ahead and move her somewhere, it doesn't matter where. I'm moving her a bit on the Y axis: *G* then *Y*.

3. With your cursor within the 3D view, press *I* to pull up the **Insert Keyframe Menu**.

You're looking at a list of all the different **channels** you might want to make a keyframe for. Select **Location** at the top of the menu.

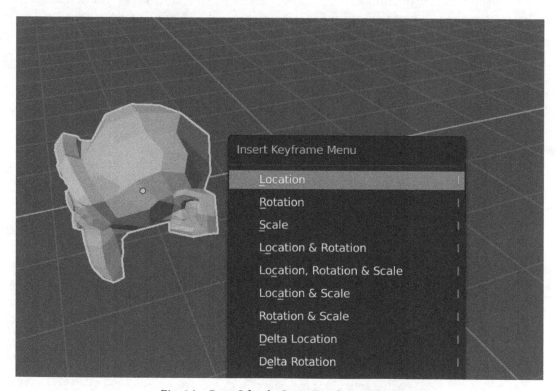

Fig. 6.8 – Press I for the Insert Keyframe Menu

You should immediately notice a change over on the right side in the Properties panel:

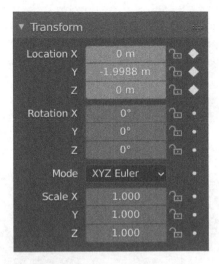

Fig. 6.9 – The Location display has changed after pressing I

You'll notice that the **X, Y, Z** values have gotten highlighted and the dots to the right have become diamonds.

The diamonds are an alternative way of setting keyframes and a filled diamond indicates that the channel contains a keyframe at the current frame of the playhead.

The color of the channel indicates its state as explained below.

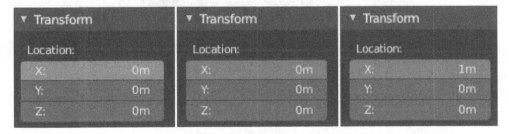

Fig. 6.10 – Properties have different colors and menu items for different states

Fig 6.10 can't show you this information, so refer to your computer screen to see that the state colors for a channel are:

- Gray – the channel is not animated (default).
- Yellow – the channel is keyframed at the current frame.
- Green – the channel is keyframed at a different frame.
- Orange – the value has changed from the keyframed value.

In order to not have to specify what channels you want to capture every time you add a keyframe, you can choose a **keying set**, which allows you to set the channels you are interested in once. You can choose this from the top of the Timeline panel by clicking **Keying** and then, from the popup, clicking within the space next to the keys on the left and selecting **Location, Rotation & Scale**. See *Fig 6.11*. Note that you can change your keying set at any time:

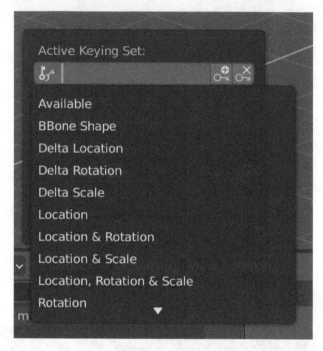

Fig. 6.11 – Keying set options

Now then. Your mission is to go to several different points in the timeline and create new keyframes to get some practice. Go to a frame, change some combination of location, rotation, and scale and then press *I* to create a keyframe. Do this four to five times or so. If you are daring, you can use the multi-transform tool from the Toolbar.

Tip: Two Common Mistakes to Watch Out For

The two most common animation mistakes are: 1) Forgetting to set a keyframe. This can happen when you concentrate so much on adjusting the transforms and moving the playhead that you forget to press *I* to create a keyframe. 2) Overwriting a keyframe. This often happens when you make lots of changes and press *I* to keyframe, but you forget to move the playhead. Beware!

Once you have some keyframes created, use the arrow keys to jump around between frames and keyframes, scrub the playhead to preview your beautiful animation, and try playing your animation by pressing the play button or the spacebar.

> **Tip: Disappearing Keyframes**
>
> Huh? What happened? You might find that you can still scrub the animation and play it, but your keyframes seem to have disappeared. Don't panic! You have probably unselected your animated object by accident. Just re-select it again and your keyframes should re-appear.

Keyframes can be manipulated like many other objects in Blender. They can be copied, cut, pasted, and duplicated. They can be selected with the *A* key. They can be moved with (*G*)rab. They can even be (*S*)caled! Experiment until you are ready to move on.

Auto-keying

If you refer back to *Fig 6.6*, which showed the transport controls, I mentioned that the circle marked as **1** is the toggle for **auto-keying**, which is a convenience feature to help you avoid making the mistake of forgetting to add keyframes. With auto-keying on, any change you make to an object's location, rotation, or scale will create a keyframe. The potential downside is that it is very easy to create keys that you don't mean to. It's recommended that you get comfortable with manual keyframing before you use auto-keying.

When you're ready, here is one more thing besides keyframes that can be added to the Timeline: **markers**.

Markers

Markers are a label for a point in time that has whatever meaning you assign it. They are like a reminder or a signpost for you and they don't actually affect anything. You might, for example, create a marker where a foot contacts the ground, so you know where you want to add a sound effect.

Markers appear at the bottom of the timeline panel.

You can create a new marker at the current frame of the animation by hovering over the timeline and pressing *M*. The default name is just going to be the frame number, so you'll want to select the marker and rename it with *Ctrl + M*.

Fig. 6.12 – A marker is selected when its triangle is filled. You'll want to change the default name

With a marker selected, you can also (*G*)rab it to move it to a different frame and you can delete it with *X*.

We have covered a lot in this section and hopefully your head is not spinning (other than the 30 km per second the Earth spins at). We examined the Timeline panel and learned the basics of working with keyframes as well as some of the gotchas to watch out for. We also learned about frame rate and the conveniences offered by Auto-Keying and Markers.

Are you ready to dig into something more concrete—er, metal? I thought so!

Creating Animated Blastdoors

We are going to make two blastdoors. The first version will be a simple one that is a single piece we animate on the Timeline. In our Unity minigame, these will be portals that automatically open and close based on the player's proximity. The second version will look a lot cooler and have multiple pieces that move. This version will be used to create puzzle obstacles in Unity that stay closed until a certain action is performed.

In this chapter, we will focus on modeling both versions, texturing them, and animating them, with the emphasis on the animation.

To create the blastdoors, we are going to follow the same basic process we went through with creating a wall in *Chapter 3, Entering the Blender Zone for the First Time*, but we will learn about a new workspace and use some new tools along the way! We'll break down the creation of the doors into little steps and learn about Modifiers, gain practice with Loop Cuts and using the Timeline, and apply other techniques. Let's do it!

Blastdoor creation scheme

The first thing we will do is create a doorframe that will be shared by both versions of the door. The simple door will only have one part. The more complex version will have three sections and subparts: a top, middle, and bottom that we will animate in more interesting ways.

Creating the Blastdoor Doorframe

There are a lot of steps to creating our cool little blastdoors, but there is nothing too complicated and nothing you can't handle. Go slowly and be thorough. A lot of the steps should be familiar to you. Learn and have fun! Here's how to start:

1. Open your `SpaceEscapeObjects` project, the one that has the floor and walls. Be sure all objects are hidden in the Outliner.

2. Import the human reference model from the book resources and back it away from the origin a little bit (so it'll be in front of the door). Use *G*, then *Y*, then `-1` to move the object -1 units along the Y axis.

3. Add a cube with *Shift + A* then **Mesh | Cube**. Name it `Doorframe` in the Outliner.

4. Let's set dimensions and the location. Open the sidebar with *N* and be sure you have the **View** tab selected.

5. Set the X, Y, Z dimensions to be `4, 1, 2.5` so we'll have a wide door with a good amount of headroom to pass underneath. Set the X, Y, Z location to be `0, 0, 1.25` so the door is sitting exactly on the floor.

6. *Tab* into Edit mode and create a single loop cut in the center with *Ctrl / Command + R*.

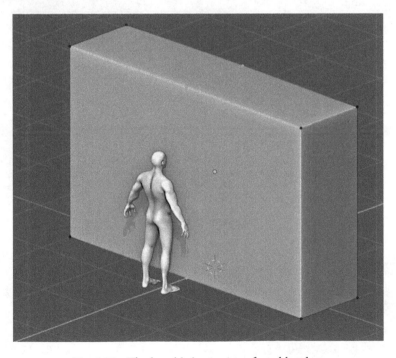

Fig. 6.13 – The humble beginning of our blastdoor

To save us a lot of effort, we are actually only going to model half the door, then use a **mirror modifier** to create the symmetrical other half.

> **Tip: Modifiers**
>
> Modifiers are an extremely powerful feature of Blender that you will use over and over again. They are a way to perform all sorts of *non-destructive* edits and transformations. "Non-destructive" means you aren't actually changing the underlying geometry, so you can always back out of your changes if you need to. Modifiers can also be "stacked up," with the output of a modifier on top affecting the one underneath. Different effects can be achieved by rearranging the modifier stack for an object. When you are finally happy with your creations, you can **Apply** some or all of your modifiers to bake them permanently into your mesh.

By default, the mirror modifier will mirror your geometry around the correct axis. Let's continue on to see how all this works…

7. Turn on X-ray (*Alt* + *Z*), box select all the vertices on the right, and delete them (*X*). Your door will now be cut in half.

8. Turn off X-ray, return to Object mode, and open the **Modifiers** tab of the Properties pane.

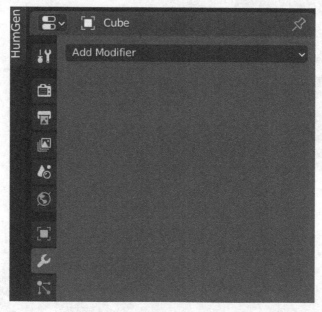

Fig. 6.14 – Choose the wrench icon to open the Modifiers tab.

We're about to take a big step into the wonderful world of Modifiers. There's no going back now!

9.   Choose **Mirror** in the modifier pop-up window (*Fig 6.15*).

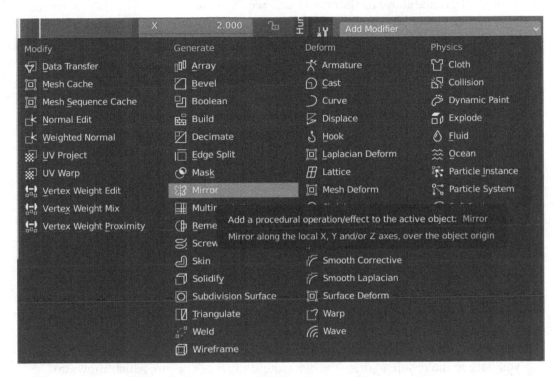

Fig. 6.15 – There are a lot of modifiers to choose from!

Like magic, it will seem that the right side of your door has been restored. This is half true. What's happening is that everything on the left side of the door is being mirrored around the X axis onto the right side.

We're going to add some **loop cuts** that will allow us to shape a doorframe. Toggle into Edit mode and *Ctrl / Command + R* to create two edge loop cuts, one horizontal and one vertical. Slide them to match the image. Make sure the horizontal one leaves enough clearance above the human's head. See *Fig 6.16*.

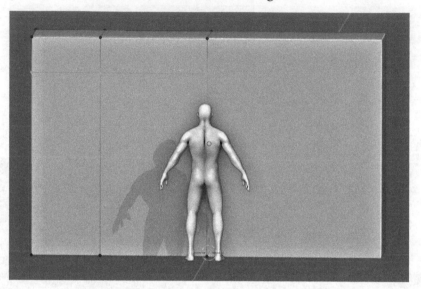

Fig. 6.16 – The loop cuts will be mirrored because of the modifier

10. Toggle X-ray and then, in the middle, **box select** the front, back, and bottom faces. Box select is the default selection mode of the selection tool. In order to select a face, you have to make sure to draw the box around the face's origin, which shows up as a dot. So, to select the three faces, you need to draw around the three dots. See *Fig 6.17 A*.

11. Delete the three selected faces (front, back, and bottom). Notice how the mirror modifier has completed your doorframe! See *Fig 6.17 B*.

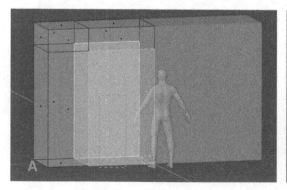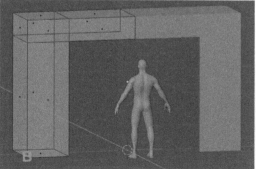

Fig. 6.17 – Box select around the three origins (A), then delete the faces (B). It gets mirrored!

Our doorframe is almost complete, but by deleting those faces we have created a gap that will be visible in gameplay. We need to fill that.

12. Turn off X-ray and move your view to see the inside of the archway. Press *Ctrl + 2* to enter Edge selection mode and select the bottom edge of the archway (*Fig 6.18 (A)*).

13. Press *F* to create a new face, *Fig 6.18 B*. Notice how Blender was smart and was able to figure out how to make a face from only one selected edge!

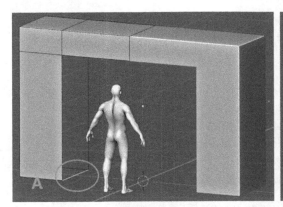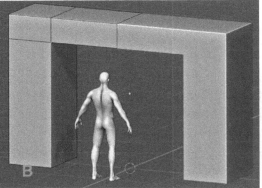

Fig. 6.18 – Select the bottom edge (A) then fill in the missing face (B)

Okay, one final tweak and then we can move on. See how the top piece of the door is split? There's no need for that. We'll get rid of the division and have it be sort of a lintel.

14. Use *Alt* + right-click to **loop select** the edges at the top (*Fig 6.19*).

Fig. 6.19 – Top edge loop selected (back edge is not shown)

If you're not sure if you've selected all three edges, you can swing your view around to the other side to see or you could toggle X-ray. And remember, loop selecting is just a convenience. You could always shift select each edge to add it to your selection. Blender gives you options!

15. Right-click to open the context menu and choose **Dissolve Edges**.

16. Save your file (hopefully you're in the habit of saving as you go!).

We're done with the doorframe for now. We'll come back to unwrap and texture it later.

Creating the Simple Door

To fill up our doorframe, we are going to create an extremely basic mesh in the interest of getting to more interesting topics more quickly. You know enough from *Chapter 3, Entering the Blender Zone for the First Time*, to make it much more visually compelling if you like. Since we have covered some of the following commands several times, I am not going to be as explicit as previously. (You can use this task as a good test of how much you have internalized. You should practice until most things in this section come easily.)

1. From Object Mode, enter Front view (*Numpad .*).

2. Add a cube and rename it to Door01.

3. Set the X, Y, Z Dimensions to 2.5, .5, 2.2 and the Z Location to 1.1. Your door should now fit neatly into the frame. It's okay if it sticks into the frame a bit. Choose **Object | Apply | All Transforms**.

4. Enter Edit mode and then Face select mode. Select the front face.

5. (*I*)nset the face of the door to a distance that suits you. Leave a big area in the middle.

6. Swing your view to the side and (*E*)xtrude the face a short distance inward. We did something very similar when hollowing out the turret tube in *Chapter 3, Entering the Blender Zone for the First Time*.

7. Swing your view all the way around and give the same treatment to the back face of the door, which is to say, inset it and then extrude it inward.

8. Return to Object mode.

9. Save your work.

It doesn't get much more basic than the door we just made, so let's move ahead quickly and get it animated.

Animating the Simple Door

Remember all that time we put into learning about the timeline and keyframes? It's time to put that knowledge to use in a very basic way. Let's go!

1. Enter the Animation workspace and enlarge the Timeline panel just as we did earlier. Make sure the playhead is on frame **1**.

2. In the Output tab of the Properties pane, set your FPS to 30.

3. Select your door in the 3D View and press *I* to create a keyframe. Choose **Location** from the popup.

4. Skip ahead to frame **15** using either the right arrow or setting the value at the upper right of the Timeline.

5. Set the Z Location of the door to be the negative of whatever it is now. In my example, this is -2.1. This will make the door flush with the floor.

6. Add a keyframe with *I*.

7. Preview (scrub) your animation.

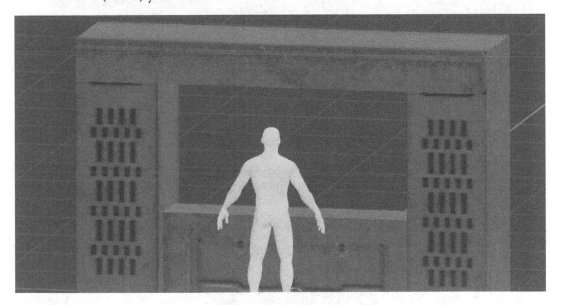

Fig. 6.20 – The single middle piece sinks into the floor. (Busted! We haven't textured it yet!)

Your door now zips open over half a second. Yay!

Creating the Complex Door

The complex door is going to have three sections--top, middle, and bottom—that will each have sub-parts, and the whole thing will look much more interesting when opening and closing. Here's what we're going to do:

1. Start again in the Layout workspace and hide `Door01`.

2. Create another cube and name this `DoorTopA`.

3. Set its X, Y, Z Dimensions to `2.5`, `.5`, `.2` and the Z Location to 2. This should create a thin bar at the top of the doorframe. >> Be sure to **Apply** your transform! <<

4. Press *Shift* + *D* to Duplicate the object and (*G*)rab it on the (*Z*) axis to move it below the first object with just the tiniest bit of overlap. Name it `DoorTopB`.

5. Scale the object `.9` on the Y-axis and apply your transform.

6. Repeat *steps 4* and *5* to create `DoorTopC`. Don't forget to apply your transforms!

You should now have this:

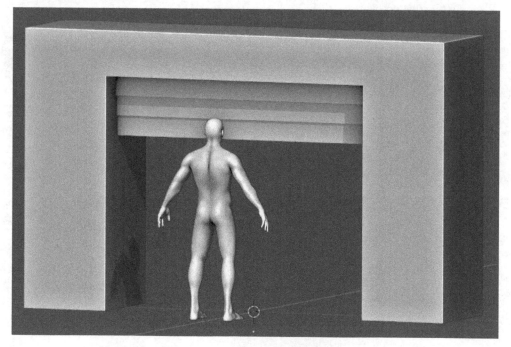

Fig. 6.21 – The three sections of the door top

Parenting these objects together will make animation easier, so do this:

7. Select `DoorTopC` then shift select `DoorTopB`. Then press *Ctrl / Command + P* then **Object** to set the parent relationship.

8. Select `DoorTopB` and shift select `DoorTopA`. Then press *Ctrl / Command + P* then **Object** to again set the parent relationship.

The top piece (A) now has a child (B), which has a child (C). All of these will animate upward.

Creating the middle of the door

The middle of the door will eventually wind up having four pieces. Two will retract to the left and two to the right. First, we need to create the basic shape, which will give us both the middle and the bottom of the door. To do that, follow these steps:

1. Create another cube and name this `DoorMidA`.

2. Set its X, Y, Z Dimensions to `2.5`, `.4`, `1.6` and the Z Location to `.8`. (Careful you are setting Dimension and not Scale! It's an easy mistake!)

3. This should fill the lower region of the door. We will go on to carve this into smaller pieces. Be sure to **Apply** your transform.

4. Enter Edit mode and press / on your Numpad. This will enter **Local** view mode, which shows you *just* the object being edited. It is similar to the hide functionality but separate and more convenient. We are going to need to remember to leave the Local view when we're done.

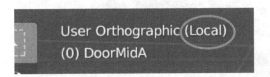

Fig. 6.22 – Local viewing is indicated at the upper left of your display

We're going to explore a different type of mirroring than the mirror modifier we used to create the simple door. For the complex door, we are going to first create all the left side pieces we need and then, at the end, create copies that we flip with the **mirror command**. (It's a command, not a modifier.)

5. With Face select, select the front face and press *Ctrl / Command + R* to add a vertical loop cut down the middle of the face.

6. Switch to vertex select and delete (*X*) the vertices on the right, just like we did with the first door. Select the new right-side vertices and create a (*F*)ace to cover the gaping hole.

Fig. 6.23 – Cover the hole with a new face

7. We are going to add two loop cuts, one vertical and one horizontal, so that our door piece is divided into quarters.

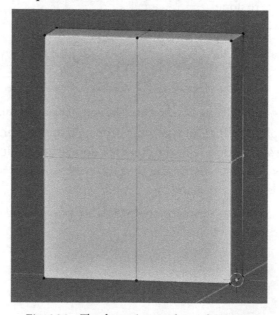

Fig. 6.24 – The door piece with two loop cuts

8. To create a more interesting sci-fi shape, we are going to perform an **edge slide**. In Edge select mode, select the edge on the left edge of the door. Press *G* two times in rapid succession and slide the edge downward close to halfway:

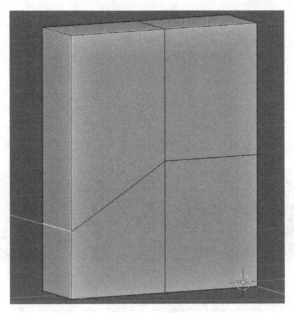

Fig. 6.25 – The door after the edge slide

9. Now we are going to perform a maneuver that we've done before: we're going to duplicate the lower elements and separate them out into their own object. To begin, toggle X-ray (*Alt + Z*).

10. Select all the edges from the middle downwards. Duplicate them with *Shift + D*, then right-click to **Separate | Selection**. Name the new object DoorBottom and hide it using the eye icon toggle in the Outliner.

11. Back on DoorMidA, select everything on the very bottom and delete the *vertices*, which should leave you with this:

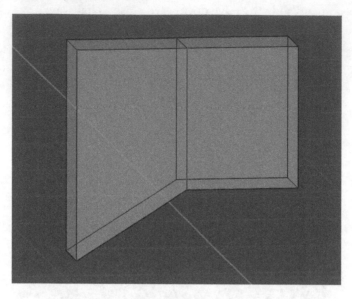

Fig. 6.26 – The middle section is nearly done

12. Select all the vertices from the middle to the right, duplicate them, and separate them into their own object, which you name DoorMidB and then hide. Do you remember how to do all that?

13. Back on DoorMidA, select the right-hand vertices and delete. Exit Local view with *Numpad /*.

14. Unhide DoorMidB and go back to Solid view by toggling X-ray off. Select DoorMidB first, then shift select DoorMidA, making it the active object. Right-click and choose **Parent | Object**. The small right piece should now be the child of the left piece.

15. Here's where we copy everything and flip it. With A and B still selected, *Shift + D* to duplicate and immediately right-click and choose **Mirror | X Global**. The cool thing is that the correct parent-child relationships will also be mirrored.

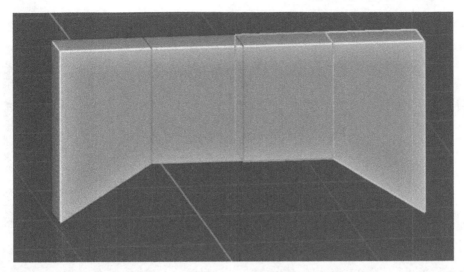

Fig. 6.27 – The middle door parts: DoorMidA_L, DoorMidB_L, DoorMidB_R, and DoorMidA_R

16. For sanity's sake let's do a little renaming, distinguishing left-side parts and right-side parts. Refer to *Fig 6.27* to rename the parts: `DoorMidA_L`, `DoorMidB_L`, `DoorMidB_R`, `DoorMidA_R`. The big idea when we animate is that the B parts will first slide into the A parts and the A parts will slide into the frame.

17. Save your work.

Well, we finished the middle (which you could make a lot more complex if you wanted to), but we are more than two-thirds done, and the hardest parts are behind us.

Finishing the bottom of the door

We are very, very close to *finally* being ready to animate the complex door. We just need a tiny bit of work on the door bottom. Patience, grasshopper.

1. In Object mode, make sure `DoorBottom` is visible and select it.

2. *Shift + D* to duplicate, then right-click and **Mirror | X Global** just like we did with the middle door. What we are going to do differently this time is select both pieces and *Ctrl / Command + J* to **join** them into one object.

What's this, though!? Yeccch! It looks kind of funky!

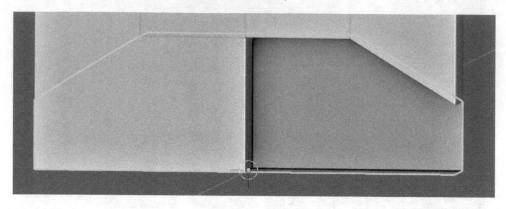

Fig. 6.28 – Gadzooks! What's going on with this object?

What's happened is that Blender has gotten confused about what is the inside and the outside of the object and the **face normals** have gotten messed up. Luckily, this is very easy to fix.

> **Tip: Normals**
>
> Normals are a huge topic in 3D modeling and texturing and we will only scratch the surface here. Basically, normals have to do with the calculations of how light bounces off of an object. They can be used to indicate what the "front" of a surface is and they can also be cleverly manipulated to seem to add "detail" to a surface without actually adding any geometry.

To fix this, follow these steps:

1. *Tab* into Edit mode and select (*A*)ll.

2. Now choose **Mesh | Normals | Recalculate Outside**. Yay! Problem solved! Save your work!

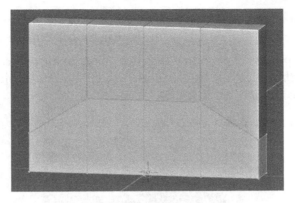

Fig. 6.29 – Normals fixed. That looks much better!

Believe it or not, we are *finally* ready to animate the complex door.

Animating the complex door

Okay, I lied.

A tiny bit more organization before we animate. (Email your complaints to my secretary.)

First, let's admire our handiwork so far. Follow these steps:

1. In Object mode, make everything visible except `Door01` and your walls and floors. You should have something looking very close to this:

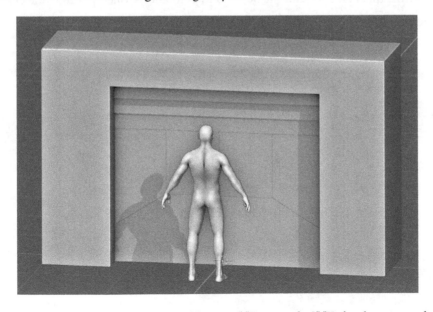

Fig. 6.30 – "Knock, knock." "Who's there?" "Doctor." "Doctor who?" "Yeah, what a great show!!"

2. Let's create a parent object to keep things tidy. Create a plane. Make its dimensions `3, 2, 0` and name it `Door02`. Hide the human model to make animating easier.

3. Go through the process of parenting each door piece to the plane. Remember, first select the piece *then* select the plane, right-click, and **Parent | Object**. Do this for `DoorTopA`, `DoorMidA_L`, `DoorMidA_R`, and `DoorBottom`.

Our collection now has a very clean top level. I approve.

Fig. 6.31 – Good organization increases productivity, leads to success, and cures baldness

4. Choose `Door02` and enter the Animation workspace. Be sure you can see the Timeline panel (the one with the clock icon) across the bottom of your screen.

What we are going to do is set a small number of keyframes on each piece of the door. The top pieces will fold up into each other, as will the left and the right pieces. The bottom will just sink down similar to the simple door. Our animation is going to be 60 frames long because we will show it opening then closing again. Later in Unity, we will turn this into two separate 30-second animations: one opening, one closing.

5. Set the length of the animation to `60` frames.

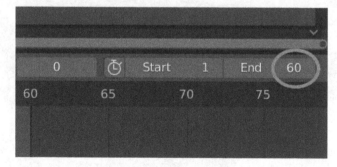

Fig. 6.32 – Set the number of frames at the top right of the Timeline

6. As we did earlier, (*I*) to insert a keyframe on frame 1 and in the Keying popup, choose **Location**. Those are the only keys we care about.

7. Working in Front view (*Numpad 1*) is easiest, so choose that then select DoorTopC.

8. Move to frame 1. Open the sidebar with (*N*). Right-click and **Insert Keyframe**. Move to the last frame (**60**) and add a keyframe there too. This way we will start and end in the same place.

9. Move the playhead to frame **10**.

10. In the 3D view, press *G* then *Z*. Move the door part up so that it is flush with its parent, DoorMidB. Be sure to create a keyframe with *I*.

11. In the Timeline, click to select just the keyframe on frame **10**. Copy it with *Ctrl / Command + C*, move the playhead to frame **50**, and paste it with *Ctrl / Command + V*. Remember we are creating an opening *and* a closing animation so all the keyframes will be mirrored.

Fig. 6.33 – The orange bar shows that the same keyframe is held. The parent's motion will still apply

12. Get used to this process because we are going to do it a lot. Now select DoorTopB.

13. This piece will start moving later. Go to frame **10** and add a keyframe from the sidebar. Go to frame **50** and add another one. This is its twin.

14. Move to frame **20**.

15. In the 3D view, press *G* then *Z*. Again, move the part up so that it is flush with its parent, this time DoorMidA. Again, be sure to create a keyframe with *I*.

16. Any guesses on what's coming up? Select DoorTopA. This will have delayed movement as well. Set a keyframe at frames **20** and **40**.

17. Go to frame **30**. Move the piece up so that it is flush with the doorframe and set a keyframe.

18. Test your work by either scrubbing the playhead or pressing play. All the pieces should fold up out of sight on frame 30.

Fig. 6.34 – By frame 30 all the top parts are nestled in the doorframe

19. Save your work.

Next we'll see how we can animate the middle part of the door.

Animating the door middle

This will be the most time-consuming part, but it is not that long, and it is practically an identical process to animating the top. We will work on the pieces going from the middle out to the sides. Follow these steps:

1. Select DoorMidB_L. Add a keyframe to frames **1** and **60**.

2. Move to frame **20**. G then X and move the part *left* until it is flush with its parent, DoorMidA_L. Add a keyframe.

3. Copy that keyframe and paste it onto frame **40**.

4. Here we go again… Select DoorMidA_L. Add a keyframe to frames **20** and **40**.

5. Move to frame **30**. G then X and move the part *left* until it is flush with the doorframe. Add a keyframe.

We are going to mirror the animation for the right-side parts. You should almost be able to do this on automatic.

1. Select DoorMidB_R. Add a keyframe to frames **1** and **60**.

2. Move to frame **20**. G then X and move the part *right* until it is flush with its parent, DoorMidA_R. Add a keyframe.

3. Copy that keyframe and paste it onto frame **40**.

4. Select DoorMidA_R. Add a keyframe to frames **20** and **40**.

5. Move to frame **30**. G then X and move the part *right* until it is flush with the doorframe. Add a keyframe.

6. Scrub the timeline.

Voila! The middle door sections should separate and move in opposite directions. Save your work.

Animating the door bottom

This will be a piece of cake and we basically already did it with the simple door. We are going to add a "stutter" to its movement just to make it slightly more interesting.

1. Select DoorBottom. Add a keyframe to frames **5** and **55**.

2. Move to frame **15**. Press *G* then *Z* and move the part *down* about halfway to the floor. You can eyeball this. Add a keyframe.

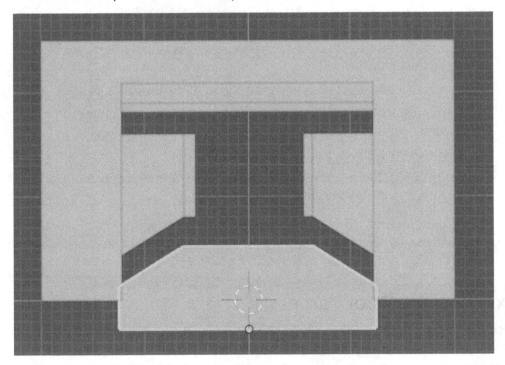

Fig. 6.35 – The bottom will "stutter" or pause in its motion

3. Copy that keyframe and paste it onto frames **20**, **40**, and **45**.

4. Move to frame **30**. *G* then *Z* and move the part the rest of the way *down* until it is flush with the floor. Add a keyframe.

5. That's it! Test the whole thing and save your work.

Well, then. We've hit a milestone. At long last, we have finished modeling and animating the three sections of the complex. Just one major task remains. I'm sure you know what. We must make everything pretty!

Texturing the Blastdoors

It's all coming together as we approach the end of the chapter. This section is only going to be a refresher on UV-unwrapping and texturing. If you are struggling to get the parts unwrapped, go back and review *Chapter 3*, *Entering the Blender Zone for the First Time*, but here is an overview of the whole process:

1. Make sure the object you want to texture has a material slot. Do this from the **Materials Property** tab.

2. Create a new material, if necessary. Set the **BaseColor** type to be an image and select or open that image.

3. In the UV Editing workspace in 3D view, delete faces that will never be seen, then mark the seams on your mesh by selecting edges and right-clicking to **Mark Seam**. It is better to err on the side of having too many seams as that will reduce face distortion/stretching.

4. When you are ready, select everything and choose **UV | Smart UV Project**.

5. To see your textured object, you need to switch your Viewport Shading to Material Preview.

6. Select faces in the 3D View to see them in the UV Editor.

7. Work in the UV Editor to move, rotate, and scale the vertices, edges, and faces until they are covering the texture areas you want.

The following sections, which deal with each piece of the doors again, will be very brief and just call out any particular issues to be aware of as you apply the 7 steps above to each section.

Texturing the Doorframe

Before you can take the frame through the process outlined above, you need to **Apply its mirror modifier** to make the changes permanent. You do this in the Properties Modifiers tab in Object mode:

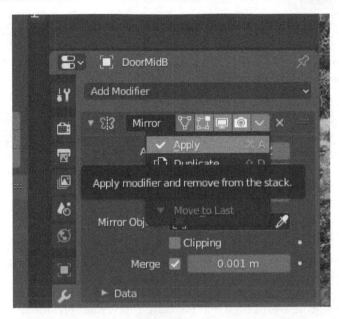

Fig. 6.36 – Modifiers are automatically applied when you export, but don't rely on this

I created a `Doorframe MAT` material and used the same `eU_wallpanel4_BaseColor.png` that we previously used. Follow your own tastes and experiment. Here is what I came up with:

Fig. 6.37 – Use your imagination

Remember, if the overview steps listed above don't help you enough, refer back to the relevant parts of *Chapter 3, Entering the Blender Zone for the First Time*. Go slowly. There are lots of fiddly little bits and it's easy to miss a step and not have anything show up and get frustrated. Stick with it. You can do it!

Don't Freak Out

If you ever go back to Object Mode and it seems like some of your pieces have outright disappeared, make sure you are not in the local viewing (isolation) mode. You can tell because it will say **User Perspective (Local)** on the screen. You can exit with *Numpad /*.

Texturing the Simple Door

Create a `Door MAT` material. You can use the same texture image or a different one of your choosing.

Once in UV Mode, select All and then enter isolation mode with *Numpad /*.

The UV-unwrapping was super-straightforward, and I wound up with this:

Fig. 6.38 – My final simple door

One door down, one to go. The process for the complex door will be exactly the same.

Texturing the Complex Door

I used the same Door MAT material for this door. The parent object, the plane, is just a square, so unwrapping couldn't be easier. If you are feeling ambitious, create a new material for it and use one of the floor textures we haven't used. Keep track though, because we need to know the textures when we are back in Unity.

If you ever have difficulty selecting an object, first go out to Object mode, then re-enter Edit mode and select. This usually works.

One great tip is that in Object mode, you can select multiple objects such as all the top pieces and then jump into the UV Editor to work on them all simultaneously.

Texturing the Bottom

Before unwrapping, first do some cleanup. There are some faces that will never be seen. Then get to work tweaking your UVs. I settled on this:

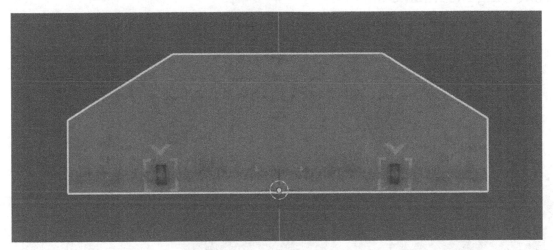

Fig. 6.39 – Nothing too exciting, but—hey!—whaddya want from a bottom piece?

Texturing the Top Parts

There are plenty of faces you can get rid of before unwrapping. Edit all the parts together for convenience. With some UV rotation I did this:

Fig. 6.40 – There are so many different ways you could go with this

Texturing the Middle Parts

Again, editing all the parts simultaneously helps greatly. I came up with this:

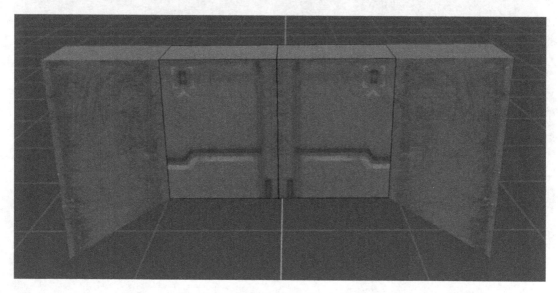

Fig. 6.41 – Is this a-door-able? <groan>

And now, here is everything in all its splendor:

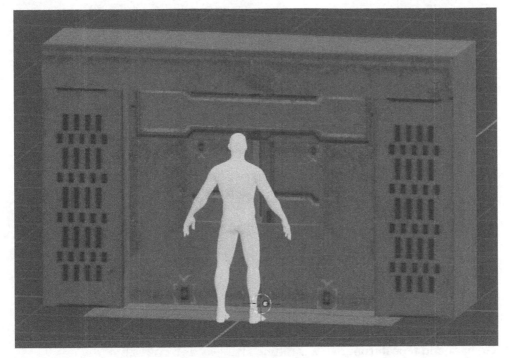

Fig. 6.42 – The final result. Works for me

So we've now textured all the pieces of both doors, which provides us with a single cool look, but you could get a lot more bang for your buck… With all that you know now and all the free textures available, you could make a million cool door variations! In fact, go do that. I'm exhausted!

Exporting Your Goodies

And for our final magic trick, we need to get all our stuff out of Blender so we can get it into Unity. Follow these steps:

1. Enter Object Mode. Remember to leave isolation mode if you are in it.

2. Hide your human figure if it's visible.

3. Let's start with the animated doors. Select **Door01**, make it visible, then press / to enter isolation view.

4. Make sure everything is selected with (*A*).

5. Select all and choose **File | Export FBX**.

6.   Choose **Limit to Selected Objects** and **Forward: Z Forward**.

7.   To export the timeline correctly, make sure to uncheck these two settings:

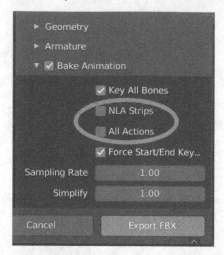

Fig. 6.43 – Don't forget this step. Uncheck these

8.   Click **Export FBX** and save as `door01.fbx`.

9.   Exit isolation, hide **Door01**, and reveal all the parts of **Door02**. Enter isolation.

10. Go back and repeat from *step 5*, this time saving as `door02.fbx`.

11. Continue to do this process. Export `doorframe.fbx`, `wall01.fbx`, `wallcorner01.fbx`, and `floor01.fbx`.

That's it! <sniff> Our babies have left the nest!

Summary

Is it just me or is it every time we reach the end of a chapter it feels like we ran a marathon?

At any rate, CONGRATULATIONS AGAIN! We covered a lot. We learned some basic animation concepts including frame rate, keyframing, and dope sheets, and explored how they are implemented in Blender with the Timeline (one of Blender's several animation tools). Then we went ahead and put that knowledge to practical use by creating cool animated blast doors, planning out how to model them in detail and then animating each piece in the Timeline. Finally, we added some textures to spice up the visuals and exported them for use in our Unity minigame.

I can't wait to see our creations in action back in Unity. Next chapter, we will return to Unity and continue to incorporate what we've built, as well as adding some new game functionality. All systems go!

7
Prep Work: Materials, Grids, and Snapping

"You can't mix matter and anti-matter cold!"

– Starfleet Engineer Montgomery Scott

Here we are, about halfway through our journey, which makes it a moment to look back and to look forward. Paradoxically, we have unlocked an incredible amount of game development capability, yet at the same time we have not really scratched the surface of what we can do.

You now have many options from which to get your game resources: you can work with an artist, you can get them from the Asset Store, or you can create your own simple assets. In this chapter, we will pause to bring together and shape the assets we have created so far, then in the chapters that follow, we will 'up our game', so to speak, and learn how to create more complex things than we have learned so far.

Specifically in this chapter, we will do the following:

- Import all the assets we have created so far and turn them into prefabs.
- Improve the materials of the walls, doors, and floors.
- Explore Unity's Grid and Snap settings.

By the end of the chapter, you will have a much better understanding of what modular level design is all about, and you will have gained confidence and had practice of importing and detailing your own assets. This chapter is the preparation you will need to lay out your level in the next chapter.

Technical Requirements

This chapter will focus on the Unity editor. We will be making use of textures from two different free asset packages available on the Asset Store. If you don't already have these from *Chapter 2, Gathering Our Resources*, download them and import them into your SpaceEscape Unity project:

- **eU Sci-Fi textures set Volume 1**: We used these for the walls and doors.
- **Yughues Free Metal Materials.**: We will use some of these great materials to create different floors.

The supporting files for this chapter can be found here: `https://github.com/PacktPublishing/Mind-Melding-Unity-and-Blender-for-3D-Game-Development/tree/main/Chapter07`

Getting Our Act Together: Collecting Our Great Stuff in Unity

Okay, previously we focused on learning how to create new assets. In this section, we are going to start making use of them. We'll review the import process, then improve the asset materials, then learn how Unity's grid and snap systems are a big help. We wind up laying out a level of our mini-game with the assets we have been working with so far. Here is the asset list to refresh your memory:

- Blaster turret
- Floor
- Wall section
- Wall corner
- Door frame
- Door 1
- Door 2

As I mentioned previously, since the floors are just simple quads, we could've easily made them in Unity.

The blaster turret, which we worked with extensively in *Chapter 4, Asset Assimilation : Returning to Unity*, should already exist as a prefab in your SpaceEscape unity project.

Let's review and expand upon the Unity import process.

Importing into Unity

You have two options to get your `.fbx` file into Unity. As we have covered before, you can simply choose **Assets | Import New Asset** and select the file from the filesystem. A shortcut, though, is to simply drag the file right into Unity and release it in the `Assets` folder of your project window:

1. Regardless of how you import the file, move your mesh file into your `Models` folder. Then you will need to change the import settings in the **Inspector** window.

2. Select the file and in the **Model** tab, check **Bake Axis Conversion**. Scroll further down and click **Apply**. (See *Fig 7.1* for reference).

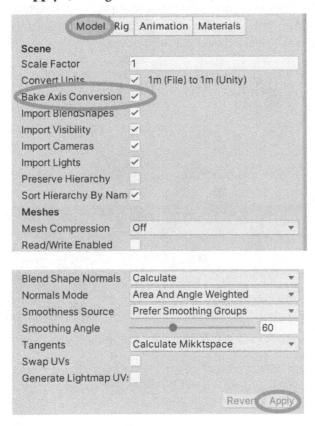

Fig. 7.1 – Check Bake Axis Conversion then click Apply (middle of image omitted)

3. If you want to be completely thorough, you could uncheck **Import BlendShapes**, **Import Cameras**, and **Import Lights** since we don't have any of those. If you do that, click **Apply** again.

4. In the **Animation** tab, uncheck **Import Animation** if there are no animations (for the wall, corner, and doorframe) and then click **Apply**. Otherwise, leave it as is. We will talk about how to import the door animations in a moment.

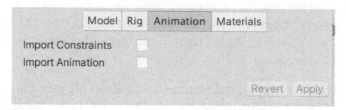

Fig. 7.2 – Toggle animation import based on each model

Lastly, in the **Materials** tab you don't have to change anything, but I want to draw your attention to the fact that if we *had* created a more sophisticated material in Blender, it would be embedded within the .fbx file and we could choose to extract it and work on it in Unity. But like I said, leave this alone right now.

Fig. 7.3 – We could extract sophisticated embedded materials if we had them

So now, go ahead and import everything into your Models folder:

1. If you have not imported your human reference model, you might as well import that. Remember, you can drag .fbx files directly into Unity if you prefer that to using the menu.

2. Import your floor as floor01 exactly as described previously. We will texture this soon.

3. Import `wall01` the same way and while you are at it, bring in `wallcorner01` as well.

4. Importing `doorframe` should be no problem.

5. For `door01` be sure **Import Animation** is *checked* in the **Animation** tab in the **Inspector**. Turn *off* **Model | Bake Axis Conversion** to get the animations to orient right.

Bear in mind that for a commercial project, it would be a good idea to explicitly set some import settings that we are ignoring for our simple project. For example, under **Model**, you could uncheck **Import Cameras**. Under **Rig**, you could set the **Animation Type** to **None**. You can set **Animation** according to whether you had any, and likewise for **Materials**. For all of these, remember you need to click **Apply** to save any changes.

All these things will create minor efficiencies that you might need in a commercial product.

Turning the models into Prefabs

It wouldn't be a bad habit to start turning every model into a prefab as soon as you import it. There isn't really any downside, and you may benefit from its "prefab-ulousness" later even if you don't think you will need it. In just about all but the most trivial scenes it is a Unity best practice to work with prefabs or prefab variants in your scene, as opposed to individual models. This is due to the ability to have changes to a prefab propagate to all its instances.

Prefabs

Many of you are no doubt already familiar with the Unity concept of a **prefab**, or prefabricated game object, but let's quickly recap. A prefab can be thought of as a recipe or a blueprint—changes to the prefab affect every **instance** created from the prefab. If you take a regular model and drag it into your scene five times and then change the material on one version of it—the other four game objects are unaffected. But if you create a prefab and drag five instances of it into your scene, any changes to the prefab will immediately be seen in all the instances.

Unity recently added the ability to create prefabs that are themselves composed of prefabs. This was a feature the dev community had been begging for years and it finally got implemented. Many consider it a 'game changer' in terms of flexibility and productivity.

Turning a Model into a Prefab

To create a prefab from a model imported into your project, first drag the model into your scene hierarchy, making sure the position is at **0, 0, 0** (and it should be, by default).

For Blender-exported models you may find that your model looks okay in the scene, but its X rotation is set to **-89.98**. This is an artifact of the conversion process and rarely, but sometimes, causes difficulty under certain circumstances. Usually, you can safely ignore this.

In an ideal world, your prefab would have no transformations by default (similar to when you **Apply** all transforms to an object in Blender). Some people use the following 'hack' to fix that. For simplicity, we are not going to do this, but until there is a perfect import solution, it is good to be aware of.

First, they create an empty, *untransformed* game object to serve as the root parent of the prefab. Next, they drag the model with the transformation into the parent as its only child. Lastly, they drag the parent into the **Project** window to "prefab-itize" it. Any transformations from that point on happen to the root object and behave normally.

So, we are not going to use this empty game object hack, but still go ahead and turn each model (the wall, floor, and so on) into a prefab by dragging it from the **Hierarchy** window into your Prefabs folder in the **Project** window. When prompted by a popup menu, choose to create an Original Prefab.

The two doors that you import are going to need some special treatment, so that is what follows.

Defining the Door Animations

The process for dealing with imported animation is the same for both doors and you will find that you can generalize it for working with any imported animation. What we are starting out with is one long keyframe sequence, which was our timeline in Blender. What we want to do is define *subsections* of that to become individual animations. In our case, we want an Open and Close animation for each door. When working with third-party character assets, especially older ones, you might often find subsections defined as Idle, Attack1, Attack2, Wounded, Die, and so on.

In the **Inspector**, when you click on the **Animation** tab for one of the doors, you will see a display very similar to *Fig 7.4*.

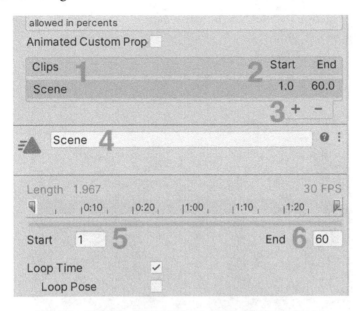

Fig. 7.4 – Details of imported animations in the Inspector

Let me draw your attention to some important details:

1. Below the area labeled **Clips** is a list of named animations imported from your .fbx file. In this example, there is a single sequence named **Scene**.

2. The starting and ending frames of each animation clip (sometimes called a 'take') are listed here.

3. You can add a new clip to the list with the + button. The – button will delete the currently selected clip.

4. You can rename the currently selected clip by clicking here. Be sure to hit *Enter* to save your change.

5. Set the start frame of the current clip here.

6. Set the end frame of the current clip here.

If you scroll down, you can see the animation preview area (you can grow or shrink the height by dragging the handle).

You can play the animation by clicking the arrow button or you can scrub forward and backward by dragging the white line:

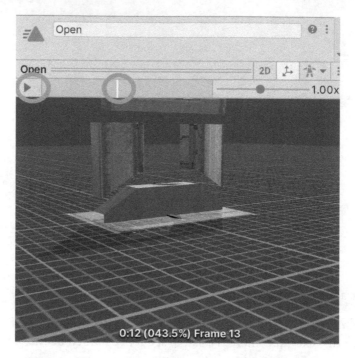

Fig. 7.5 – The animation preview area (with textured door)

So, what you should now do for both of the blast doors is to split the single imported sequence into Open and Close clips:

1. First, create a second clip with the + key. Name the second clip `Close` and set the start frame to **31** and leave the end frame as **60**.

2. Now select the first clip and rename it to `Open`. Leave the start frame as **1** and change the end frame to **30**.

3. Use the scrub bar to preview the clip then be sure to click **Apply** to save your changes.

The following figure shows the two clips that have been created from the total number of animation frames available. Some files you encounter could have many, many more.

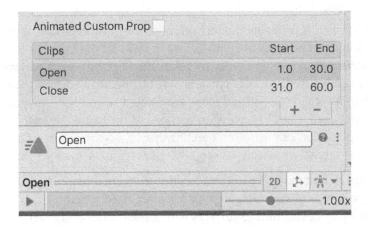

Fig. 7.6 – Be sure to create Open and Close clips for each of your doors

Now that we have everything imported successfully, it's time to spruce things up a bit visually. We're ready to take our visuals to the next level.

Living in a Material World: Materials for Walls, Doors, and Floors

In this section, we'll learn about what goes into a Unity material and then apply that knowledge (and our free texture maps) to make the materials of our assets more visually appealing than just a single flat-looking texture. Unity can create some very sophisticated materials. We are just going to scratch the surface of what you can do and primarily concern ourselves with the following material properties (refer to *Fig 7.7*):

- **Standard shader**: Shaders are an enormous topic. Basically, they are a programmable way of displaying your object and can produce stunning visuals. The Standard Unity shader is versatile and can produce some great looking materials, so we will stick with that.

  There is a big properties section labeled Main Maps. These are texture maps that are used and combined in different ways

- **Albedo map**: The name "albedo" is yet another reason why the people of Earth should be subjugated. "Albedo" does not communicate well what it is. Another name is **diffuse map**, but I prefer a third alternative, **color map**. This is what most people mean when they say "texture map". It most often resembles photographic or painterly surface detail.

- **Metallic map:** This is basically the 'shininess' of the surface. You can control it with a slider. If you specify a grayscale texture map, you can vary the shininess in different areas of the material.

- **Normal map:** This is probably the second most common type of map to specify. We had a brief discussion of normals before in *Chapter 5, On the Level: Making Modular Scenery*. Normals are a way to define how light strikes a surface at a given point. They can be used as a very efficient way of making a surface seem to be more detailed than it actually is. Normal maps are created from high-polygon models and then "texture baked" onto low-polygon versions of the same models. A very good and brief explanation can be found here: `https://cgcookie.com/articles/normal-vs-displacement-mapping-why-games-use-normals`.

- **Height map:** Height mapping is a similar idea to normal mapping, but more expensive computing-wise. Height maps are often used together with normal maps to give extra definition to surfaces with large bumps and protrusions. Height maps are grayscale images, with white areas representing the high areas and black representing low areas.

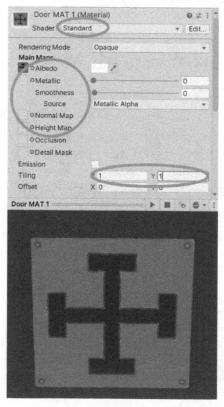

Fig. 7.7 – A material seen in the Inspector and the properties we are concerned with

- **Tiling and Offset**: You may recall from *Chapter 5, On the Level: Making Modular Scenery*, that the UV space used for texture-mapping is a two-dimensional space with a 0, 0 origin in the lower-left corner, ranging up to 1, 1 in the upper right. **Tiling** is how many times your texture repeats in this 0 to 1 range and **Offset** is where your texture begins within this space. Just to purposely confuse you, instead of referring to U and V, Unity uses X and Y for tiling and offset. Or maybe that's actually clearer after all? You decide.

In *Fig 7.7*, in the preview pane at the bottom, the texture appears in its basic state with **Tiling** set to **1, 1** and **Offset** set to **0, 0**, meaning that the texture will display one time across the U and V axes and it will start at its normal origin point with no offset.

In *Fig 7.8*, the left-hand side shows the texture with a 50% offset on the X (or U) axis, while the right-hand side shows a tiling of 3 on both the X and Y (U and V) axes.

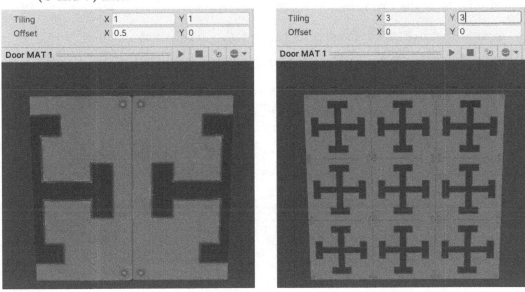

Fig. 7.8 – Examples of offset and tiling in UV space (labeled X and Y in Unity)

Materials are defined primarily by a combination of different types of texture maps. Next up, we will look at the most common map types and how to apply them to our assets.

Creating our new materials

We are going to use four materials for the objects we have so far. They will be created from the free Asset Store packages I mentioned in the *Technical Requirements* section: **eU Sci-Fi textures set Volume 1** and **Yughues Free Metal Materials**, so you should have them imported into your project. To keep things tidy, I moved their folders into the Third-Party folder we created earlier.

First, we'll create materials for the walls, corner, door frame, and doors. Then we'll adapt some existing textures for two floors. You may want to create a ton more floor varieties once you see the process we're using.

In your `Materials` folder, create two materials by right-clicking and choosing **Create | Material**. Give them these names:

- `frame Wall MAT`: For the doorframe, the wall and corner piece.
- `door MAT`: Heh. Doormat. Get it? This is for both door models.

For each of these we are going to specify an **Albedo** map, a **Metallic** map, a **Normal** map, and a **Height** map. The slider settings for **Metallic** and **Height** are a matter of personal preference.

For **frame Wall MAT**, use the dot selector next to the **Albedo Map** label to open the **Select Texture** chooser (see *Fig 7.9*). You can resize the chooser window to get a good preview of the textures.

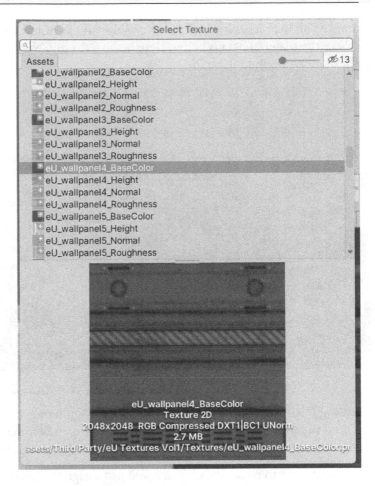

Fig. 7.9 – Click the dot selector to open the Select Texture window

Assign eU_wallpanel4_BaseColor to the **Albedo** map. For the **Metallic** map, assign eU_wallpanel4_Roughness. I put the slider at 0.36, but go with your own tastes. Assign the **Normal** and **Height** maps with the corresponding eU_wallpanel4 textures. I set the height slider at 0.02.

Open your Prefab folder and one-by-one select the wall, the corner and the doorframe and drag frame Wall MAT into the **Element 0** slot of the Prefab's **Materials** section. Alternatively, if you are a more advanced user, you could drag the material onto an instance in the scene and then apply the override back to the prefab in the Inspector.

I dragged all the pieces into my scene, positioned them, and created some point lights to show the material details better. Here is the test I did. Notice how the textures seem to have more depth to them:

Fig. 7.10 – Testing the frame Wall MAT material

Creating the `door MAT` material is ridiculously similar to `frame Wall MAT`. In fact, we used the same texture image when UV-mapping in Blender. I'm creating a separate material in case you want to use a different texture at some point.

If you just want to move ahead, you could just assign the doors the same `frame Wall MAT` and be done.

If you would like a challenge, go back to *Chapter 5, On the Level: Making Modular Scenery*, and remap one or both doors to a new texture such as `eU_wallpanel6_BaseColor` (or any of the others). You would then come back here to Unity, create a new material, and assign all the new texture slots (roughness, normal, and so on).

I went ahead and remapped the doors to `eU_wallpanel6`. Here are my results:

Figure 7.11 – The two doors with improved textures

Now let's deal with floor textures. It's very simple, but slightly tweaky.

Let's create two different floors. You'll see the process quickly and can create as many floors as you like. There are over 40 textures in the Yughues textures pack, many of them excellent, so feel free to go crazy beyond the two I'll use:

1. In your `Prefabs` folder, select `floor01` and press *Ctrl/Command + D* to duplicate it.

2. Rename the new prefab—wait for it!—`floor02`.

3. Put one of each prefab into your scene.

    I chose to use materials **M_YFMM_01** and **M_YFMM_16**. You can find them in the `Materials` folder beneath **YughuesFreeMetalMaterials**.

4. Drag one material to each floor in the scene. Be sure to apply the override in the **Inspector**.

    The new materials look cool, but you'll see an immediate problem: they are too big. Here's where tiling comes in.

5. Choose each material in the Project view and in the **Inspector** set the **X** and **Y** **Tiling** to 4. These numbers can be anything you like. Note: Make sure you are *not* setting the tiling for **Secondary Maps**, which is further down the material's properties. You won't see any changes if you do.

6. If you feel like it, create a test in your scene:

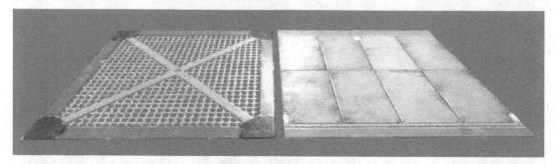

Fig. 7.12 – Two floor tiles illuminated by an invisible point light. Your materials will vary

When you are happy with your floors, we can move on. We're done with improving the materials of our assets, and next, we'll learn some essential tools for laying out levels before we actually go ahead and do it.

Snapping and the Scene Grid

Before we can lay out our mini-game level, we're are going to learn about some Unity features that will save us a lot of hassle and frustration.

Modular mesh creation and level design would not be half as efficient if you had to try to eyeball the correct distances and angles to place things at. Luckily, you don't have to, as all modern 3D software has snapping features to a greater or lesser degree. We have already briefly encountered snapping in Blender, where it can be a huge convenience when modeling. Now it's time to learn about Unity's robust snapping features and how they can help in the level creation process.

To get a feel for snapping, create a new scene. I populated mine with a plane, two cubes, and a cylinder. Then I created four super-simple color materials (gray, red, blue, green) and assigned them, so this is what I am working with:

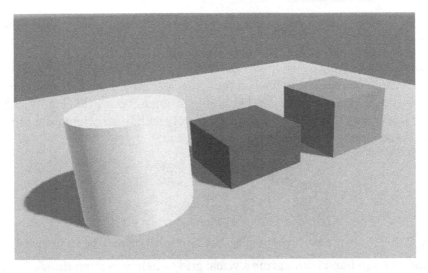

Fig. 7.13 – The plane is bisecting the shapes, which are their default sizes

At the most basic level, you can engage snapping by holding down *Ctrl/Command* and using one of the transform tools via either the gizmos on the upper left of the scene view or the hotkeys. With the translation (move) tool (hotkey: *W*), for example, a selected object moves smoothly when you drag it around with nothing pressed, but with *Ctrl/Command* held down, it 'stutters' as it snaps to the space in predefined increments in all three dimensions.

Just as handy is rotation snapping. With the rotation tool selected (hotkey: *E*) you can freely turn an object on any axis, but if you hold down the modifier key you will see a custom rotation gizmo that will let you snap in increments. Here it is in action:

 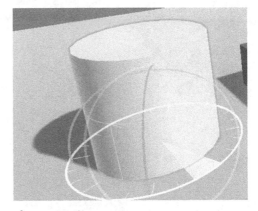

Fig. 7.14 – Free rotation and snap rotation

Like the other transformations, the scaling tool will function in increments if you hold down the modifier, allowing you to grow or shrink an object accordingly.

Take a moment to move some objects around with the snapping modifier held down and get a feel for it.

Instead of constantly holding down the modifier key to snap when you move an object, you may find it more convenient to turn on the Auto-Snapping feature. The icon for this toggle is above the Scene view and looks like a little magnet over a grid (*Fig 7.15*). Note that this only works for the Move transform and the object handle orientation must be set to **Global**, as shown in the following screenshot:

Fig. 7.15 – The toggle for Auto-Snapping. Handle orientation must be set to Global

Snapping goes hand in hand with having a visual grid to help you align things. By default, the Scene view will display a grid along the Y axis, but you can change the display axis at any time. Also, if you are in orthographic (isometric) view, Unity will automatically choose the right view to display. You can toggle grid visibility with the button on the Scene Toolbar (*Fig 7.16*). The letter appearing on the button corresponds to which axis is visible. Take a look at that here:

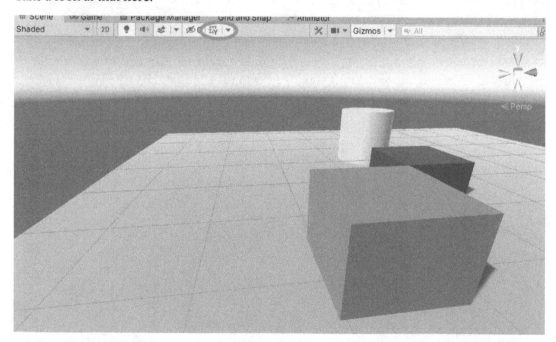

Fig. 7.16 – The grid visibility button. Click the icon to toggle it, NOT the down arrow

The grid is, in fact, very customizable. At the simplest level, you can change the display axis and the grid line opacity. But you can go much farther and specify things like the gridline spacing along each axis, the unit size of the increments at which objects will snap to the grid, and the color and position of the grid itself (moving it closer/farther, higher/lower).

To make the simple changes click the down arrow next to the toggle icon (*Fig 7.17*). The panel that drops down lets you select an axis and there is a slider to control the opacity.

To get much finer control over the grid, you can open up the **Grid and Snap** settings panel by either going to the main Unity menu and choosing **Edit | Grid and Snap Settings**, or by selecting the "overflow" (dots) menu in the **Grid Axis** dropdown (*Fig 7.17*). **Note**: The **Grid and Snap** settings are global to all Scene views.

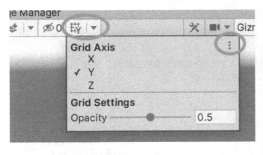
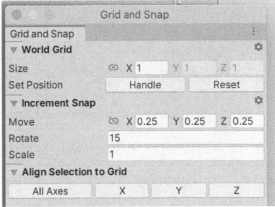

Fig. 7.17 – Open the Grid and Snap Settings window (right) by choosing the dots (overflow) menu from the dropdown (left)

Moving from top to bottom, the **Size** setting below **World Grid** controls the spacing of the main grid lines in terms of 3D units (in Unity it's meters, remember?). By default, the spacing is uniform across all axes, but if for some reason (boredom, perhaps? Or space madness?) you want different spacing on the different axes, you can click the icon that looks like a chain link to set the spacing of each axis independently.

You can also use keyboard shortcuts to increase and decrease the size of the grid:

- To increase grid size: *Ctrl/Command +]*
- To decrease grid size: *Ctrl/Command + [*

The **Set Position** settings change where the grid center is. The handle position for your objects can be set to either the object's Pivot point or its Center (*Fig 7.17*) and pressing the **Handle** button in this window will move the grid center there. The **Reset** button changes the grid center to be the world origin.

The **Incremental Snap** settings are reasonably straightforward. To the right of the **Move** label you can set whatever fraction of a grid unit you want your objects to incrementally move by. It's worth making this distinction here: changing these values does *not* affect the grid *display*, it just changes the size of the incremental snapping movement of an object. If the chain link icon is toggled on, there will be one uniform setting for all three axes, otherwise you can set them individually.

The **Rotate** setting specifies the number of degrees to incrementally rotate.

The **Scale** setting changes snap values for the Scale tool. Remember that a value of 1 really means 100% of normal size. So, if you uniformly snap scale an object with this setting it will get 100% bigger, which is to say, twice its original size.

The **Align Selection to Grid** section allows you to align an object to either the closest grid point on a single axis, or on all axes at once:

- To align an object to the closest point on a grid for a specific axis, click the *X*, *Y*, or *Z* button that matches the axis you want to 'push' to.

- To align an object on *all 3* axes at once, click **All Axes**. Alternatively, you can use *Ctrl / Command* + \ to do the same thing.

Occasionally you may want to change how near or far the grid is, for example, if you have objects spaced far apart from each other but you want to align them. You can use the following shortcuts to move the grid backward and forward along its axis:

- To nudge the grid backward, use *Shift* + *[*.

- To nudge the grid forward, use *Shift* + *]*.

That is almost everything there is to know about the grid system, except for one last thing that is strictly a matter of personal preference.

Changing the color of the grid lines

I found this option useful because the default grid lines were too indistinct for me. I changed my grid color to magenta so there was absolutely no mistaking what I was looking at. That might be too extreme for you, but you should be aware of how to change the colors in Unity anyway.

Go to **Edit** > **Preferences** (or **Unity** > **Preferences** on a Mac) and click on the **Colors** category to see the **Colors** page:

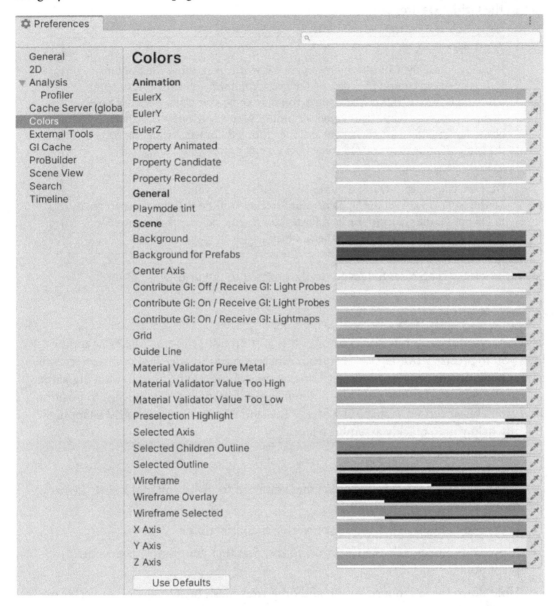

Fig. 7.18 – You can really go nuts customizing the colors in Unity

Scroll down to locate the **Grid** property and set it to whatever you like. Remember that you can set the alpha transparency for a color, so this is an alternative to using the **Opacity** slider in the **Grid Axis** dropdown.

Color Preferences

While you have the **Colors** window open, it is worth examining what other features you can control the color of. One very common adjustment is to apply a tint to playmode. This is a safeguard. You may know that Unity does not save changes you make while your game is running. Many developers have been burned by making a lot of changes and then losing them when they stopped the game. Tinting playmode to some obvious color gives you a safeguard against losing changes.

Here are two things NOT to do unless you want to give yourself Space Madness: 1) Do not set the alpha of your Selected Outline to fully transparent. 2) Do not set the colors of the X, Y, Z axes to the same color. Sheesh, seriously. Why do they even let you touch these values?

Last, but not least, is an essential layout tool unrelated to the grid…

Vertex Snapping

I've saved one of the most useful features of this section until the end. Vertex snapping allows you to precisely overlap vertices from different meshes—the snapped vertices will occupy the same position with no gaps. For example, this could be used in a racing game to precisely align road sections, or in a different style of game you might want to position power-up items at certain vertices of a Mesh. This ability combined with grid snapping can really help you to quickly assemble a level.

Here's how to use vertex snapping:

- Select the mesh object in the scene that you want to move and make sure the Move tool is active.
- Press and hold the *V* key to turn on vertex snapping mode.
- Move your cursor over the vertex on your object that you want to use as the pivot point.
- Hold down the left mouse button and drag your mesh next to any other vertex on another mesh.

- To snap a vertex to a surface on another mesh, add and hold down *Shift + Ctrl/ Command* while you move over the surface you want to snap to.
- To snap the pivot to a vertex on another mesh, press and hold the *Ctrl/Command* key while you move the cursor to the vertex you want to snap to.
- When you're happy with the results, let go of the mouse button and the *V* key.

This is a little tricky to get the hang of, so I suggest you practice with the primitive objects in the scene. But the practice is totally worth it.

Summary

Yay! You made it to the end of our middle-of-the-book chapter! Congrats!

Once again, we covered a lot of ground. We gathered together all the pieces we made in Blender into our Unity project, covering exporting and importing in the process, with a special look at animations.

We improved the look of all our assets by understanding the basics of what goes into Unity materials and then we improved our materials with Metallic maps, Normal maps, and Height maps.

After that, we took an in-depth look at Unity's Grid and Snap settings, which improve efficiency, help us to avoid frustration, and no doubt keep you hirsute lifeforms from pulling your hair out.

After all this preparation, you will finally have the chance to put your new skills and knowledge to use in the next chapter, when you will lay out the level of your mini-game.

8
Laying Out the Level

"I love it when a plan comes together."

—*Hannibal Smith, The A Team*

Okay, it's game time. (Although in game development, I suppose it's *always* game time.)

You spent the last chapter learning how to improve the materials of your objects and how to precisely align and place them using Unity's grid and snapping system. Now it is time to put together the majority of our level according to the rough plan we made in *Chapter 5, On the Level: Making Modular Scenery.*

In this short chapter, we will cover the following topics:

- Level layout: We'll lay out the level area by area. We'll spend most of the chapter's focus here, calling out anything that requires particular attention.

- Skyboxes: We'll add some atmosphere (literally) by adding a Skybox to the level.

- Ambient and Soundtrack audio: We'll add some atmosphere (figuratively) by adding some ambient sound effects and music.

Little details and small bits of work add up over time. Once we have laid out the level and given it some "flavor," by the end of the chapter, it will start to feel like we have a real game level on our hands!

Technical Requirements

This chapter stays focused on the Unity editor. We will make use of some free art and sound assets from the Asset Store at the end of the chapter, but I will provide those references when we get there.

The supporting files for this chapter can be found here: `https://github.com/ PacktPublishing/Mind-Melding-Unity-and-Blender-for-3D-Game- Development/tree/main/Chapter08`

Laying Out the Level

Armed with the modular pieces we've created so far and your new knowledge of snapping and grids, it's time to lay everything out according to the rough plan we made back in *Chapter 5, On the Level: Making Modular Scenery*. Do you remember that? Here it is again, and the areas are labeled for easy reference:

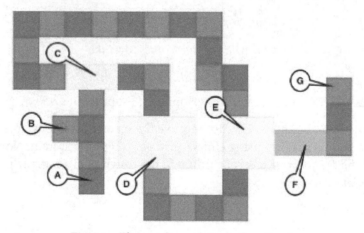

Fig. 8.1 – The rough area layout of our level

In actually laying this out and seeing how it looks relative to the size of the human reference model, I generally increased the amount of floorspace for each area. Also, I am placing doorframes, but not yet placing doors.

Remember, this is all modular. You do not need to follow my design exactly. You may want to make something simpler or more complex. I would suggest, however, that you create some kind of linear flow for the rooms and corridors such that the player winds up in a final area, such as Area G in the preceding layout.

We'll start by covering a few general layout tips and then proceed area by area, calling out anything of note.

Level Layout Tips

Even a simple level is composed of a huge number of parts. The following tips may make the difference between finishing your level layout or running off screaming into the darkness (although you should try that at least once. It's fun!):

- The Duplicate action, *Ctrl / Command + D*, is your BFF. In most cases, do not be an insane person who uses cut and paste.

- Group prefabs into larger prefabs. Analyze what you want to build. Do you have a long corridor to lay out? Create a big section with both walls and floors and duplicate *that* prefab to lay out the corridor.

- Create a good folder organization. I made an empty game object to use as a "folder" for each area and beneath that, I had three child folders: `walls`, `floors`, and `misc`. You can see it here:

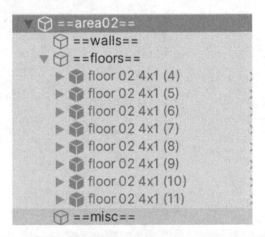

Figure 8.2 – The folder structure I used for areas

This is a common way to organize. It is an excellent way to focus on an area or small section at a time because you can disable the top-level object to hide all the children.

- Grid snapping and vertex snapping. Forget BFFs, these features are your survival tools. I find myself not really using Auto-Snap, but instead using *Ctrl / Command* to toggle snapping very often.

- Isometric mode. Viewing your level in orthographic mode can prevent a lot of alignment headaches, but you do want to keep flipping back and forth with perspective mode to make sure everything looks good.

Those tips will get you 99% of the way to the finish line. Here are some notes on individual areas. Level creation is, of course, a huge topic, but what you want to focus on here is looking for ways to make your workflow easier, simpler, and faster. Think lazy. In this case, it's not only excusable, but also a good thing!

Areas A and B

This area is 8 units wide and 16 long. The floor we made in Blender is 8 x 8. As an exercise, you may want to create smaller floors in Unity with the Plane primitive.

You may want to build in Area B as a nook to hide a turret in.

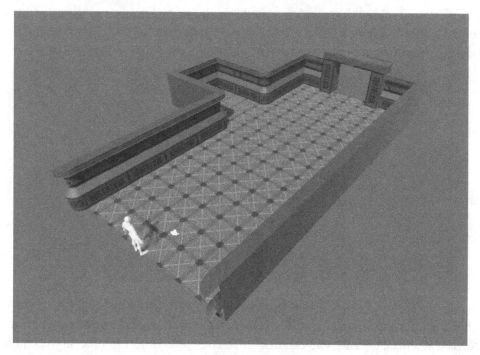

Fig. 8.3 – How I laid out Area A

I didn't do it, but you may want to create two prefab versions of the doorframe. Later on, you can add the appropriate door prefab to the frame prefab and the doors will automatically appear throughout the level!

Area C

The missing near wall (the south wall?) is shared between areas A and C.

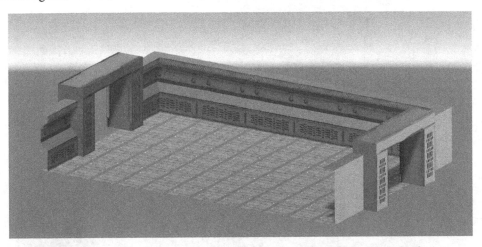

Fig. 8.4 – Area C without the shared wall. The grid has been toggled off

Area C2

This is an optional long corridor. In a real game, you would want to make some sort of trade-off for taking this route, such as it is longer but safer than going to the right in Area C. In that case, you might want to build in a time limit, such as the spaceport is about to self-destruct!

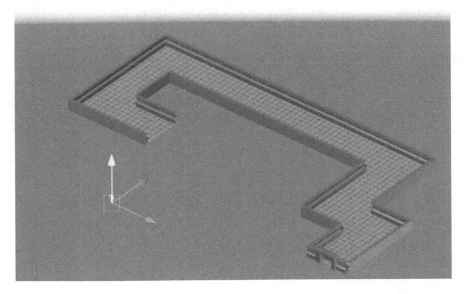

Fig. 8.5 – Now that is one long corridor!

Area D

Area D is just a big, open room. Are you starting to feel comfortable with snapping yet?

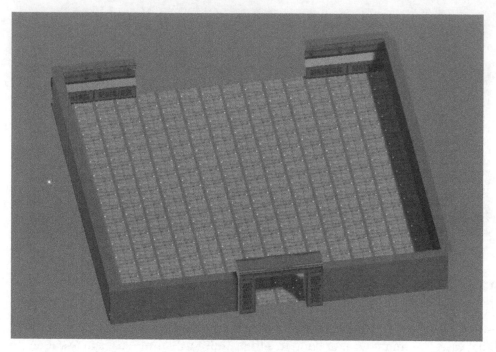

Fig. 8.6 – There's no cover here and just one way across

The Space Marine's armor better be charged up when he runs through here.

Area E

This area is just before the bridge. In a more fleshed-out game, you would want the player to have to solve some sort of puzzle in this room to extend the bridge to the next one. And you should complicate this by having lots of things shooting at them at the same time.

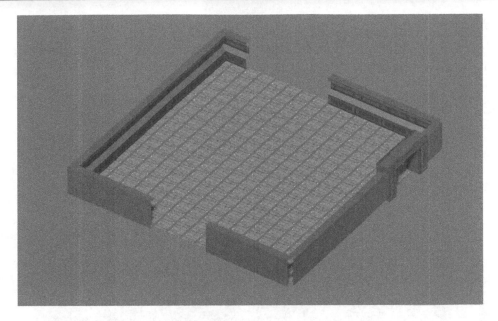

Fig. 8.7 – Plenty of room to add danger

Area F

We are going to start building more interesting custom scenery beginning in the next chapter. For now, just put in a placeholder floor.

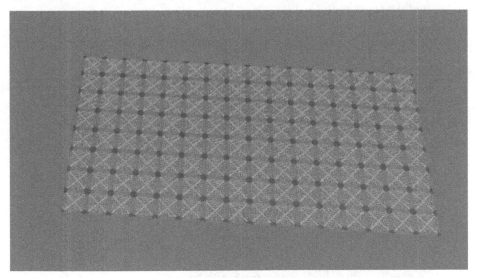

Fig. 8.8 – This is just a placeholder

Don't spend a lot of time here. Just get the sizing right.

Area G

We're in the home stretch now. Area G has two parts. If you had power-ups, you might put some in the antechamber:

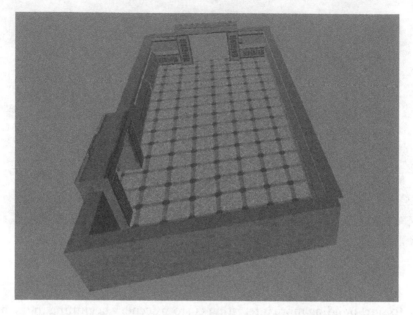

Fig. 8.9 – An antechamber after the bridge

We will put something special in the final area:

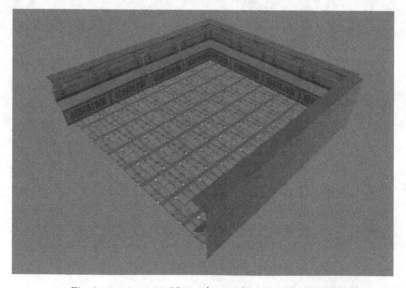

Fig. 8.10 – Area 10. Not to be confused with Area 51

Can our intrepid marine survive long enough to reach the final area and make his space escape?

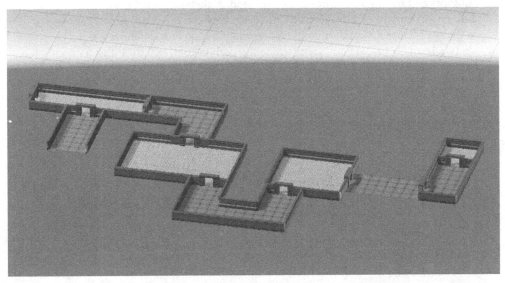

Fig. 8.11 – All areas laid out and visible. Your results will vary

Here is the big picture (*Fig 8.11*). Did you decide to follow along? Or did you do your own thing?

One thing I can guarantee if you've laid out your level is that in addition to the duplication, prefab, and folder tips I offered at the beginning, you are certain to have found your own unique workflow that will serve you well in future games. Continue to refine it!

So, we now, for the first time, have the foundation of our level laid out. It's not terribly fun yet, but it's a good start. Next, let's add a couple of simple touches that will go a long way toward giving it a "feel" even before there's any gameplay.

The Sky's the Limit: Adding a Skybox

You've got a first pass at a level layout. Fantastic. But raise your hand if you're tired of looking at the default Unity scene background.

Just for fun and to add a bit of flavor to our level, let's add in a *free* sci-fi skybox. In your browser, go to the Asset Store and search for *FREE* Skyboxes - Sci-Fi & Fantasy. Go ahead and select **Add to My Assets**, then **Open in Unity** and **Import** it into your SpaceEscape project.

Er, what's a skybox?

A skybox (and its sibling the **skydome**) is a visual effect that simulates being outdoors and having a huge open sky overhead. A skybox is a cube with a different texture on each *inside* face. The seams between the textures don't show, so the sky texture looks continuous. When you use a skybox to render a sky, Unity essentially places your Scene inside the skybox cube exactly at the center. Unity renders the skybox first, so the sky always renders in the background.

In order to add a skybox to your scene, you need to open up the lighting panel via **Windows | Rendering | Lighting**. Go ahead and dock the panel if you feel like it. Here is the panel:

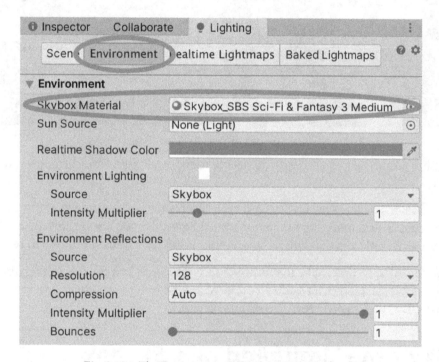

Fig. 8.12 – The Environment tab of the Lighting panel

Choose the **Environment** tab in the panel and then assign a skybox material. I chose **Skybox_SBS Sci-Fi & Fantasy 3 Medium** but follow your preferences and also remember there are a million free skyboxes out there *plus* they are not that hard to make/customize yourself.

Here's a view of my level now:

Fig. 8.13 – Star light, star bright, first star I see tonight…

What's that you're asking? Shouldn't the space station really have a roof to, you know, keep the air in?

Well, Mr. Smartypants, there's, uh, an, uh, energy field thing that contains the atmosphere. And it's decaying rapidly. Yet one more reason the space marine better get out of there in a hurry. (Thought you had me, didn't you?)

Sounds Like Trouble: Adding some Audio Effects

Now to add a little more atmosphere to the level (so to speak): looping ambient audio and a musical soundtrack. I can't stress this enough, people constantly underestimate how much "life" audio can add to a game. Don't skimp here!

We are going to start out incredibly simply and get a bit more sophisticated in later chapters.

To begin, create an empty game object in your Hierarchy and name it `SoundManager`. In the Inspector, go ahead and add *two* **AudioSource** components to it.

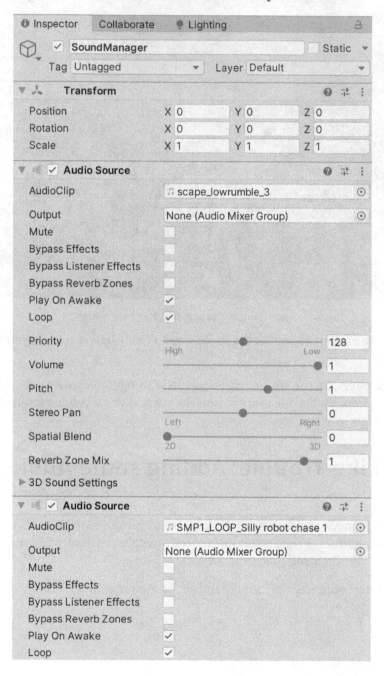

Fig. 8.14 – Add two AudioSource components to your SoundManager

The first **AudioSource** will be for our ambient sound. I used the free Asset Store **Sci Fi World Sounds - Free Package** package. As I've said before, there are many other excellent free assets available in the store. You would be doing yourself a favor to explore what's there.

From that package, I chose the **scape_lowrumble_3** audio clip. I felt this had some nice tension, which is the feel I was going for.

The second **AudioSource** will be for our soundtrack. For this, I used the free **Sci-Fi Music Pack 1** package from the store. From that package, I used the **SMP1_LOOP_Silly robot chase 1** clip. Despite the name, I thought the clip had the right amount of tension and energy.

Be sure to check the **Loop** checkbox for both AudioSources so you will have endless audio accompaniment.

Go ahead and play your level to hear the sounds. Lots of energy and tension in the air, right?

Summary

Finally, in this chapter, we called upon everything that came before and applied that to lay out our level pieces according to the plan we created earlier.

Hopefully, you have begun to create your own personalized workflow and are learning how to make your process more efficient. Have you imagined or created new prefabs to help you out?

After laying out the level, we quickly dropped in some A/V (audio/visual) effects—a skybox, an ambient loop, and a soundtrack loop—that go a long way toward defining a "feel" for our game.

In the next chapter, we will continue to breathe life into our level, and we will introduce the built-in ProBuilder tool, which is fantastic for prototyping and creating additional scenery and props. How exciting!

Onward!

9
Secret Weapon #1: Deploying ProBuilder

"The ability to destroy a planet is insignificant next to the power of Unity and Blender combined." —Someone on the Internet (maybe)

If you've worked with Unity for any amount of time, you know one thing: that it just keeps getting better. The company, Unity Technologies, listens to and works with real-world developers to learn how the Unity engine is being put to practical use and where workflows could use some improvement. This results in them making improvements and additions several times a year. (And, no, I don't work for them! *g*)

Sometimes, an independent developer will release a tool on the Asset Store that is so awesome the company sits up, takes notice, and actually *purchases* the tool and incorporates it into the Unity engine. This has happened with TextMesh Pro, the Bolt visual scripting system, and some tools we will focus on in this book—specifically, ProBuilder (this chapter) and Cinemachine (a later chapter).

In this chapter, we will focus on one of Unity's most recent major features that is very often unknown, underutilized, or misunderstood by both those new to Unity *and* long-time users: ProBuilder, a built-in package that is very useful for prototyping, modeling, and game development.

This chapter will cover the following topics:

- An Introduction to ProBuilder
- History of ProBuilder
- Installing ProBuilder
- Exploring the ProBuilder Toolbar
- Bridgework: Making Movable Scenery

By the end of this chapter, we will have covered the following:

- What ProBuilder is and the many different applications it can have
- Some of ProBuilder's history
- All the objects ProBuilder can create and the ways it can edit them
- How to create scene objects in ProBuilder suitable for using as is or refining further in Blender or another 3D program

I know I've said this before, but the capabilities you unlock in this chapter will open up incredible new creative possibilities, as well as making your workflow much more efficient. You trust me, right? I wouldn't say it if it wasn't true! Let's get cracking!

Technical Requirements

This chapter will focus on working in Unity and will only utilize elements in your work-in-progress SpaceEscape project.

The supporting files for this chapter can be found here: `https://github.com/PacktPublishing/Mind-Melding-Unity-and-Blender-for-3D-Game-Development/tree/main/Chapter09`

The code in action video for this chapter can be found here: `https://bit.ly/3oHNpmo`

An Introduction to ProBuilder

ProBuilder is an extremely useful built-in Unity package that lets you build, edit, and texture custom geometry. It is often described as a hybrid tool for 3D modeling and level design, optimized for building simple meshes but capable of detailed editing and UV unwrapping too. ProBuilder is great for in-scene level design, quick prototyping of structures, terrain features, vehicles, and weapons, as well as custom collision geometry, trigger zones, or nav meshes. Whew! That's a lot of versatility.

ProBuilder also has advanced features that include UV editing, vertex coloring, and parametric shapes. You can also export your meshes to tweak them in any external 3D modeling suite (Blender, of course, being our first choice!).

As if all that wasn't enough, ProBuilder has its own Scripting API to let you take advantage of many of its features from your own C# scripts. Mamma mia (as all Earthlings say)!

ProBuilder vs. Blender

ProBuilder definitely has some overlap with some Blender features we have encountered before, but Blender ultimately offers a lot more fine-grained and detailed tools. Knowing how to use ProBuilder greatly increases the flexibility you have in approaching design and knowing how to use this tool, and Blender lets you choose the right tool for the right job when the need arises.

ProBuilder has so many different applications that we can't possibly cover them all, but once we have covered what the available tools do, we will use some ProBuilder shapes to create a new piece of scenery for our level.

So, let's get to know this great tool, starting with where it came from and how to install it.

History of ProBuilder

ProBuilder was originally one of three tools offered by ProCore in the Asset Store. The other two were called ProGrids and PolyBrush. Unity bought either the company or the three tools, I'm not sure which. Since then, the functionality of ProGrids has largely been absorbed into Unity's Grid and Snap system, which we explored in *Chapter 7, Prep Work: Materials, Grids, and Snapping*. ProBrush is a terrain- and level-painting/populating tool. It is available from the Package Manager under the Unity Registry tab. Here's how to start using ProBuilder.

Installing ProBuilder

ProBuilder, like any other built-in package, is easy to install. To do so, follow these steps:

1. Open the **Package Manager** window and select the **Unity Registry** option, as shown in the following screenshot:

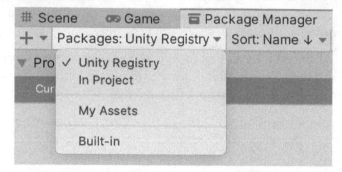

Fig. 9.1 – From the Package Manager, select Unity Registry in the dropdown

2. Search for `ProBuilder` in the search bar and then select **Install**:

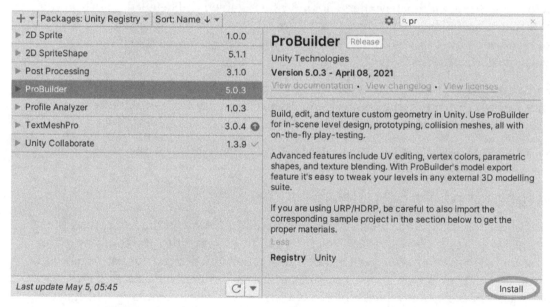

Fig. 9.2 – Search for ProBuilder in the Package Manager and Install

Once installed, you should now have a **Tools** option available in the top editor menu. (It's possible the **Tools** option was already there depending on other packages you may have installed.)

3. Next, select **Tools | ProBuilder | ProBuilder Window - P-Bold**:

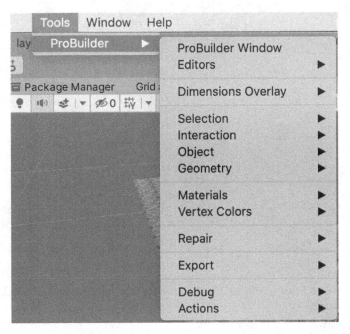

Fig. 9.3 – Open the ProBuilder window from the drop-down menu

By default, you will get a new dockable window that appears, which contains the ProBuilder Toolbar. You can go ahead and dock it somewhere, but many developers prefer to have it floating over their Scene view. If you want that too, follow the next step.

4. From the dots menu in the upper right of the window, choose **Open as Floating Window**.

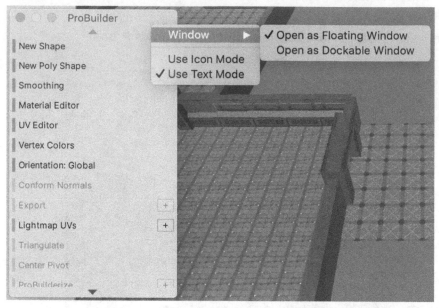

Fig. 9.4 – The ProBuilder window in floating mode

Notice also that you can choose either **Use Icon Mode** or **Use Text Mode**. Although Icon mode has tooltips that can help you out, I recommend starting out with Text mode until you become more familiar with the options.

We are going to spend a huge amount of time examining the ProBuilder Toolbar, but one other thing happens when you open the window, and we will quickly look at that: at the top center of your **Scene** view, you will now have a little floating **Edit** mode toolbar that looks like this:

Fig. 9.5 – The ProBuilder Edit mode toolbar appears when you open the ProBuilder window

Pat yourself on the back: you are already very familiar with this functionality because we learned about it in Blender. From left to right, the four edit modes available from this toolbar are as follows:

1. **Object edit mode:** Select objects, modify their normals and pivot points, and merge objects together.

2. **Vertex edit mode:** Select vertices (vertexes!) and make edits such as transformations, vertex splitting, and connecting.

3. **Edge edit mode**: Select edges and make edits such as adding edge loops.

4. **Face edit mode**: Select faces and perform basic tasks such as moving, extruding, and deleting them.

Sounds familiar, right? (If not, please review *Chapter 3, Entering the Blender Zone for the First Time*.)

There are also some keyboard shortcuts for the edit modes:

- *Esc* switches to **Object** mode from any other mode.

- *G* toggles between the **Object** and **Element** modes. For example, if you are in Vertex mode, press *G* once to return to Object mode, and press it again to switch back to Vertex mode.

- *H* toggles between the three Element modes.

If you want to change these key assignments, you can use Unity's **Shortcuts Manager**. Access this through **Unity > Shortcuts** on Mac or **Edit > Shortcuts** on Windows, as shown in the following screenshot:

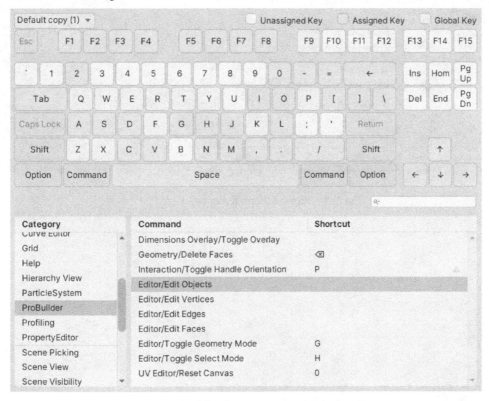

Fig. 9.6 – ProBuilder shortcut customization options

Now, I know you hardly know anything about ProBuilder yet, but you should be aware that there is quite a lot you can customize about it once you are more familiar and would like to make your workflow process even more efficient. To change ProBuilder settings, go to **Unity > Preferences > ProBuilder**, seen here:

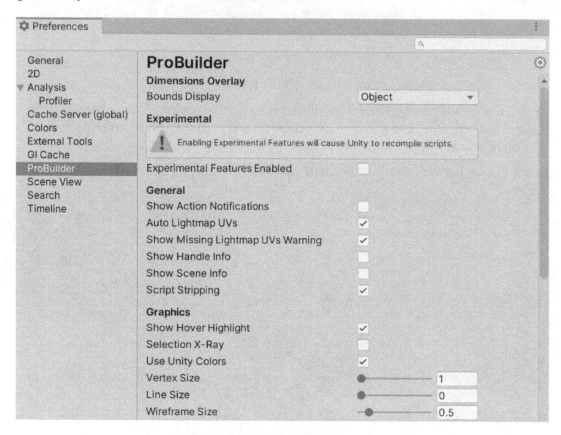

Fig. 9.7 – ProBuilder preferences – part 1

But wait, there's more once you scroll a bit more…

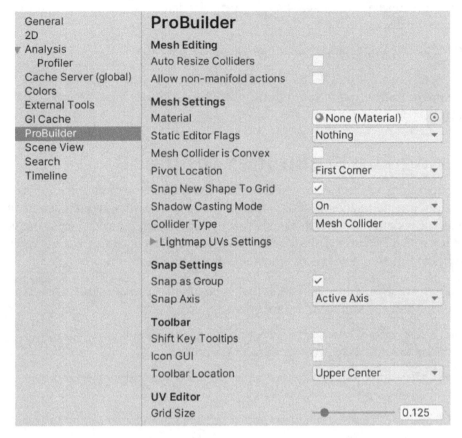

Fig. 9.8 – I told you there was a lot you could customize!

There is too much here to go over individually, and many of these settings are for advanced users, so I will just call out a few things of note and leave the rest for you to explore (or at least read the tooltips of!):

- **Bounds Display**: This is turned on with **Tools | ProBuilder | Dimensions Overlay | Show**. You can toggle whether the bounds of the entire object are shown or just an element.

- **Experimental**: At the time of writing, you can experiment with creating objects with Bezier curves and editing objects with **Constructive Solid Geometry (CSG)**.

- **Selection X-Ray**: Similar to Blender's X-Ray mode.

- **Use Unity Colors, Vertex Size, Line Size**: I, personally, was not happy with how ProBuilder displayed selected shape elements by default. Use these settings to change the display.

- **Material**: Use this to set a default material for new shapes.

We've now seen how to install ProBuilder, how to call up its window, and how to customize many of its settings. Now it's time to take an extensive look at ProBuilder object creation and manipulation.

Exploring The ProBuilder Toolbar

The ProBuilder Toolbar is the heart of ProBuilder and it has a ton of options. You can use the ProBuilder toolbar to access editor windows as well as selection, creation, and editing tools. The toolbar options will be dynamically active or not based on what object(s) you have selected in the **Hierarchy**. The toolbar options are color-coded to group them by similar types of functionality. Here is what the color groupings mean:

- **Orange**: These are editors and tools that open up in a separate panel. The shape creation tools you will often use are grouped here.

- **Blue**: These options are used for selecting things in different ways. They are functions to set and change your current selection.

- **Green**: These are mesh editing functions that affect the entire object, not its individual elements (edges, faces, vertices).

- **Red**: These mesh editing functions affect the individual elements of your object: vertices, edges, and faces.

Just ahead, we'll go through each color group and see what's available.

> **ProBuilder Tool Options**
>
> Some actions have extra options or custom settings that can change how ProBuilder performs by default. If options are available, a clickable indicator appears in the top-right corner of the button. In text mode, this is a + character, and in Icon Mode, it is a gear icon.
>
> NOTE: When you change an option, those changes become the default settings for that action in the scene until you change them again.

Since each color group has a number of options, even just giving most of them a quick summary is going to turn into some long sections, so here is the game plan: first, we will look at a short list of high-level, orange-grouped tools to get ourselves oriented. After that, we will take a detour to dive into how to create objects with ProBuilder, since that is probably the main thing and certainly the first thing you will want to do with the tool.

After that detour, we will return to look at the remaining color-coded tools of the toolbar.

Orange-Colored Options – Tools and Editors

At the top of the ProBuilder toolbar are the options that mostly pop open their own work panels. The exceptions to this are the two shape (object) creation tools.

| New Shape | New Poly Shape | Smoothing |
| Material Editor | UV Editor | Vertex Colors |

Fig. 9.9 – The orange-color group is the shortest of all the groups

Note that the following tools are also available from the ProBuilder main menu under **Tools | ProBuilder | Editors**. (There is one additional editor that is available only from that menu: the Vertex Position Editor, but we will not cover that.)

The orange-colored tools are as follows:

- **New Shape**: This creates a new type of ProBuilder mesh. Many of these are shapes you are already familiar with from the built-in Unity selection (cube, sphere, and so on), but some are new, such as arch, prism, torus, and the awesomely awesome customizable Stairs mesh.

  The options to customize your shape appear in a panel in the lower right of your scene view. One thing that is very cool is that you can change these options on the fly and see your object update in the scene. You can even change the shape type over and over!

- **New Poly Shape**: Use this tool to create a custom two-dimensional shape and extrude that shape into a three-dimensional mesh.

- **Smoothing**: Use this editor to give a smooth, rounded look to faceted, jaggy shapes. Blender has this functionality as well. You can define different **smoothing groups** to mix the two looks. Smoothing is outside of what we will cover but is not very complex.

- **Material Editor**: This popup has presets to allow you to apply materials to objects, individual faces, or face groups.

- **UV Editor**: Use the UV Editor window to apply textures to objects or faces. You can also use it to manually or automatically wrap and unwrap textures. It is powerful and perhaps suitable for quick fixes, but I think overall, Blender is a better environment to do this in.

- **Vertex Colors**: This editor allows you to paint vertex colors onto your meshes. Setting vertex colors is a great way to colorize levels for prototyping, team layout, zones, and so on. You can also apply vertex colors to faces or objects in order to easily identify where they begin and end.

  Note: Click the **Apply** button next to the color you want to apply or select the preset from the ProBuilder menu: **Tools | ProBuilder | Vertex Colors | Set Selected Faces to Preset <number>**. **Note #1**: To remove a vertex color, apply the white vertex color (#FFFFFF). **Note #2**: Not all shaders display mesh vertex colors. However, you can see vertex colors on your meshes as long as you use a material that supports vertex colors.

Okay, one toolbar group down and three to go. But as I said earlier, let's take a detour and do something hands-on, that is, learn how to create objects with ProBuilder.

Creating Objects with ProBuilder

There are two main ways to create objects with ProBuilder (the others are currently experimental features): you can use the **Shape** tool or the **Poly Shape** tool.

The Shape tool provides presets for some familiar primitive Unity objects, as well as some specialized ones. The primitives that are similar to what Unity already offers are the Cube, the Cylinder, the Plane, and the Sphere. ProBuilder has some good additional primitives, such as the Cone, the Prism, the Sprite, and the Torus. Lastly, there are some presets that are highly useful when **grayboxing** buildings: the Arch, the Door(way), the Pipe, and the Stairs.

If none of the existing primitives are suitable for your needs, you can create a custom shape with the Poly Shape tool. This is a good strategy for quickly building an irregular structure, such as if you wanted to model the Pentagon building.

> **Tip: Graphboxing**
>
> Graphboxing is a term both from the software engineering world and the game dev world. In software, it means testing techniques halfway between "blackbox" testing and "whitebox" testing. (Look those up if you want.)
>
> In game dev, graphboxing is a traditional technique game developers use to prototype level designs. You block out levels with simple (gray-colored!) shapes, not final assets. Graphboxing allows you to start outlining and planning your levels early, try out ideas, and see whether the level design supports the right gameplay before creating final art assets.

To try out shape creation, I telepathically command you to create a new Unity scene in your SpaceEscape project to use for testing.

Creating a Pre-Defined Shape

You can create a new shape object from the first option in the ProBuilder toolbar. When you choose **Create Shape,** you will see in the **Inspector** that ProBuilder immediately creates a new GameObject that has these components: a **MeshRenderer**, a **MeshCollider**, a **ProBuilder Mesh Filter**, and a **ProBuilder Shape** (Script).

ProBuilder builds new mesh shapes inside of a bounding box you define. The bounding box determines the size of each new shape relative to the "first corner" of the box. To define the bounding box, you can either draw it in the **Scene** view or set the dimensions on the **Create Shape** panel and then click in the **Scene** view to indicate where you want to place the new shape. The following two figures illustrate the two steps of shape creation:

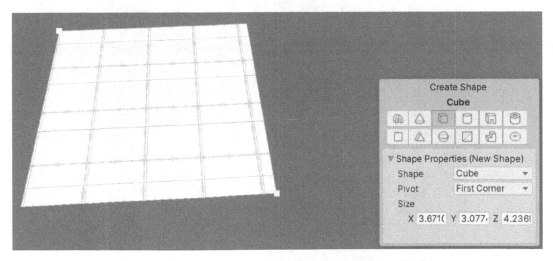

Fig. 9.10 – Creating a new shape by first defining a bounding box

Once you have a bounding box, you can give it depth by dragging it in the direction you want to extrude.

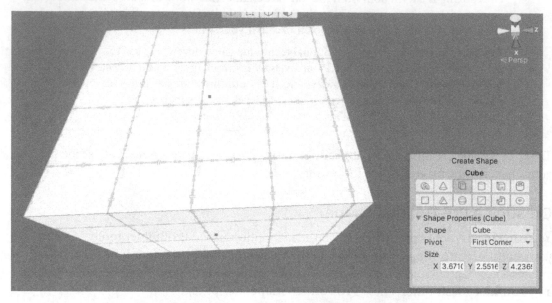

Fig. 9.11 – Dragging your mouse to extrude your shape

Create Poly Shape works in a nearly identical fashion. First, you define points along the perimeter of your shape, and then you extrude it. The two steps are nearly identical to what we've seen for creating a preset shape.

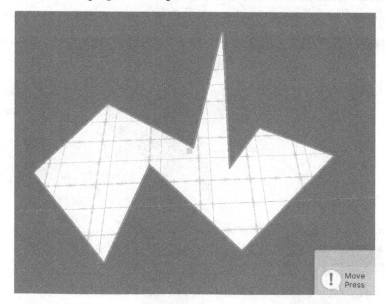

Fig. 9.12 – Defining points on the perimeter to create a Poly Shape

Just as before, you drag to give it depth.

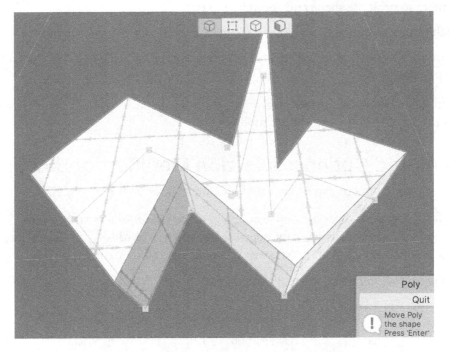

Fig. 9.13 – Dragging to extrude your Poly Shape

Once you have extruded your shape within its bounding box, you can set shape-specific options (width, height, radius, and so on) in the **Create Shape** panel.

Go ahead now and try creating some different kinds of shapes yourself. That's the real way to get a "feel" for the tool. It's actually kind of fun. Did I mention how awesomely awesome the Stairs shape is?

Additional shape creation tips

Here are a few more miscellaneous things that will help you with ProBuilder shapes:

- You can switch between primitive shape types when drawing or editing a shape and ProBuilder instantly adjusts the dimensions of the new shape to fit within the bounding box.

- ProBuilder builds new shapes on top of any pre-existing scene mesh or, if there is no mesh under your mouse, on the plane defined in the settings for Unity's Grid Snapping.

- While the Shape tool is active, you can't use the transform tools, but you can use the Camera to orbit the shape and zoom in and out.

- Enable auto-snapping to set a more accurate size than drawing freehand.

- To modify the last shape you created, you can change the properties on the Create Shape panel.

And that concludes our detour into creating ProBuilder shapes. Do you remember what we took a detour from? The ProBuilder toolbar!

Blue Colored Options: Selection Modifiers and Actions

Okay, we are back from our exploration into creating shapes with ProBuilder.

The tools for this part of the toolbar give access to selection modifiers and actions. Note that which tools/actions show up depends on which **Edit Mode** you have selected (Vertex, Edge, or Face), and you must have an object selected to use the tools.

Here are the three different contextual choices:

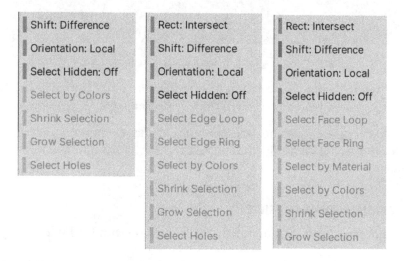

Fig. 9.14 – The choices that you see depend on the element editing mode: vertex, edge, or face

As I suggested earlier, don't just read these sections, try them out in simple tests. That is what will help the ideas stick. So, for example, when you're reading about selecting by material, set up a test case where you assign a material to only certain faces, select one, and then apply the tool to really appreciate what it does in a hands-on way.

So now, let's briefly examine the choices:

- **Rect (Edge/Face mode)**: This action defines whether drag selection should only select elements inside the drag-rect, or any intersected elements.

- **Shift (Vertex/Edge/Face mode)**: Defines how holding the *Shift* key affects your selection.

- **Orientation (all modes)**: Sets the onscreen visual orientation for object Scene handle gizmos to global, local, or normal.

- **Select Hidden (Vertex/Edge/Face mode)**: Toggles whether hidden elements are selected or ignored when drag-selecting.

- **Select Edge Loop / Edge Ring (Edge mode)**: Selects an edge loop from each selected edge. This is similar to Blender. See the following…

- **Select Edge Ring (Edge mode)**: Selects a ring from each selected edge, going in the other direction than a loop. Also similar to Blender, which actually combines these into one tool that can go in either direction.

- **Select Face Loop (Face mode)**: Selects a face loop from each selected face. This is going to be like deja vu with the preceding edge selection tools.

- **Select Face Ring (Face mode)**: Selects a face ring from each selected face. Like the Edge Ring tool, this is really selecting faces going in the other direction than the loop. Blender combines both of these functions into one tool covering both directions.

- **Select by Material (Face mode)**: Use this action to select all faces that have the same material. Go ahead and try it!

- **Select by Colors (Vertex/Edge/Face mode)**: This selects all faces on this object that have the same vertex color. It's very similar to selecting by material.

- **Shrink Selection (Vertex/Edge/Face mode)**: Use the Shrink Selection action to remove the elements on the outside (perimeter) of the current selection (this is Grow Selection in reverse). Blender has similar functionality.

- **Grow Selection (Vertex/Edge/Face mode)**: Use Grow Selection to expand the selection outward to adjacent faces, edges, or vertices. Blender has this functionality and calls it **Fatten**.

- **Select Holes (Vertex/Edge mode)**: This tool selects all elements along the selected open vertex or edge. A hole is like a removed face. This action is useful for selecting all edges around a missing face. If no elements are selected, this action automatically selects all holes in the selected object.

Just about all of ProBuilder's selection tools should seem somewhat familiar from Blender. One big difference is that Blender has functions distributed across its interface in different ways, so you don't see the commands grouped as they are in Unity.

That's it for taking a peek at the selection modifiers and actions. Time to move on to the next color grouping.

Green Colored Options: Object Editing Tools

The tools in this color group affect an entire ProBuilder object (as opposed to individual elements such as vertices, edges, and faces). Note: You must have an object selected to use a tool.

Fig. 9.15 – These actions apply to whole objects. Lightmap UVs is available by default

The object actions are a mix of things we have encountered before in Blender and things that are new and particular to Unity. I'll make the distinction between both:

- **Conform Normals**: Use Conform Normals to set all face normals to point in the same relative direction. ProBuilder uses the direction that most of the selected faces on the object are already facing. This is similar to Blender's commands: Recalculate Outside / Inside.

- **Export**: We have explored exporting meshes to `.fbx` files before, but ProBuilder can also export to `.asset`, `.obj`, `.ply`, and `.stl`. Note that as soon as you convert a ProBuilder mesh to the `.asset` format, it becomes a regular Unity GameObject, and you can't modify it with ProBuilder tools any more (unless you ProBuilderize it).

- **Lightmap UVs**: This action will generate any missing lightmap UVs for meshes. This is for Unity only and we will not be covering lighting.

- **Triangulate**: Triangulate will reduce all polygons to triangles. Blender has both a Triangulate tool and a modifier. You may recall that ultimately, all meshes will get triangulated under the hood, but that other polygons (such as quads) are easier to work with in some circumstances.

- **Center Pivot**: Moves the pivot point for the selected mesh to the center of the object's bounds. **Note:** If multiple objects are selected, each object's new pivot point becomes the center of each object, regardless of the position of any other object.

- **ProBuilderize**: You thought I made this word up before, didn't you? Nope. With this option, you can take an existing Unity object and turn it into an object that you can use with the ProBuilder tools.

- **Subdivide Object**: Subdivision divides every face on your selected objects, allowing you to add in more detail.

- **Flip Normals**: This flips the normals of *all* faces on the selected object(s) to the opposite direction. Basically, it is the same as Flip Normals in Blender and is especially useful if you want to convert an exterior-modeled shape into an interior space.

- **Mirror Objects**: You can simply flip an object around an axis or you can choose to create a mirrored duplicate of the object. We've seen this in Blender.

- **Merge Objects**: Use the Merge Objects action to merge multiple selected ProBuilder meshes into a single one. Blender calls this Join. The objects remain editable with ProBuilder.

- **Freeze Transform**: Freeze Transform sets the selected object's position, rotation, and scale to the world-relative origin. This is kind of like doing an Apply Transform in Blender.

The next toolbar breakdown section is the longest because the selections are all dynamic. Once again, I emphasize, mess around (mesh around?) with these options!

Red-Colored Options: Element Editing Tools

Almost all the Element Editing Tools available change based on the Element Editing Mode you have selected, so that is how we will tackle going over them. The following figure shows the three different contextual choices:

Fig. 9.16 – The dynamic actions available for Vertex Edit Mode, Edge Edit Mode, and Face Edit Mode

Let's look at the actions available in each contextual group.

Vertex Actions

Unsurprisingly, these actions can be performed when you have **Vertex Editing Mode** selected:

- **Collapse Vertices**: This action collapses all selected vertices to a single point, regardless of distance. Blender has similar functions. You can collapse to the first selected vertex or a central point.

- **Weld Vertices**: This action merges selected vertices within a specific distance of one another. In Blender, this is called—wait for it!—Merge by Distance.

- **Connect Vertices**: Launches a volley of photonic torpedoes at the enemy fleet… *Huh?* Okay, I was just checking whether you were paying attention. This action creates a new edge connecting the selected vertices. If you have more than two selected, ProBuilder creates as many new edges as required, and adds extra vertices where necessary in order to keep the geometry valid.

- **Fill Hole**: Use the Fill Hole action to create a new face filling any holes that touch the selected vertices. The intuitive shortcut for this in Blender was the *F* key.

- **Cut Tool**: Similar to the Knife tool in Blender, you can use the Cut tool to create a new face on an existing mesh.

- **Offset Vertices**: Use the Offset Elements action in the Vertex edit mode to move the selected vertice(s) according to the settings.

- **Split Vertices**: Use this action to split a single vertex into multiple vertices (one per adjacent face).

- **Set Pivot**: This moves the pivot point of this mesh to the average center of the selected vertices. Not quite as versatile as Blender's options.

Edge actions

Yep, you guessed it. These commands apply in Edge Editing Mode:

- **Bridge Edges**: This action creates a new face between two selected edges.

- **Bevel**: Bevel splits the selected edge(s) into two edges, with a new face between.

- **Connect Edges**: Connect Edges inserts a new edge connecting the *centers* of each existing selected edge. I haven't found this to be very useful and prefer the options in Blender.

- **Extrude Edges**: Use this action to push a new edge out from each selected edge. By default, this action only works on open edges (that is, edges that have no connected face on one side). You can override this. Extrude is our old friend from Blender.

- **Subdivide Edges**: Subdivide Edges divides the selected edge(s) into multiple edges.

- **Fill Hole**: Creates a new face that fills any holes that touch the selected edges.

- **Insert Edge Loop**: Use this action to add a new edge loop from the selected edge(s). An edge loop is a series of edges that are directly connected.

- **Cut Tool**: Use the Cut tool to create a new face on an existing mesh. Similar to the Knife tool in Blender.

- **Offset Edges**: Moves the selected edge(s) according to the settings.
- **Set Pivot**: Moves the pivot point of this mesh to the average center of the selected edges.

Face actions

I will not insult your intelligence by saying which Editing Mode these actions apply to:

- **Subdivide Faces**: This action adds a vertex at the center of each edge and connects them in the center. Blender has both a tool and a modifier for this.

- **Triangulate Faces**: Gets rid of quads, n-gons, and so on. Use Triangulate Faces to reduce the selected faces to their base triangles. (This will ultimately happen under the hood anyway.) Blender has this functionality, too.

- **Bevel**: Bevels every edge on the selected face(s). So, for example, a triangle gets three new faces, a quad gets four, and so on.

- **Merge Faces**: Merges the selected faces into a single face, and removes any dividing edges.

- **Conform Normals**: Use the Conform Normals action to set all selected face normals to the same relative direction. ProBuilder uses the direction that most of the selected faces on the object are already facing. Similar to Blender.

- **Flip Face Edge (Turn Edges)**: Swaps the triangle orientation on the selected quad-only (!) face(s). This reverses the direction of the middle edge. Use this to smooth ridges in quads with corners of varying heights. **Note**: This is often called Turn Edges in other 3D programs.

- **Extrude Faces**: Use this to pull out the currently selected face and attach sides to each edge. By default, each new face extrudes in the direction of its vertex normals, but you can change this option. As with Extrude Edges, this is our old Blender go-to command.

- **Duplicate Faces**: This action duplicates each selected face either as a new GameObject or as a sub-Mesh on the same GameObject depending on the options you select.

- **Detach Faces**: No, no, no, this is not talking about our ability to—nevermind—it has to do with modeling. Use Detach Faces to detach the selected face(s) from the rest of the Mesh. **Note**: When you detach a face, the newly separated mesh remains in place. This is basically the same as Blender's Separate action.

- **Delete Faces**: This command is top-secret. You do not need to know what it does and I refuse to even give you a hint.

- **Cut Tool**: Use the Cut tool to create a new face on an existing Mesh.
- **Offset Faces**: Use the Offset Elements action in the Face edit mode to move the selected face(s) according to the settings.
- **Set Pivot**: Use the Set Pivot action to move the pivot point of this Mesh to the average center of the selected faces.
- **Flip Face Normals**: This action flips the normals only on the *selected* face(s). This differs from the `Flip Normals` action, which flips the normals on *every* single face on the mesh.

Whew! We've actually gotten through all the ProBuilder Toolbar choices. I told you there are a lot! Do you now see what I'm talking about when I say ProBuilder is this hidden, under-utilized secret weapon? And even just knowing its tools doesn't make you a master. As you start using it more and more in real development situations, you will have "a-ha!" moments where you realize, "Hey! I can also use ProBuilder to do this!"

Just before we get into adding a bridge to our SpaceEscape project, let's take a super-quick look at some non-toolbar capabilities that are tucked under the ProBuilder drop-down menu.

Other ProBuilder options

Do you remember how we originally showed the ProBuilder Toolbar window? We first went to **Tools | ProBuilder**. There are a few other features here to take a look at.

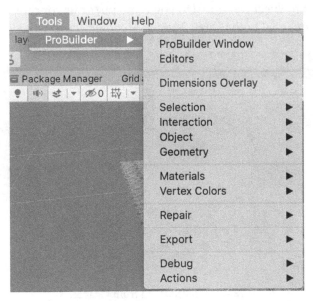

Fig. 9.17 – Remember this menu?

We are not going to go in depth into each option on this menu since many of them have overlap with what's available from the toolbar. I will, however, call out some of the most notable options:

- **Dimensions Overlay**: Shows or hides the shape dimensions for all three axes. Very useful when you need precision.

- **Repair**: This option can be a lifesaver if some things about your ProBuilder objects get wonky.

- **Debug**: The Debug submenu lets you set some options, such as what types of messages are output as well as where they go: console, log file, and so on.

- **Actions**: The Actions menu gives you the option to strip out all ProBuilder scripts from your GameObjects. You might want to do this before you ship to have the least amount of data possible. Remember: you lose the ability to edit with ProBuilder, but—if necessary—you could always "ProBuilderize" if you need to edit again.

You still out there? We made it! Your head should be dizzy with the number of ways that ProBuilder can manipulate shapes and elements, but hopefully your experience with Blender has prepared you for much of it. It's time now to flex your new ProBuilder muscles and add to our level.

Bridgework – Making Movable Scenery

Let's do some hands-on object creation. Do you remember our concept for our mini-game level layout from *Chapter 5, On the Level: Making Modular Scenery*?

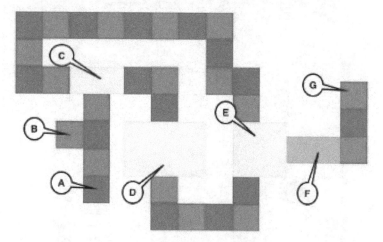

Fig. 9.18 – Our level layout from Chapter 5

When we did this, we just put in a placeholder for **Area F**, but let's start to make that a little more real. We'll create some geometry and then animate it in the next chapter.

Here is the high-level concept: the area is an abyss that you have to activate a bridge to cross. The bridge will be composed of six sections, kind of like planks, but we'll use (loooong) prisms because they're cooler and more sci-fi.

Three prisms will form the left side of the bridge and the other three the right. The prisms will start in the center of the abyss, facing vertically. The idea is that when you activate the bridge, they will extend upward and then fold over to create both sides of the bridge and allow safe (?) passage. Get it?

I'll describe what I did in a general way. It is not important that you do it exactly my way. The point is that you are learning to do this for yourself and can extend and apply this knowledge to any of your projects.

My version of the **Area F** placeholder looked like this to start:

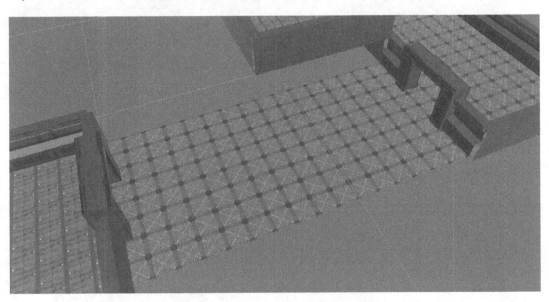

Fig. 9.19 – Hmm, not very challenging

The first thing I did was grab an *8 x 16* section of floor and drop it to *-5* on the Y axis to create an "abyss".

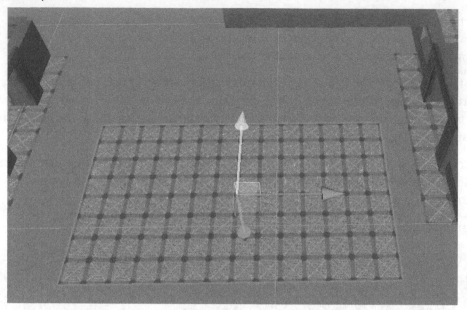

Fig. 9.20 – I moved the floor to -5 on the Y axis

Next, I created walls to surround the sunken floor. I created a north side wall from a ProBuilder cube. I gave it X, Y, Z dimensions of *16, 6, 1* and positioned it like so using *Ctrl / Command* to snap it to grid increments:

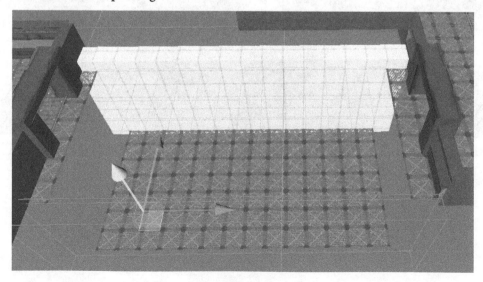

Fig. 9.21 – Using snap to help you position walls (front wall hidden)

I duplicated (*Ctrl / Command + D*) the north wall and positioned it on the south side.

For the east and west sides, I created another ProBuilder cube and gave it the dimensions of *1, 5, 8*. I positioned it on the west side and then duplicated it and positioned the copy on the east side like so:

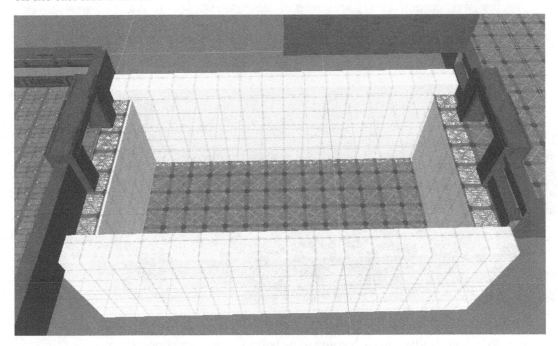

Fig. 9.22 – The four walls in place. Your mileage may vary

I kind of like the look of the default ProBuilder material for the walls, but you can easily change it to another material. You can create a new material normally, possibly using one of our excellent free textures from the Yughues metal collection we used for the floors. Then, you can assign this to the ProBuilder materials palette that is accessible via the toolbar or the drop-down menu. Finally, you can select your ProBuilder object (walls) and choose the material you want to assign from the palette.

I created a little pedestal for the bridge "planks" to extrude from. This is a simple ProBuilder pipe object. I made its **Radius** 1.5, **Height** 5, **Thickness** .5, and **Number of Sides** 16. I positioned it in the middle of the floor and also aligned it with the midpoint of the doorways.

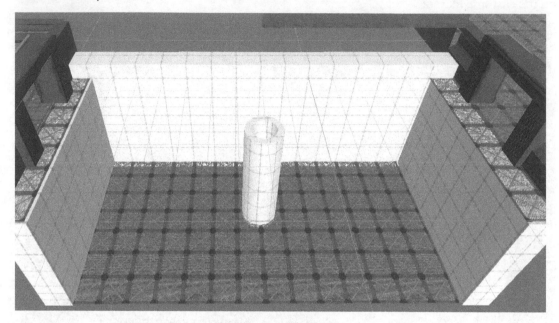

Fig. 9.23 – An "extruder" housing for the planks (front wall hidden)

The "planks" of our bridge are each going to be half as long as the floor. In my case, this is 7 units.

I went ahead and created a ProBuilder prism with X, Y, Z dimensions of .5, .5, 7. Then, I rotated it *90* degrees on the X axis and moved it to the center of the pipe (I eyeballed this). Position it on the Y axis so it is below the lip of the pipe, that is, not sticking out.

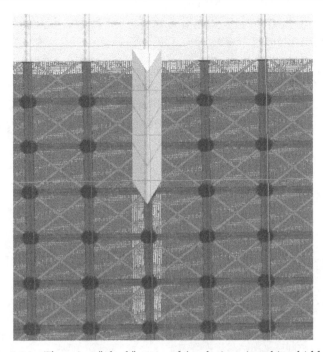

Fig. 9.24 – The prism "plank" centered (enclosing pipe object hidden)

Once you have it where you like, name it `Prism Shape`.

Save your file. We will continue to work on building out the bridge in the next chapter.

Summary

You made it! Fantastic job!

You've gotten a little bit of practice creating some "real" objects for our mini-game and hopefully, your brain is spinning with all sorts of other things you can create and add.

In this chapter, we first examined what ProBuilder is, where it came from, and the most common ways to use it. It is a powerful yet under-utilized built-in Unity tool.

Then, we went on a deep dive and had at least a cursory look at all of the many tools, commands, and actions available. There are a lot! It is my hope, however, that a lot of this seemed familiar from our time spent learning the tools in Blender. I believe that seeing how different applications tackle similar tasks will help you better plan how to tackle your own tasks.

We finished this chapter by further developing one of the later rooms of our mini-game by adding some simple ProBuilder objects (but, sadly, no Stairs).

In the next chapter, we will get to know Unity's secret weapon #2: Timeline. *Wait, what?!* We already covered Timeline in Blender! Well, not exactly. Unity has its *own* tool called Timeline and it's really cool! Timeline, as you will see, is a new way to animate, but the better idea is that it helps sequence things. We will use Timeline to start to give some life to our level.

Andiamo!

10
Secret Weapon #2: Animating with Timeline

"The best way to predict the future is to create it."

—Peter Drucker

What's that? You want even more cosmic power than you already have? Are you sure? It might be dangerous. After all, you can now create new objects in Unity and Blender, you can animate them in both apps, you can UV unwrap, you can texture, you can code abstract classes, and you can do other things as well.

Remember: absolute power corrupts absolutely. But if you're sure you want to learn more powerful ancient galactic secrets, who am I to say no? (Just don't start wearing a shadowy hood and cackling "Muhahaha!" all the time.)

In this chapter, we will learn about and explore a built-in Unity package called Timeline (as opposed to Blender's tool of the same name!). We'll cover two main topics:

- An introduction to Timeline where we learn what Timeline is good for and when to choose it over other Unity systems
- Using Timeline to animate the bridge prop we began in the last chapter

By the end of this chapter, you should have a working knowledge of how to use Timeline for animation and audio and you will have added a major new feature to our minigame level. We are barely going to scratch the surface of what Timeline can do, but you will be aware of other powerful capabilities you could harness if you need to.

Is that enough to satisfy your unending, ravenous curiosity? At least for now, I hope. Let's go.

Technical Requirements

This chapter will concentrate on awesome stuff entirely in Unity. We will use a sound effect, `ch 10 bridge.mp3`, available from the GitHub repository for this book.

The supporting files for this chapter can be found here: `https://github.com/PacktPublishing/Mind-Melding-Unity-and-Blender-for-3D-Game-Development/tree/main/Chapter10`

The code in action video for this chapter can be found here: `https://bit.ly/3Hw0Tu8`

Introducing Timeline

The Timeline system is a built-in Unity tool. The Unity Timeline is a way to play (and blend) content in a linear sequence. The easiest way to think about this to begin with is to imagine an animation clip or an audio clip. Both are examples of content that plays linearly. But Timeline can do more. Imagine, for example, you wanted to execute a series of scripts in order over a period of time. Timeline can do that, too.

Chiefly, you would use Timeline to create and edit cut scenes, cinematic content, gameplay sequences, audio sequences, and complex particle effects. You can move different types of **clips** around the Timeline, change when they start and end, decide how they should blend and behave with other clips on a **track**, and other things as well. In this chapter, we are just going to focus on creating a simple animation with a sound effect.

"But wait," you may be saying, "I thought Unity already has an animation system." Yes, you are correct. In fact, Unity already has *two* animation systems. The original one, referred to as the **legacy** system, and the current **Mecanim** system that was introduced way back in Unity 4.

So why would you want to use another animation system? Let's see.

When to use Timeline for animation

Let me first say that you *could* achieve any animated sequence using Mecanim (the earlier system) or Timeline (it's best to leave the original legacy system alone unless you have a specific reason for it). It is just a question of how much pain and hassle you save yourself by choosing one system over another.

The Mecanim system can animate any game object, but it is ideal for working with humanoid characters. The **avatar system** is optimized for this and Mecanim specializes in having *retargetable* animations—that is, you can, for example, use the same attack animation on many different humanoid character meshes.

Mecanim is a **state-based** system. To use it, you create an AnimationController object and you define different states for your character: idle, run, walk, jump, sneeze, curtsey, and so on. After defining states, you then define rules (logic) for the state transitions, which can happen dynamically during gameplay. For example, if speed is greater than 0, then enter the walk state, and if speed is greater than 4, move from walk to run. This logic also defines which states can interrupt other states, for example, sneeze might be able to interrupt any other state, but curtsey cannot.

AnimationController logic can get quite complex and to use Mecanim to create a scripted scene (cutscene) involving multiple characters can be quite challenging and time-consuming. Enter Timeline.

Everything about Timeline is about linear progression; it is not state-based. To use Timeline, you work with different kinds of tracks, stack some of them, and arrange them in a left-to-right fashion, which is how they will play back at runtime. Timeline is ideal for cutscenes. It simplifies scene coordination, for instance, when you want one object to animate, then wait 3 seconds, then play a sound, turn on a light, play a different animation, and so on.

Additionally, Timeline has a super-cool feature that takes the idea of "retargetable" to another level. Suppose you have a team-based game with a boss-fight at the end of every level. When the boss is defeated, the whole team is supposed to do some kind of victory dance. The challenge is that the team members can change from level to level and game to game. With Timeline, you can define the victory sequence once and then dynamically **bind** different members to different dance roles at runtime.

Timeline is also suitable for simple to moderately complex individual character animations.

So, the question you need to ask yourself when deciding what system to use is whether the solution you need is more state-based or sequence-based. State-based? Use Mecanim. Sequence-based? Use Timeline!

Timeline Tracks

Timelines are composed of "stacks of tracks." The easiest way to understand the idea of tracks in Timeline is to draw an analogy. If you have ever worked with a video production program such as Premiere or Camtasia, you should have a pretty good idea of what a track is: it's a piece of content that gets combined with the content of other tracks and played back in a linear fashion. The two most common types of tracks from the A/V world are audio and video.

Here is an overview of the basic types of tracks that Timeline supports by default:

- **Animation track**: There are two flavors of content that can go here. The first is a standard `.anim` clip. The second is called an Infinite Animation.

- **Audio track**: This allows you to import existing audio clips and alter playback properties over time. At the simplest level, it just plays a sound at a certain point. This is exactly what we want in this chapter.

- **Activation track**: This is a very simple track that sets whether an object is enabled or disabled at different points in time. It is very useful when you need to control the visibility of a GameObject.

- **Signal track**: This is basically an event system that allows communication (signals) between the Timeline and your other game systems in a clean, elegant, and flexible way. For example, it would be useful if you have a Timeline cutscene and when it ends you want to load a new scene.

- **Override track**: These tracks are used to override or mask out certain parts of animations with other animations, such as overriding a running torso with one that's waving its arms.

- **Control Track**: Control tracks are a cool, versatile, and super-powerful advanced feature of Timeline. They control time-related elements of another GameObject and in particular, they allow you to do things such as manipulate particle systems at runtime and instantiate objects on the fly.

- **Playable Track**: This track type allows C# scripts to extend Timeline with new track types. I won't sugarcoat it and say that this is a super easy thing to do, but it *can* be done, even if you are not a hyper-intelligent, pan-dimensional being.

For our purposes in this chapter, we will just make use of the first two track types: Animation and Audio, but first, a slight detour…

Prepping the Prism: Getting our asset ready to animate

You may recall from *Chapter 9, Secret Weapon #1: Deploying ProBuilder,* that we began work on creating a bridge out of a ProBuilder prism element in what we labeled Area F in our level layout. The idea is that six of these prism "girders" will form the walkway of the bridge.

We created a central "pipe" (for lack of a better name) in the middle of the room's sunken floor, like so:

Fig. 10.1 – The "pipe" that will house the prisms

The idea is that the prism girders will start out hidden within the pipe, but when activated will extrude up and then fold over, forming the walkway. So, first, they would go up:

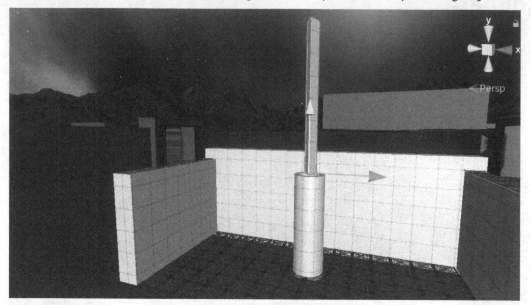

Fig. 10.2 – The prisms will first extrude up the Y axis

Then they would fold over and level out. This screenshot shows a single prism extruded and folded over:

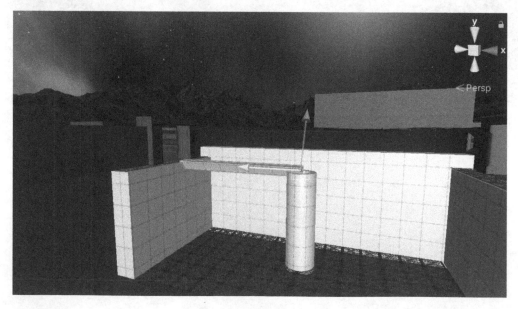

Fig. 10.3 – Eventually, three prism girders will form the left side of the walkway and three the right

Does this plan start to make sense to you? Thinking back to the initial position of things, the six prisms will begin overlapped in the center of the pipe. Here is a top orthographic view:

Fig. 10.4 – This is the overhead of the initial position of the prisms

The prisms will start out below the lip of the pipe, something like this:

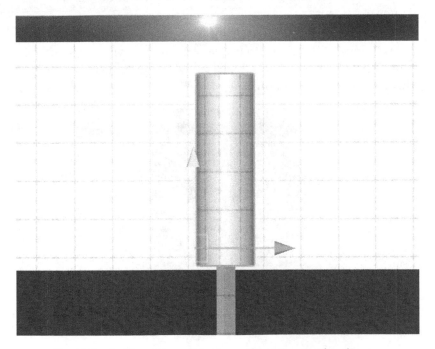

Fig. 10.5 – A side orthographic view of the prisms within the pipe

Easy peasy, right? Well, okay, now for the bad news. To achieve the kind of animation we've described, we need finer control over the prism *pivot points* (that is, centers of rotation) than ProBuilder can give us. We want the pivot to be at the bottom center of the prism so it can easily rotate, as in *Fig 10.3*. This is a perfect example of one reason you might want to create an object in Blender that gives you total control of pivot placement. But I wanted to demonstrate ProBuilder shapes, so we'll live with this situation.

In order to deal with this, we are going to use an old Unity pro-tip: we are going to create an empty parent game object, add our shape to that, and align the shape so that the place we want the pivot is at the **0, 0, 0** origin of the parent—this means that it will pivot from its bottom, which is what we want. So that's the first order of business.

> **Tip: Orthographic versus Isometric versus Perspective**
>
> This is a difference I didn't understand for a long time and I still mix up sometimes. I think you know by now that in a **Perspective** view, parallel lines will converge the farther into the distance you go. In an **Isometric** view, parallel lines stay parallel. (Unity has an onscreen toggle for this. See *Fig 10.6*.) An **Orthographic** view *is* isometric, but it is viewing an object straight-on down one of the three axes (giving us front, top, side views, and so on). So, in an orthographic view, you can only see and manipulate objects on two planes because you are looking straight down one of the XYZ axes. Now you are smarter. You're welcome.

Before you start, be sure you know how to toggle orthographic views (front, top, and so on) on and off in your **Scene** view with the axes gizmo. Aligning objects while in iso mode will help prevent **Space Madness**.

Fig. 10.6 – Use the gizmo to enter and exit isometric mode as needed

If you don't already recall, clicking **Persp** will toggle to Iso mode and back. You can click on the colored axes cones to jump to an aligned view (Y for top view, and so on).

Right-clicking on the **Persp** text will give you a popup to directly select an orthographic view.

Creating the Prism Prefab

We are going to create a prefab object that we will wind up instantiating six times to create the bridge walkway. Follow these steps:

1. In your **Hierarchy**, rename your existing ProBuilder prism to `Prism Shape`.

2. Create a new empty game object named **Prism** and drag **Prism shape** to be a child of it.

3. Add an **Animator** component to the *parent* **Prism** object you just created.

4. Drag this parent **Prism** object from the **Hierarchy** into your project `Prefabs` folder to change it to a prefab.

5. Open the prefab for editing (double-click in the project folder).

6. First, we want to work with the parent object, so disable the **Prism Shape** child to hide it. (Uncheck the checkbox next to its name. See *Fig 10.7*.)

7. Set an icon at the parent origin. We want to be able to identify the origin of the empty **Prism** object and this next tip is a great trick if you don't already know it: you can create custom icons to display for your game objects by clicking the cube icon near the object name:

Fig. 10.7 – Setting a custom object icon (you can even choose a custom sprite in your project!)

I chose a little blue diamond. If you are insane, you can make these icons huge by choosing **Gizmos** at the top of your **Scene** view and then moving the slider:

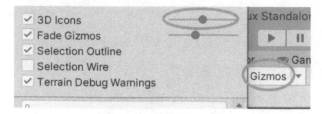

Fig. 10.8 – How to adjust icon size

At any rate, if you click somewhere in your **Scene** view so that nothing is selected, you should see just your icon showing the parent origin:

Fig. 10.9 – The diamond icon is difficult to see if you have something selected

What you now want to do is re-enable your prism shape and align it so that it rests right on the origin point. That will be the pivot point of the parent. It will help to switch to the Right Iso view. You may have to zero-out the prism's location and adjust the rotation:

Fig. 10.10 – Center the bottom of the child prism shape at the origin. The icon can be your guide

Once you get the pivot point right, you are ready to rock and roll so you can exit prefab-editing mode and return to your normal **Scene** view.

Captain to the Bridge!—Animating our Bridge with Timeline

Okay, with the prism walkway good to go, let's get our feet wet, or our hands dirty, or—let's just get on with it already!

Creating a Timeline

The first question to answer is where you should place your **PlayableDirector** component. If your Timeline will control multiple scene objects, the best practice would be to create an empty game object in your Hierarchy and add a **PlayableDirector** to it. If your Timeline will be focused on a single game object, you might decide to add the **PlayableDirector** right on that object.

In our example, we are going to have a Timeline that controls six prism walkway objects and plays a sound effect, so here's how:

1. In the Hierarchy, create an empty game object and name it `Bridge TL`.
2. Select this new object and open **Window | Sequencing | Timeline** from the top menu.
3. In the Timeline window, you will see a nice big empty window. Click the **Create** button. You will be prompted to create a `.playable` asset. This is just your Timeline as a file. Give your **Timeline** a name and choose where to save it:

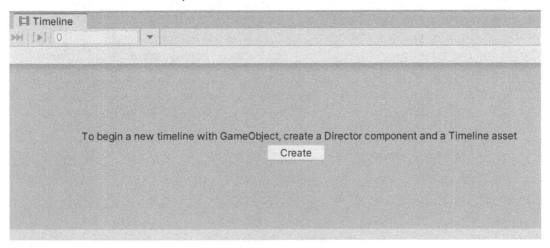

Fig. 10.11 – The first step in working with a Timeline

4. If the Timeline window is floating, dock the window somewhere convenient (often the bottom of the screen).

You now have an empty **Timeline Editor** window where you can add tracks to control assets and sequences. The **Create** button also added a **PlayableDirector** component to your GameObject. This connects the object to the Timeline and gives access to some properties you can control.

You'll see that the Timeline has three main areas:

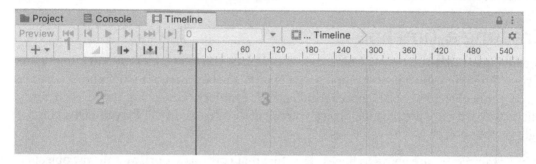

Fig. 10.12 – The main areas in an empty Timeline window

- **Controls (Area 1):** Here there is a mix of controls, many of them playback controls for when there are keyframes to navigate. When there are no keyframes, many controls are grayed out.

- **Tracks (Area 2):** All existing tracks get stacked up here.

- **Keyframes (Area 3):** All existing keyframes get displayed here. Similar to animation windows we've seen before, the frame numbers are displayed across the top.

It is a best practice to lock the **Timeline** window while you are using it (see *Fig 10.13*). The reason to do this is if you don't lock it and then click on a different game object, the focus switches and the **Timeline** window will go blank because there is no associated Timeline asset to edit:

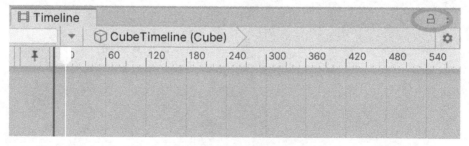

Fig. 10.13 — Click the lock icon to keep the window focused on one Timeline

Creating an Animation Track

Creating tracks is easy. We will wind up with about a half dozen, but let's start with one.

1. Create a new **Animation Track** by right-clicking in the empty tracks area (*Fig 10.12*, area 2) and choosing from the pop-up menu (or click the big + button):

Fig. 10.14 – The default track types. More are available

A brand new, empty track should look like this:

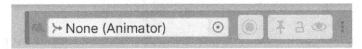

Fig. 10.15 – An empty Animation track

You can't use the track until you **bind** a game object to it. To do so, all you have to do is drag a game object into the slot (or choose one from the circle selector dropdown).

Additionally, the object *must have an* **Animator** *component*.

That last point tripped me up several times so I will repeat it: *to use a game object with Timeline animation it must have an Animator component.*

Read that last sentence again to be sure you've got it.

Aaaaaaand one more time really wouldn't hurt. **Animator** component. Comprende? Good.

The missing **Animator** component issue tripped up enough people that Unity added a helper function. If you drag in an object without an **Animator** component, the editor will prompt you to create one:

Fig. 10.16 – An auto-prompt to create an Animator component on a game object

2. Start with a single instance of your prism prefab in your **Hierarchy**. I named mine `Prism 1.1`.

3. Drag the instance into your animation track (the space where it says **None (Animator)**) or use the circle selector on the track to select it. When prompted, choose to have an **Animator** component added.

Once you have bound a game object to a track, you can move on to animating it. Timeline actually gives you two different ways to animate: with **standard animation clips** or **infinite clips**.

If you have a little Unity experience, you might be familiar with standard animation clips, which are the `.anim` assets created in the Animation window or from externally created animations.

Infinite clip is the default mode for a new animation track. It's called infinite because unlike a regular animation clip, it has no set duration (that is, no fixed length): whatever the farthest keyframe you place is, that is the length of the infinite clip. So, if you put a keyframe on frame 20, you have a 20-frame clip and if you put a keyframe on frame 10,000, you have a 10,000-frame clip!

Infinite clips done in the **Timeline** window are good when you want to make simple, basic animations on a scene object, changing its position, size, rotation, or some other big obvious change. More subtle animations are better done through the **Animation** window or even in another program (such as Blender!).

We will make an infinite clip for our bridge.

You should also note that an Infinite clip *cannot be positioned, trimmed, or split* because it does not have a finite size. (To do those things, you have to convert the infinite clip into a standard clip.)

The Plan for the Bridge

We are going to take the single instance of our prism prefab and keyframe it extending upward and folding over to bridge the gap.

Having done that, we will create a new instance, pop it into a new duplicated **Animation Track**, adjust it, then rinse and repeat until we have all six girders in place. Are you with me? My organization scheme in the **Hierarchy** wound up looking like the following figure:

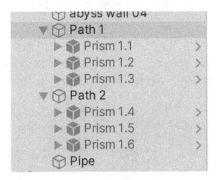

Fig. 10.17 – My girders are organized into two groups: Path 1 (left walkway) and Path 2 (right walkway)

At the end of this process, you will have something that looks like *Fig 10.18*, but **go one track at a time** (!) because we will duplicate as we go, saving a lot of effort. We want to create three keyframes for each track: an initial position with the girder hidden within the pipe, a position where it fully sticks up out of the pipe, and a final position where it is folded over.

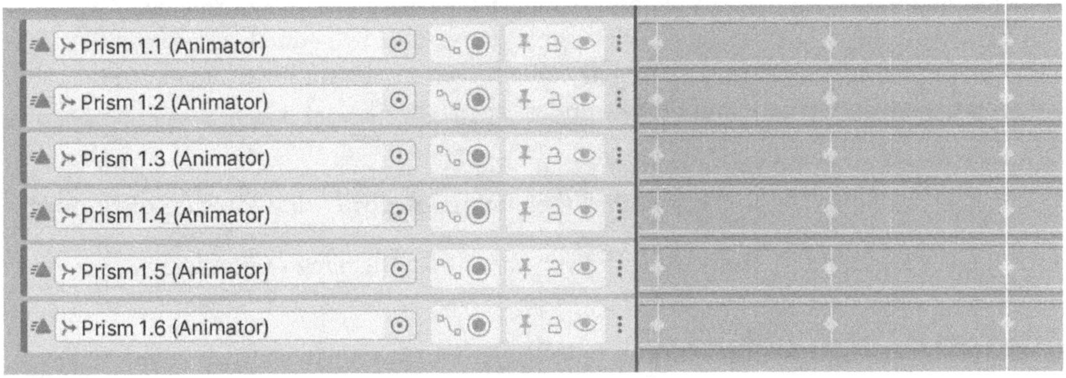

Fig. 10.18 – Finish the first track completely before duplicating anything.
Note the three keyframes for each

That's the plan, got it?

Recording an Infinite Clip

I want you to understand this process before we actually do it. Don't worry, it's short.

To create an infinite clip, you use the red record button on the track pane to start recording:

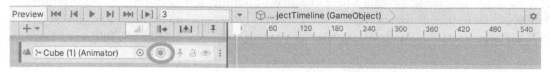

Fig. 10.19 – Click the round red button to start recording

When a track is in Record mode, the clip area of the track is drawn in red with the message **Recording…** displayed in the track and the **Record** button blinking:

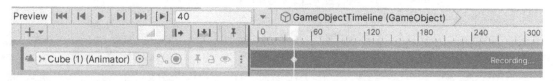

Fig. 10.20 – An animation track recording an Infinite clip

The basic workflow when recording an Infinite clip is as follows:

1. Position the white playhead at your desired keyframe.

2. Change an object property (which will create a keyframe if none exists). You can either manipulate the object in the scene via the gizmos or change properties from the **Inspector** window. Any change to a property will create a key. (You can also click **Add Key** from the right-click context menu. This will add an animation key for the property without changing its value.) A white diamond will appear in the clip to show the position of the key under the playhead.

3. Repeat steps 1 and 2 as necessary.

4. When you finish the animation, click the blinking **Record** button to stop recording.

The process is actually straightforward and you should get the hang of it quickly.

Animating the prism walkway

So here we go. You should already have a single animation track that is bound to a prism instance (**Prism 1.1**) in your **Hierarchy**.

1. Make sure the playhead is on frame 0 and click the red dot to begin recording the track.

2. Select **Prism 1.1** in the **Hierarchy**. You should now see its info in the **Inspector**.

3. In the **Inspector**, right-click on the **Position** property and choose **Add Key** from the popup. This will capture the prism's initial position:

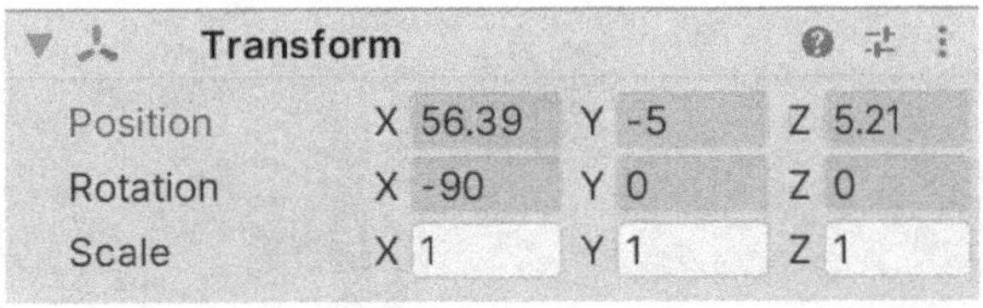

▼ ⋏	**Transform**		❷ ⧾ ⋮
Position	X 56.39	Y -5	Z 5.21
Rotation	X -90	Y 0	Z 0
Scale	X 1	Y 1	Z 1

Fig. 10.21 – The transform is now keyframed. Ignore the exact numbers shown here

4. In the **Timeline** window, move the white playhead to the next position. I chose 2 seconds later at frame **120**.

    This keyframe will be the upright position of the prism. Refer to *Fig 10.2*. Adjust the Y position of the prism and then keyframe the position again just as you did in step 5. *Be sure you are adjusting the parent object and not Prism Shape!* You might want to lock the **Inspector** so you don't accidentally adjust **Prism Shape**. For safety's sake, right-click **Position** and choose **Update Key**.

5. Move the playhead to the final position. I chose 2 seconds later at frame **240**.

6. This is the trickiest part of this whole process. Refer to *Fig 10.22*. What you want to do is use the transform tools to rotate and level out the prism, so it has a flat surface on the top. You can eyeball this, making good use of orthographic views. (Note to noobs: if your movement placement is jerky, be sure you don't have snapping on!)

7. Keyframe the Transform you just changed. Right-click both **Position** and **Rotation**. Choose **Add Key** if prompted for either of those. (Note to noobs and pros: if you need to tweak a Transform after keying it, change it, then right-click and choose **Update Key**.)

8. Scrub your animation to check it. The prism should rise and then fold over.

9. Turn off recording by clicking the blinking red dot. Here is a screenshot of the bridge in progress:

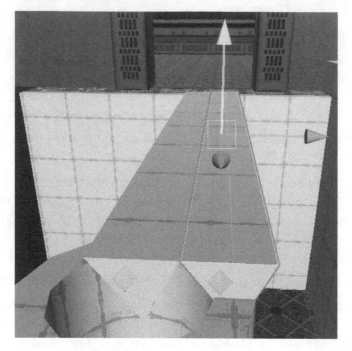

Fig. 10.22 – Two of the prisms in their final positions, rotated and leveled

Previewing your Animation

You can preview your Timeline animation without actually running your game, which is pretty cool. You use the controls in the upper left of the window.

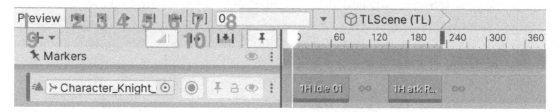

Fig. 10.23 – The Timeline window controls

Let's examine the controls available:

1. **Preview**: This toggles your ability to move through your keyframes and see the results in your **Scene** view. I've never had a reason to turn this off, but you know, never say never.

2. **Start**: Goes to the beginning of the Timeline.

3. **Previous frame**: How shall I put this? This button goes to the previous frame. There, I said it.

4. **Play**: Starts the playhead moving from wherever it is. You will see your animation(s) in the **Scene** view assuming that the **Preview** button is down.

5. **Next frame**: Goes to the next frame in the sequence.

6. **End**: Goes to the end of the Timeline.

7. **Play range**: This will toggle whether you are seeing only a group of frames you have defined.

8. **Current frame number**: You can also enter a frame number here to jump there.

9. **Track selection**: This will open a menu to select a track type to add.

10. **Edit Mode buttons**: These three buttons allow you to choose between Mix mode (the default), Ripple mode, and Replace mode. We'll stick with the default.

Use the Timeline Play button to preview your prism animation and make any adjustments as necessary.

Also, remember you can drag the white playhead to "scrub" through frames.

Finishing the bridge animation

One prism down, five to go! Here is how to deal with the rest of the prisms:

1. Create a new Prism prefab instance in the **Hierarchy**. (Continue to use a good naming scheme such as **Prism 1.2**, and so on.)

2. Duplicate your previous Animation Track in the Timeline (select the track, then right-click and choose **Duplicate** or press *Ctrl / Command + D*).

3. Assign your new prefab instance to be the game object for your new track. (This is **binding** it, remember?)

4. Enable recording for the new track (the red button).

5. Go to the final keyframe. (In my example, this is frame 240). This is the only keyframe you have to adjust because the prisms all occupy the same place starting out. Move the new prism to one side of the pre-existing one (*Fig 10.22*).

6. Save the keyframe and turn off recording.

7. Return to *step 1* and continue to do this until you have three girders that extend to the west (left).

8. We need to make a slight change to the process for the girders that will extend to the east (right). Start by duplicating a prism and naming it `Prism 1.4`. You can put it under **Path 2** if you are following my organization scheme.

9. Change the **Y Rotation** to **-180** so that it faces the opposite way than the other girders. Switch to Top iso view to get this right. You will also need to adjust the X position to account for the offset of the pivot point:

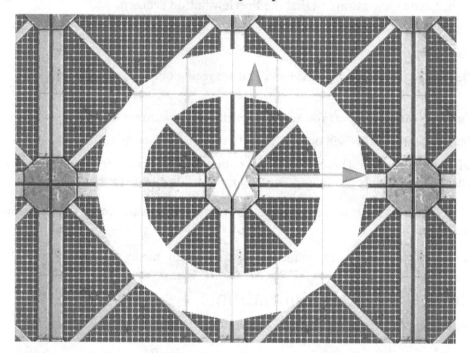

Fig. 10.24 – Rotate the prism in the opposite direction and adjust the position

10. Be sure you are on frame 1 and that the prism is in a good starting position, then start recording.

11. Put a keyframe for its **Position** and **Rotation**.

12. Move to frame 120 and make sure it rises on the Y like the others. Keyframe that **Position**.

13. Finally, move to frame 240. Rotate the prism 90 degrees on the X and it should folder over nicely. Keyframe the **Position** and **Rotation**.

14. Scrub your animation and when you are satisfied stop recording.

15. Two more to go! Create a new instance called `Prism 1.5`.

16. Duplicate your animation track for **Prism 1.4** and drag 1.5 into the **Animator** slot so it is bound to the track.

17. The only keyframe that has to change is 240 where you scoot it to the side of the previous prism and then you should keyframe the **Position**.

18. One more to go! Go back to step 15 and call the instance `Prism 1.6`.

When finished, you should have something that looks approximately like this on the final keyframe:

Fig. 10.25 – The fully extended bridge on the last keyframe

Go ahead and scrub the playhead across the Timeline and admire your handiwork. You have taken a huge step towards mastering Timeline as well as making our mini-game cooler!

If you've gotten this far, you now understand how to animate multiple objects on a Timeline using the record mode to create Infinite clips. If I'm guessing correctly, you're probably now also an expert at using orthographic views to line up objects.

You can earn bonus points by investigating how to use Track Groups to organize and tidy up the tracks pane.

Adding Audio

As a final touch, let's breathe some more life into the bridge by adding a sound effect when it unfolds. I created a sound effect, `ch 10 bridge.mp3`, from the free ones available. It's on GitHub. The effect goes well with the 4-second animation. You may want to create or find your own.

1. In the Hierarchy, create a new empty game object named `Bridge SFX`. In the **Inspector**, add in an **Audio Source** component. Uncheck **Play On Awake**:

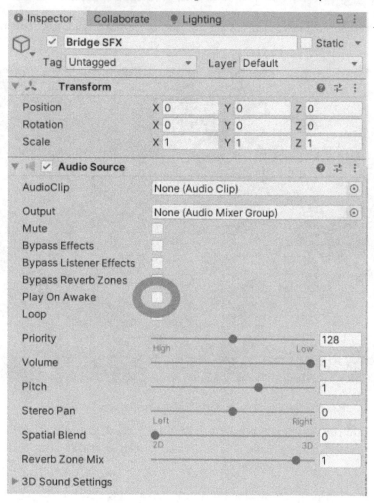

Fig. 10.26 – Uncheck Play On Awake; the other default settings are fine

2. Create a new **Audio Track** in the **Timeline** either with the dropdown or a right-click:

Fig. 10.27 – Add a new Audio Track from the menu

You should now have a new track below the others:

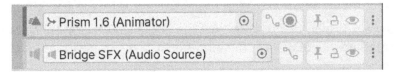

Fig. 10.28 – Audio track added

3. To the right of your new track, in the clip area right-click and choose **Add From Audio Clip**. From the selector, locate `ch 10 bridge.mp3`:

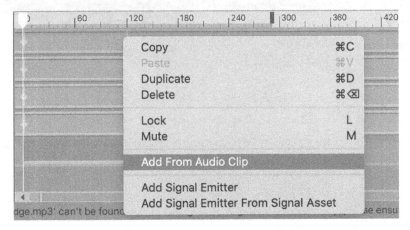

Fig. 10.29 – This will bind a clip to the track

The waveform should appear in the clip area:

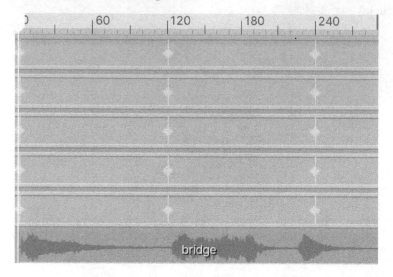

Fig. 10.30 – You see the waveform once you add the clip

Unfortunately, the Timeline preview mode does not support audio scrubbing so to hear your sound you need to play the game, but this isn't so bad.

4. Switch to your **Bridge TL** object that has the **Playable Director** on it. Change **Update Method** to **DSP Clock**. This allows better synchronization between sound and audio.

Fig. 10.31 – Change Update Method of your Playable Director

Go ahead and play the game and admire your handiwork. We're done! Don't forget to uncheck **Play On Awake** on your **Playable Director** when you are through previewing.

Summary

So many secret weapons, so little time.

In this chapter, we learned what Timeline is and when it may be the best choice for what you want to animate/sequence. We also took a super-brief look at all the different types of tracks that Timeline supports: Animation, Audio, Signal, and others. The point of this was to give a taste that Timeline is a very powerful system, and we are just scratching the surface of what it can do.

Next, we unleashed Timeline on our minigame level. We took an object that we created with ProBuilder in the previous chapter and individually animated instances of it to create a cool bridge unfolding effect that can be the result of the player solving a puzzle, blasting the right thing, or whatever you decide.

We'll investigate triggering Timelines further down the, er, line.

Coming up next: our triumphant return to Blender! This will be the most complex thing we've tackled yet. We're going to model the tough-as-nails Space Marine!

11

We Could Be Heroes: Blender Character Modeling

"I think that we all do heroic things, but hero is not a noun, it's a verb."

—Robert Downey, Jr.

Well, well, well. If it isn't time for our old friend Blender. We meet again.

This time, Blender will help us to fill in a key game element that's missing: the hero! What's a game without a protagonist? In this chapter, we will model our formidable space marine character whom we will continue to unwrap, texture, rig, and animate in later chapters.

This chapter will have three main topics:

- Blender Command Review: It's been a while since we created things in Blender. Here, we will quickly recap the most useful commands that will come in handy when you are modeling the hero.

- Prepping for the Marine: Here, we will see the output of this chapter, talk about planning, and do a little miscellaneous preparation.

- Modeling the Marine: This section is where the magic happens. We will go through creating each part of the model using all the tools at our garbage disposal, er, ignore that last bit, I seem to be thinking about garbage a lot. Can't imagine why. Just forget I said anything.

By the end of the chapter, our model will be ready to be UV unwrapped and textured, which happens in the next chapter.

Technical Requirements

This chapter will take place entirely within the space-time continuum of Blender. You may want to have your human reference `.fbx` model handy, but it's really not necessary.

The supporting files for this chapter can be found here: `https://github.com/PacktPublishing/Mind-Melding-Unity-and-Blender-for-3D-Game-Development/tree/main/Chapter11`

The code in action video for this chapter can be found here: `https://bit.ly/3Fo8pWb`

Blender Command Review

Okay, we know our mission, but it's been quite some time since we've had some Blender training. Let's have a quick, intensive overview of the most important Blender functionality that will help us build our marine with the least amount of pain.

3D View Commands

These commands will be essential to your modeling process and you will use them over and over. If this refresher is not enough for you, or if you jumped to this chapter, you may want to go back and have a look at *Chapter 3, Entering the Blender Zone for the First Time*. Here are some of the most useful commands within the 3D View pane.

Navigating the View

There are many, many ways to change what you are viewing. The basic mouse and keyboard controls are **middle mouse button** to tumble your view, *Shift* + **middle mouse button** to pan, and **scroll wheel** to zoom. There are also on-screen controls:

Fig. 11.1 – On-screen view controls

Dragging the colored axes dots tumbles the view, click-dragging the magnifying glass zooms, and click-dragging the hand pans. Clicking the grid toggles the perspective or orthographic view.

You can change the view from the top menu by choosing the options under **View | Viewpoint**, **View | Navigation**, and **View | Align View**.

Lastly, but definitely not least, you can switch the view with the Numpad. This is important enough to give it its own section.

Numpad Commands

To start with, remember that you really want to have a real number pad to use. You can turn on Blender's numpad simulation, but, frankly, it doesn't compare to using the real thing.

Orthographic viewing allows you to precisely size and align objects. The numpad commands are great for quick orthographic// viewing. The critical functions to have at your disposal are as follows:

- **Numpad 1**: Front orthographic view. *Ctrl / Cmd + Numpad 1* for back isometric view.

- **Numpad 3**: Right orthographic view. *Ctrl / Cmd + Numpad 3* for left isometric view.

- **Numpad 7**: Top orthographic view. *Ctrl / Cmd + Numpad 7* for bottom isometric view.

- **Numpad . (period)**: Frame (focus on) the selected object.

- **Numpad /**: This will put the object into "isolate" or "local" mode and focus on it. Press the slash again to leave isolation. Note that this is different from the *H* key hide options because it does not alter the visibility setting of individual objects in the view. (Visibility is controlled by the eye icons in the Outliner pane.)

If you are not yet comfortable with switching views with the Numpad, get some practice before you dive in with the marine. Create a Suzanne monkey head and make up a military-style drill: "Yer front! Yer back! Yer left, right, left!"

Miscellaneous 3D View Commands

These commands are so useful they are getting called out here, but any commands that are used less often will be specifically explained in the modeling section when we need to use them:

- **Creating Objects**: Use *Shift + A*. You can do this in either Object or Edit mode, but there is an important difference. The difference is that if you create something while in Edit mode, the thing that you create becomes *a part of* whatever you are editing—it is not a separate object that can be manipulated on its own, which is what happens when you create objects in Object Mode.

- **Selecting / Deselecting All**: The *A* key selects all objects or elements and double-tapping *A* unselects everything.

- **Transformations**: The three basic transformations are Move (*G*), Rotate (*R*), and Scale (*S*). These can be constrained by immediately entering a key for the axis: *X*, *Y*, or *Z*. You can be even more precise by entering numbers, for instance, you can set the Z scale to 2 with *S* then *Z* then *2*. Holding down *Ctrl* (Mac and PC) will engage snapping if you are transforming without numbers.

- **Toolbar and Sidebar**: *T* will toggle the Toolbar and *N* will toggle the Sidebar (you can remember: I have *No* idea why this is the hotkey). Depending on how big your screen is, you may want to always leave these open or closed.

- **The 3D Cursor**: You can place the 3D Cursor on your current viewing plane with *Shift + right-mouse button*.

Manipulating things at the Object level is all well and good, but for customizing nitty-gritty details, we need to be in Edit Mode.

Edit Mode Commands

Hopefully everything we're listing here should seem familiar. If not: practice, practice, practice!

- **Toggling Modes**: The *Tab* key switches back and forth from Object to Edit Mode. You will be doing this a lot. I mean a lot a lot.

- **Element Selection Mode**: You can change whether you are editing vertices, edges, or faces with *Ctrl / Command + 1/2/3*. You will thank yourself for practicing these key commands until they are second nature. You will switch between them a lot.

- **X-Ray mode**: Toggle this mode with *Alt + Z*. X-Ray mode is incredibly handy because it allows you to select all elements at a location, not just the ones that are visible in Solid view. For example, you might be in the Front view and want to select the overlapped vertices at the front and back of a cube. Toggling on X-Ray mode allows you to do this.

- **Inset and Extrude**: These two commands are like the bedrock of using Blender. The *I* key allows you to inset a face and the *E* key allows you to extrude any element type. You can constrain the extrusion to an axis by pressing *X*, *Y*, or *Z*.

- **Apply Transformations**: This is one command you don't want to forget. It is most useful during the modeling process and not during any subsequent manipulation, such as setting up a model in a scene. Applying Transformations takes the current transformed state of your object and makes that the base, or default, state, zeroing out the transforms in the process. This can prevent problems down the line, such as when a stack of object modifiers has trouble working on a pre-transformed object. Pressing *Ctrl / Command + A* will give you your choice of which transformations to apply. Often, it's best to apply all.

There are, of course, 4 million other things you can do from within Edit Mode (knife tool, join command, beveling, and so on and so forth) and, as mentioned, we will cover some of them as they are required during modeling.

Pro Tip: Faster Command Access

As you find yourself using certain commands over and over, you may decide to take advantage of two features designed to make your life easier: the Quick menu and custom Shortcut keys. If you press the *Q* key (and you are a new user), you will open up an empty **Quickmenu**. To add items to the menu, or to make new keyboard shortcuts, you can right-click on just about any drop-down menu command or tool icon and you will get a little popup that gives you the easy access options.

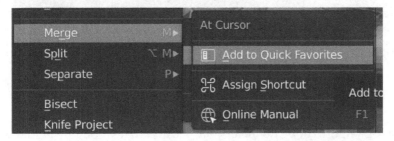

Fig. 11.2 – Here, we could add the Merge command to the Quick Favorites menu

Once you have your Quick Favorites populated and some custom shortcuts, you will find your productivity can go through the roof!

So that's it for our Blender refresher. We went over some of the most crucial commands for navigating the 3D view and for editing your model. These are the ones you should make a great effort to feel comfortable using as they form the foundation for more advanced Blender use.

Prepping for the marine

A little bit of planning goes a long way. So, let's see what we're aiming for. Although untextured, this should give you a basic idea of the type of character we are going for:

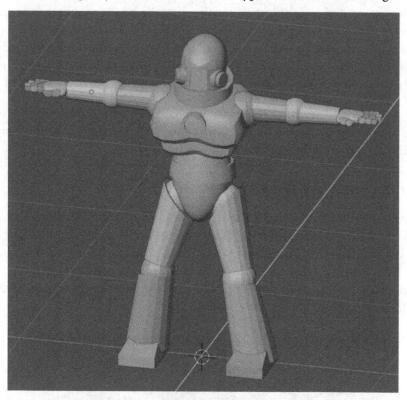

Fig. 11.3 – Untextured, but still tough as nails

Not bad for what we can do in a single chapter!

We are aiming for a figure about 1.8 meters tall, because that is roughly human height, and it will fit through the doors we've already created.

> **In-Depth Character Modeling and Animation**
>
> If you really want to take a deep dive into character modeling and animation, there are many great resources available, including Packt books. Go to `https://www.packtpub.com/` and search "blender character." Remember Blender can output AAA-quality models like the best of them. You are only limited by your imagination and the effort you want to put in.

The marine is in what's called **T-pose** because he is getting ready for afternoon tea.

Actually, you have probably already guessed that it is called T-pose because, with his arms out, the character resembles the letter T.

> **Tip: Binding poses**
>
> T-pose and the other super-common modeling pose, A-pose (where the character's arms are slanted down at the side), are called **Binding Poses**. These poses come into play when rigging a model (with **bones** or **armatures**) for later animation. Modelers choose one over the other based on where they feel they need to make trade-offs in terms of stretching during animation.

So, let's get going with this marine:

1. Start on the marine by first creating a new Blender file, a separate one from your SpaceEscape file. I chose the highly confusing name `SpaceMarine`. (Technically, we could create a new scene within the same Blender file, but I am keeping things simple.)

2. If there are any default objects in your new scene, delete them all by selecting everything with the *A* key and then deleting with the *X* key.

Images and objects will come in at the 3D cursor location, so if for some odd reason your 3D cursor is not there, press *Shift + S* for the pop-up menu and select **Cursor to World Origin**.

Organizing the objects in your scene

The marine is going to be made of lots of objects and you'll drive yourself crazy if you keep accidentally clicking on things you don't mean to. So here is a great thing to know about the Outliner panel. By default, it gives you a little eyeball icon next to each object to control its visibility, but you can also have it so that you can control an object's *selectability* in the scene. This is great because as we build pieces of the marine and move on to others, it lets us make the previous parts unselectable—we want to be able to see them, but not click on them when modeling.

The following figure and notes explain how to do this:

Fig. 11.4 – This is how to change which viewport filters are visible in the Outliner pane

The Outliner pane has some viewport filters that are not visible by default. To see the one we want, do the following (refer to *Fig 11.4*):

- At the top right of the Outliner panel, click the icon that looks like a funnel (screenshot A in the figure).

- That will open a dropdown (screenshot B in the figure) where you can toggle on the arrowhead icon. This is the icon that indicates whether something is selectable in the view.

The Selectable icon will now be visible next to all objects in the Outliner view (screenshot C in the preceding figure). An object is selectable if the arrowhead is filled in, and it is unselectable if the icon is just two angled lines.

You will notice that the arrowhead icon also appears next to the names of Collections (screenshot C in the preceding figure). This great feature allows you to toggle selectability (as well as visibility) for the collection as a whole. So, you might very well want to temporarily hide all parts of the arm and then bring them back.

Randomizing Colors

The last thing we want to do before modeling is set up a little visual convenience. We are going to have it so that each different piece of the marine (head, hand, foot, and so on) will appear as a different color in the view. This makes it a lot easier to distinguish things when you start to have lots of objects in the scene. Note that this display color will *not* get exported with your object and has *nothing to do* with vertex colors, if you know what those are.

To set this up, open the Viewport Shading dropdown by clicking the down arrow on the right and top of the screen near the **Outliner** panel (you need to have Solid Mode selected to see these options):

Fig. 11.5 – Open the dropdown with the arrow, then choose Random

Clicking **Random** will set each newly created object to be a random display color.

Okay, we're finally done with all the prep work. What is it we were going to do again? Ah, yes! Modeling!

Modeling the Marine

Are you ready, Earthling? Good. We are going to begin creating the marine starting at the top and working our way to the bottom, going through each major body part group: head, torso, arms, hands, legs, boots. As is very common in the modeling world, we start with primitive shapes and then refine them. There is so much to do that I won't waste words, and I certainly will not make any puns about getting a head start, avoiding jumping ahead, heading in the right direction, and so on.

(Sorry.)

Head

The head is going to be based on a sphere that we distort and then add some simple cylinders to. Pre-texturing, it's going to look roughly like this:

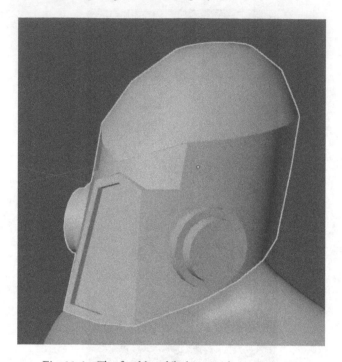

Fig. 11.6 – The final head/helmet without texturing

As we go along, we'll encounter new commands we haven't used before. I'll explain what to do with them for our purposes here, but if you have the time and curiosity, play around with the new stuff to really get a feel for it. Here we go:

1. Start from the Front Orthographic view, *Numpad 1*. Make sure your 3D Cursor is in a good starting spot. Press *Shift + S* then choose **Cursor to World Origin**.

2. Create a sphere with *Shift + A* then **Mesh | Create UV sphere.** In the **Last Operation** panel, give it **Segments:** 16, **Rings:** 8, **Radius:** 0.14m, **Location Z:** 1.66m. Focus on the sphere with *Numpad .* (period).

3. (*S*)cale in on the *X* axis to **.9** to create an oval.

4. *Tab* to enter Edit mode.

> **Big Important Note**
>
> We are going to be switching the element selection mode so often that I am going to use a special shorthand. In all of the following instructions, when you see [*V mode*], [*E mode*], or [*F mode*], that means use *Ctrl / Command 1, 2,* or *3* to enter Vertex, Edge, or Face selection mode respectively. Got it?

5. Switch to Right side view with *Numpad 3.*

6. [*V mode*]. Select the vertices at the fattest (middle) part of the sphere and scale them in slightly on the Y axis so they approximately line up with the vertices above and below; see screenshot A in the following figure. (Be sure you are in X-Ray mode to be able to select vertices on both sides of the model.)

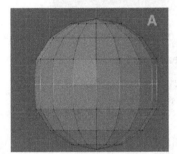 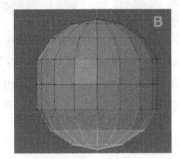 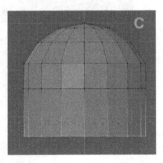

Fig. 11.7 – We're creating a kind of extended dome

7. Now drag to select the vertices toward the bottom; see *Fig 11.7*, screenshot B. Press *X* to delete them, creating a hemisphere.

8. Select the bottom vertices at the bottom of the hemisphere and move them down on the Z to create a sort of short, fat silo shape; see *Fig 11.7, screenshot C.*

   How are you doing so far? Are you getting any faster with any commands yet? I hope so! Let's keep going...

9. Put the 3D Cursor right in the middle of the neck with *Shift + right-click.*

10. With the bottom vertices still selected, (R)otate them to create an angle that slopes upward to the right; see *Fig 11.8*, image A:

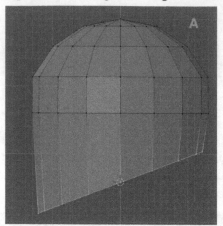 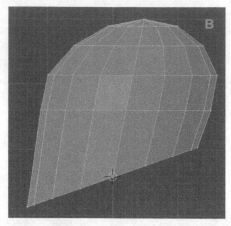

Fig. 11.8 – Rotate the bottom vertices then Shear all of them

11. Select (A)ll elements, then choose **Mesh | Transform | Shear** (see *Fig 11.8*, image B).

12. Turn off X-Ray mode (*Alt + Z*) and switch to the Front view (*Numpad 1*). We do this because we want to work with verts only on the front side of the head, not both front and back.

13. Select the vertex along the middle vertical edge (see *Fig 11.9*).

14. Tap *G* twice quickly to do a **Vertex Slide**—this will only allow the vertex to slide along a pre-existing edge as opposed to free movement. Slide the vert down to start to create the beginning of a "frown":

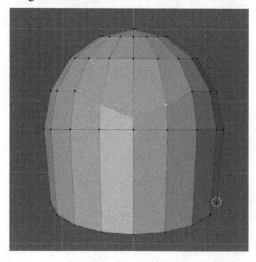

Fig. 11.9 – Slide the middle vertex and the ones to either side to create a "frown"

15. Select the verts on the left and right of the vert you just moved. Again, tap *G* twice and move the verts down to complete the frown (*Fig 11.9*).

16. Select the middle vert below the frown and slide it upward to create a pinched look:

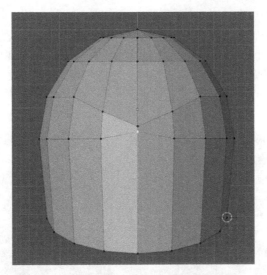

Figure 11.10 – Vertex Slide the vertex up to create a "pinch"

17. [*F mode*] Shift-select to select the two faces in the pinch area (they look like a bowtie). Then add the two faces on either side of the bowtie to your selection.

18. (*E*)xtrude the four faces inward slightly on the *Y* axis; see *Fig 11.11*. You may need to tumble your view to see and work easier:

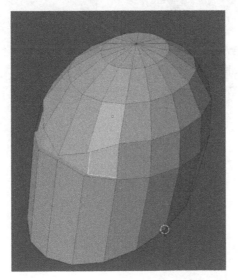

Fig. 11.11 – Push the eye area in a bit with Extrude on the Y axis

19. Let's create a sort of face grille for the helmet. [*V mode*] Switch to Front view. Select the three vertices on the bottom front; see *Fig 11.12*, screenshot A.

20. Set the 3D Cursor to the middle bottom of the helmet with *Shift right-click*.

21. (*S*)cale the vertices out on the *X* axis, creating a sort of wedge shape.

22. [*F mode*] Select the two faces that make up the wedge shape. Right-click and select **Dissolve Faces** to make them a single face; see screenshot B in the following figure. It's looking good, but there's a problem. If you tumble your view around, you will see that the face is actually bent at the center where the edge used to be. We want faces to be perfectly flat:

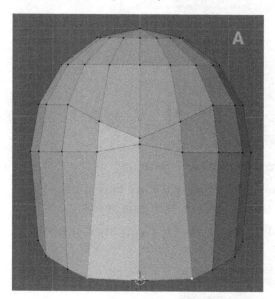 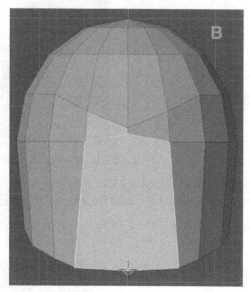

Fig. 11.12 – Widen the bottom then turn the front into a single face

23. To fix that problem, with the face selected, from the menu, choose **Mesh | Cleanup | Make Planar Faces**. You don't need to switch your view yet, but if you do, you'll see the face is now flat:

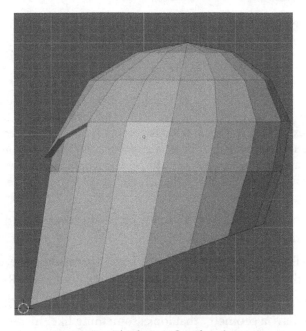

Fig. 11.13 – The front is flat after cleanup

24. If you changed your view, go back to the Front. Then, (*I*)nset the big front face slightly.

25. Next, (*E*)xtrude the face in slightly on the *Y* axis. Here's my version after extrusion:

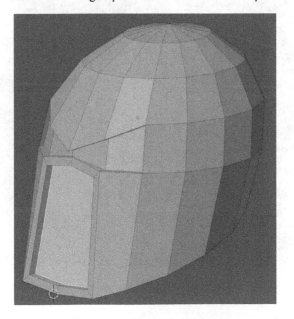

Fig. 11.14 – The grille in place

We're close to finishing the head for now, just one simple detail to add. We're going to create some geometry in *Edit* mode:

> **Tip: Creating Geometry in Edit Mode versus Object Mode**
>
> Geometry created in Edit mode is *not* a separate object from what you are already editing. This means that once you deselect the new geometry, it might be difficult to exactly select it again if it intersects with pre-existing geometry—in this case, be sure you have the Undo command handy (*Ctrl / Command + Z*). An alternative approach would be to create the new geometry in Object mode, shape it how you want, and then join the new and old objects into one.

1. Choose an area slightly away from the existing head geometry and put your 3D Cursor there with *Shift + right-click*.

2. Create a new cylinder (via *Shift + A*). In the **Last Operation pane**, set the number of **Vertices** to 16, the **Radius** to .05, the **Depth** to .04, and the **Y Rotation** to 90.

3. Select the front face of the cylinder and (*I*)nset it slightly. Then, (*E*)xtrude that face out a bit, so you have a geometry that looks something like this:

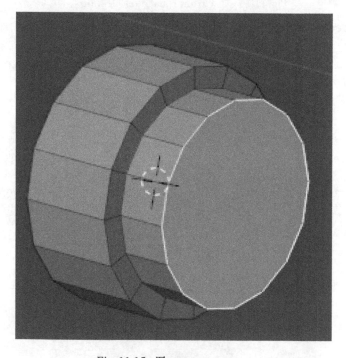

Fig. 11.15 – The new geometry

4. Now we need to place this thing correctly. Switch to Top view (*Numpad 7*) and be sure you are in X-Ray mode (*Alt + Z*).

5. [*V mode*] Drag to select all the vertices, then rotate them slightly to the right. Move them (*G*) into a good position on the cheek. You'll need to switch back and forth with the side view, *Numpad 3*. You may also choose to (*S*)cale it.

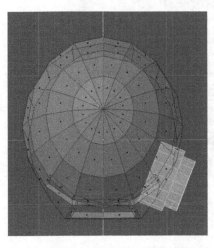
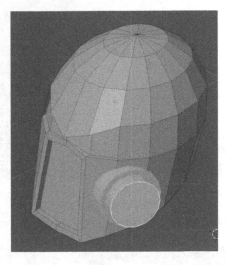

Fig. 11.16 – Rotate then align the cylinder using X-Ray mode and Top and Front views

6. Now, rather than duplicating and placing the cylinder on the other side of the head, there is a fantastic **Symmetrize** command that basically mirrors geometry around an axis. (Note: this is *not* the same as the Mirror modifier we will learn about later.) In Edit mode, make sure you have everything selected (*A*) and then choose **Mesh | Symmetrize**. In the Last Operation pane, make sure the **Direction** is set to **X to -X**. You should see new cylinder geometry appear on the other cheek.

7. Return to Object mode with *Tab*.

8. Right now, the head is **flat shaded** and showing lots of polygons. Let's improve this and make it **smooth shaded**. Right-click and choose **Shade Smooth**. I know, I know, now it looks *really* strange. We're not done. See *Fig 11.18.*

9. In the Properties pane, select the **Object Data Properties** tab and toggle on **Normals | Auto Smooth**:

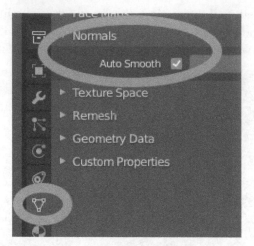

Fig. 11.17 – Select the icon tab on the left then turn on Auto Smooth

Here are the three shading stages we just went through:

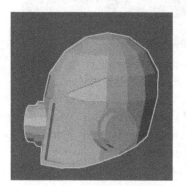 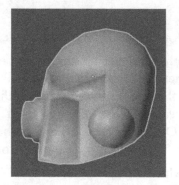 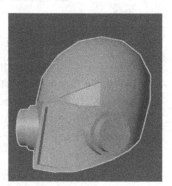

Fig. 11.18 – Left to right: flat shaded, smooth shaded, Auto Smooth turned on

So, what's all this smoothing business about? It has to do with how the renderer calculates lighting using the **normals** of all the polygon faces and the angles between the faces. For now, let's just assume you usually want smooth shading with Auto Smooth enabled:

1. For good measure, under the Object menu, choose **Apply | Rotation & Scale**.

2. In the Outliner pane, rename your object to Head.

3. Make the head unselectable by toggling the arrowhead icon off.

And that, ladies and germs, is as far as we will go with the head/helmet for now.

And now, with our plan to model from top to bottom, we will model the torso.

I guess you could say we're "heading" in the right direction! (Doh!)

Torso

We are mainly going to base the torso on a cube and cylinder. You are going to be introduced to a very important and common object Modifier called the **Subdivision Surface** modifier. The pre-textured torso will wind up looking like this:

Fig. 11.19 – The torso to be

So, let's get going:

1. The first step for modeling any part of the marine is going to be the same, so you should get comfortable with it. Make sure you are in Object mode and enter the Front Orthographic view with *Numpad 1*. Make sure your 3D Cursor is in a good starting spot. Press *Shift + S* then choose **Cursor to World Origin**.

2. Create a cube with *Shift + A* and **Mesh | Cube**. In the Last Operation panel, set the **Size** to .6 and raise it on the *Z* to about 1.26. In the Outliner pane, name it Torso.

3. Turn on X-Ray mode (*Alt + Z*). Switch to the side view with *Numpad 3*. Scale the cube by about .8 on the *Y* and move the cube forward on the Y axis so that there is more room in front of the chest area than the back. See the following figure:

 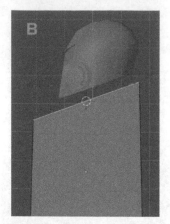 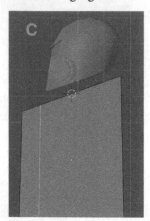

Fig. 11.20 – Position the torso, rotate the top, and add a loop cut

4. Tab into Edit mode and select the top edges. (Be sure you are in X-Ray mode to get them all.) *Shift + S* and choose **Cursor to Selected** (to set the point of rotation).

5. (*R*)otate the edges to approximately the same angle as the bottom of the helmet. If you need to, select all and move everything down on the Y axis, leaving room below the helmet (see *Fig 11.20,* screenshot B).

6. Add a vertical loop cut with *Ctrl / Command + R* and position it toward the front of the chest (see *Fig 11.20,* screenshot C).

7. In Front view, turn off X-Ray mode (*Alt + Z*) and add four vertical loop cuts (*Ctrl / Command + R, mouse wheel* to increase count):

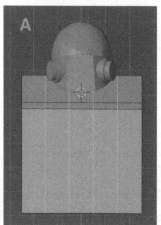 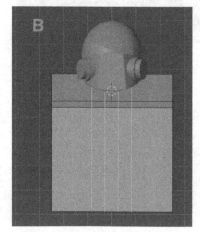 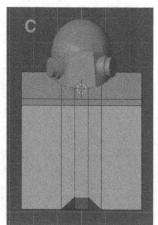

Fig. 11.21 – Adding a notch to the chest area

8. Scale the cuts in on the **X** axis.

9. Select the front edge and move (1) it up on the **Z** axis to add some definition.

10. The upper chest area is looking a bit too long, so let's scale it. I'm not giving you any keys here; can you do this? Enter side view and turn on X-Ray. Grab all the bottom vertices and lift them up on the Z by almost 50% (see *Fig 11.21*, screenshot A).

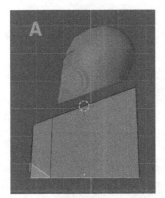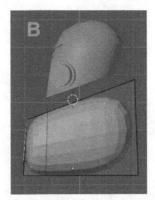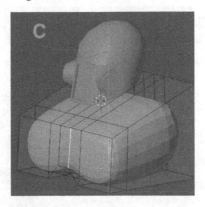

Fig. 11.22 – The upper torso shortened, then subdivision applied

11. Select the Modifiers tab (the wrench icon) in the Object Properties pane on the lower right. Add a **Subdivision Surface** modifier and increase the **Levels** to 2:

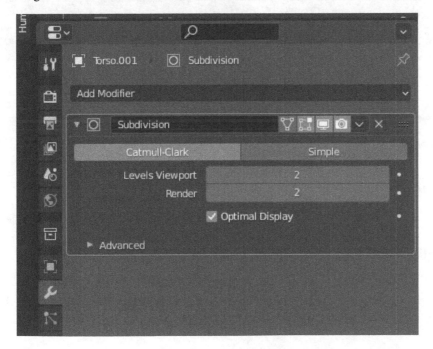

Fig. 11.23 – Add Modifiers from the Modifiers panel in the lower-right screen

12. Scale and position this chest area so that it approximates *Fig 11.22*, screenshots B and C.

13. We're going to duplicate this to make another section of the torso. Back in Object mode, select the torso and use *Shift + D* to duplicate. Move it down on the Z axis and scale it down slightly: . 8 seems pretty good:

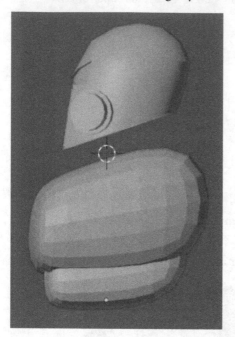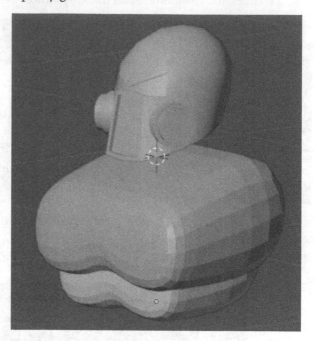

Fig. 11.24 – The upper torso duplicated, scaled down, and positioned lower

Now, how about giving the marine a way to defend himself?

Chest Blaster

Our marine is going to have a chest blaster that looks sort of like Iron Man's reactor. It's quick and easy to create:

1. In the Front view, put the 3D cursor to one side of your figure and create a new circle with *Shift + A* then **Mesh | Circle** with **Vertices:** 16, **Radius:** . 05, and **X Rotation** 90.

2. In Edit mode [*E mode*], select (A)ll and (E)xtrude on the (Y) for . 04.

3. Switch to [*F mode*], select (A)ll, and choose **Face | Solidify Faces**, and in the Last Operation panel, set the **Thickness** to . 02.

4. Back in Object mode, use the Top and other views to position the blaster on the chest. See *Fig 11.25*:

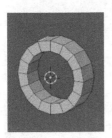 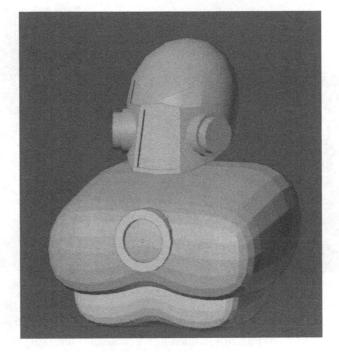

Fig. 11.25 – I am not Iron Man

Moving right along, I'm not much of a fan of heads floating in space, so let's take care of that now.

Collar

The protective neck collar is also easy to make. We'll again use a circle to start:

1. Begin in Object Mode so you are creating a separate object.
2. Press *Shift + A* and then create a **Mesh > Circle**. Give it **Vertices:** 16 and **Radius:** .16.
3. *Tab* to Edit, [*E mode*], select (*A*), then extrude the circle by .1. (Be sure you are in Edge Edit Mode—the circle has no faces!)
4. Switch to [*F mode*], select (*A*)ll, then **Face > Solidify Faces** to .02.

5. Use the Top and side views to position the collar around the head. Note the slope to the collar that we will create in the next few steps:

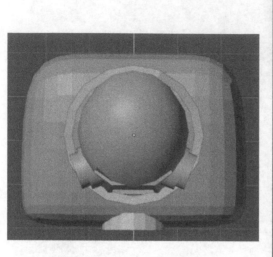
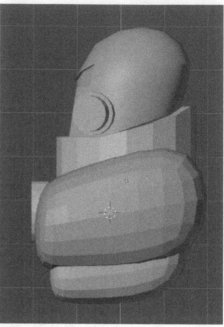

Fig. 11.26 – Positioning the collar and previewing the slope to create

Almost done, just gotta work on that slope.

6. In the Back view (*Numpad 1* then *Numpad 9*), enter [*F mode*] and select the top two faces of the back collar. Raise them up. See *Fig 11.27*, screenshots A and B:

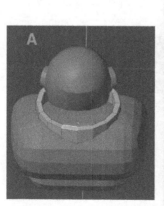
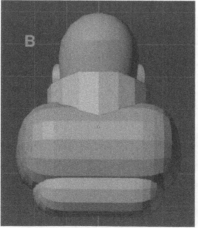
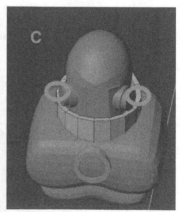

Fig. 11.27 – Raise the back faces (A and B), then select pairs of edges to shape the slope

7. Switch to [*E mode*]. By selecting pairs of opposite-side edges (see *Fig 11.27*, screenshot C), go through and raise them on the *Z* axis to create the slope seen in *Fig 11.26*.

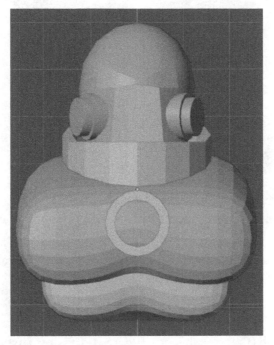

Fig. 11.28 – Our hard-as-nails work in progress

Our collar is good to go for now. Now for the last part of the torso.

The Bottom Bits

To finish off the rough torso, we'll now add the abs and groin area, starting with our good friend, Mr. Cube. Here's how:

1. Reset your 3D Cursor if you need to. Press *Shift + S* and click **Cursor to World Origin**.

2. Create a new cube. You gotta remember by now, yes? Give it a **Size** of .5m. and a **Z Location of** 1.

3. (*S*)cale it on the *Y* axis by .8 to make it skinnier front to back.

4. Use *Tab* for Edit mode, then turn on X-Ray (*Alt + Z*, but you knew that, right?).

5. Add two horizontal loop cuts and position them toward the top of the cube (see *Fig 11.29*, screenshot A):

Fig. 11.29 – Shaping the lower torso by scaling vertices

6. [*V mode*] Select all the top vertices and scale them in on the X axis (see *Fig 11.28*, screenshot B).

7. Select all the vertices below the top and scale them in on the X axis as well (see *Fig 11.28*, screenshot C).

8. Select all the bottom vertices and drastically scale them in on the X axis (see *Fig 11.29*, screenshot C).

9. In the Modifiers tab (the wrench icon), add a **Subdivision Surface** modifier and set it to **Level 2**.

Fig. 11.30 – The lower torso before and after Subdivision is applied

10. *Tab* for Object mode. **Apply** the modifier by choosing the drop-down arrow and **Apply** (see *Fig 11.30,* screenshot C).

11. Use the scaling tools to shape the lower torso as you see fit (see *Fig 11.29*, screenshot D). You may or may not want to make it skinnier, and so on.

Belt

The final touch we will add is a belt:

1. In [*F mode*], *Alt + right-click* a face to select a face loop above the widest part, then *Shift + Alt + right-click* to add the face loop below that to your selection (see *Fig 11.30*, screenshot A). To get this to select horizontal loops, you need to have the cursor toward the left or right edge of the face.

2. Choose **Face | Extrude Faces Along Normals** and extend the faces out very slightly (see *Fig 11.31*, screenshots B and C):

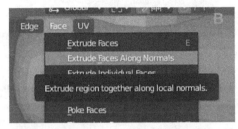

Fig. 11.31 – Extruding the belt faces

With the belt out of the way, we'll do some final cleanup before moving on.

Finishing Up the Torso

Do you remember what the final torso is meant to look like? Here's a refresher:

Fig. 11.32 – What we're aiming for

Here is the tweaky stuff we need to do:

1. Back in Object mode, with the lower torso (bottom bits) selected, right-click and **Shade Smooth**. Remember to turn on **Auto Smooth** in the **Object Properties | Normals** section.

2. Moving upward now to the two chest/rib pieces, I decided that I prefer a more angular look. Choose *each* object and change the Subdivision Surface modifier **Level** back to **1**. Then, **Apply** the modifier from the little drop-down arrow.

3. **Join** the two chest pieces together by selecting them and press *Ctrl / Command + J* to Join them.

4. Select the chest blaster circle and then **Shade Smooth** and **Auto Smooth**.

5. Do the same thing for the neck collar.

Lastly, select the collar, the blaster, the chest and the lower torso and join everything together with *Ctrl / Command + J*.

You did it! You made the most complicated part of the marine. The rest is all downhill from here.

Who's better than you? No body.

Torso? *Body*? Get it?

<sigh> I think I have a parasite. Let's just keep going…

The Arm

I had this great thing I was going to say about the marine being ready for *unarmed* combat even though he's completely h-*armless*, but seeing as how that last joke bombed, I'll just skip it.

Here's the plan: we will create the arm on one side and then symmetrize it as we've done before.

We'll start modeling by creating a shoulder joint, and for this, we will use a sphere.

Create a UV Sphere with 16 **Segments**, 16 **Rings**, and a **Radius** of .1. Position it at **Z** 1.43 and **X** .2. This will get it in approximately the right position and then you can use this figure to eyeball a better position:

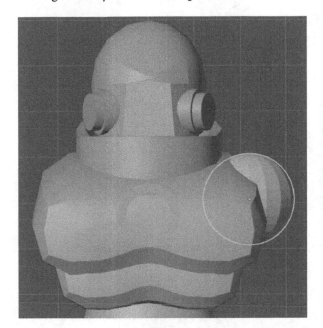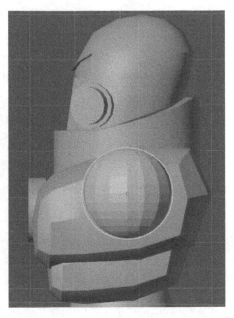

Fig. 11.33 – Use the top and side views to better place the joint

1. For the length of the upper arm, let's create a cylinder. Give it 16 **Vertices**, a **Radius** of .07, a **Depth** .25, and **Rotate** it 90 on the **Y** axis.

2. Move it up and over so it protrudes from the ball joint:

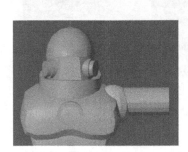

Figure 11.34 – Position the upper arm then scale the front face to taper it

3. Enter Edit mode [*F mode*] and select the front face. Scale it ever so slightly to create a taper; see *Fig 11.33*. Return to Object mode.

4. Select the shoulder joint sphere and duplicate it with *Shift + D*. Scale it to about .75 and position it at the end of the upper arm cylinder.

5. Select the upper arm cylinder, duplicate it, and scale it to about .80. Position this at the end of the arm you have so far.

6. Join the shoulder to the upper arm by selecting each and using *Ctrl / Command + J* to Join them.

7. Join the elbow joint to the forearm in the same way.

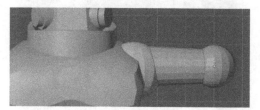 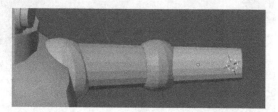

Fig. 11.35 – The forearm elements are just the upper arm elements scaled down

Okay, if you've gotten this far with the arm, you should give yourself a hand. Literally…

The Hand

Ready for some new techniques that should come in handy? I bet you are. Let's get busy:

1. Start by positioning the 3D cursor at the end of the arm with *Shift + right-click*:

 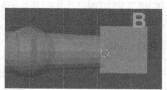 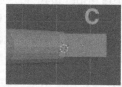 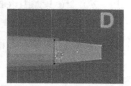

Fig. 11.36 – Position the cursor (A), then position and shape the cube from the front

2. Refer to *Fig 11.36*. In the Front view, create a cube with **Size** .14 and reposition it at the end of the arm (B). Scale it down on the Z axis to .5 (C).

3. Enter Edit mode and [*V mode*]. Turn on X-Ray and select the rightmost vertices. Scale them down on the Z axis to create a wedge (D).

4. Refer to *Fig 11.37*. In the Top view, select the leftmost vertices and scale them down on the Y axis (A).

5. Create three horizontal loop cuts (*Ctrl / Command + R*) (B).

6. Select each vertex on the right and shape them into a gentle arc (C and D):

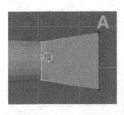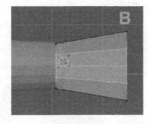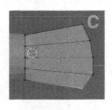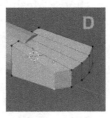

Fig. 11.37 – Shape the hand from the Top view

7. In the Front view, add two vertical loop cuts; see *Fig 11.38*, screenshot A.

8. Enter Isolation mode with *Numpad /* and be sure X-Ray is on.

9. Still in [*V mode*], select the leftmost vertices and scale down on the Z axis to taper the wrist area; see *Fig 11.38*, screenshot B:

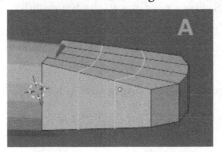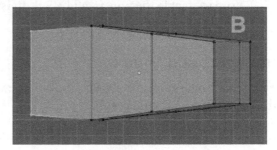

Fig. 11.38 – Insert the loop cuts then taper the wrist

10. Switch to side view and add a horizontal loop cut; see *Fig 11.39*, screenshot A.

11. Select the vertices on both sides of the hand and scale them down a little on the Z axis to create some roundness; see *Fig 11.39*, screenshots B and C:

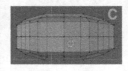

Fig. 11.39 – Adding roundness to the hand, looking straight on from the side

12. In [*F mode*], select the eight front faces and (*I*)nset them slightly; see *Fig 11.39* (D). The fingers will attach here.

13. Let's work on the thumb a bit. In the Front view, select the four leftmost faces as the beginning of the thumb and (*E*)xtrude them; see *Fig 11.40* (A).

14. Using [*V mode*], move the vertices of the face into a roughly circular shape; *Fig 11.40* (B).

15. In [*F mode*], select the four faces again and right-click to **Dissolve Faces**. Then, choose **Mesh | Clean Up | Make Planar Faces** as we've done before.

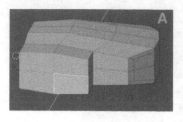
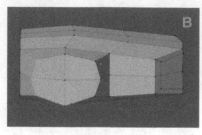
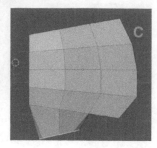

Fig. 11.40 – The beginnings of the thumb

16. With the face selected, scale it down a bit. Switch to Top view and rotate and move it to get a more natural-looking angle; see *Fig 11.40* (C).

17. Before we tackle the fingers, add a **Subdivision Surface** modifier to the hand with its default **Level** of **1**.

The Fingers and Thumb

Creating the fingers is relatively straightforward: we create a single finger, then duplicate and scale it to make the others. Here's how:

1. Set the 3D cursor at the tip of hand with *Shift + right-click*:

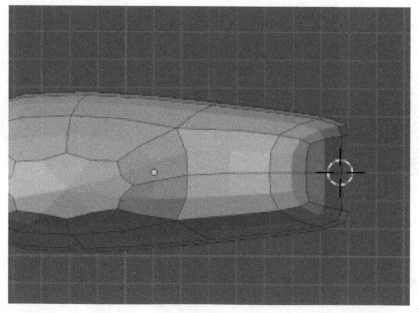

Fig. 11.41 – Position the cursor *roughly* where the first finger will begin

2. Return to Object Mode.

3. Create a cube for the first finger segment. Give it a **Size** of . 04. Scale it on the **Z** axis to . 7, then scale it on the **Y** axis to . 7 also.

4. We're going to create two more segments: the middle and the tip. Duplicate (*Shift + D*) the segment you have, move it on the X axis in front of the previous segment, and scale it to . 9. Repeat that exact process to create the tip. You should wind up with what is shown in *Fig 11.42* (A):

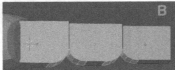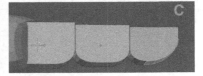

Fig. 11.42 – Create all the segments, then bevel the edges

5. Did you know Blender allows you to edit multiple objects at the same time? Select all three finger segments and enter Edit mode.

6. In [*E mode*], turn on X-Ray and select the four bottom edges: the inside one of the base segment, both edges of the middle, and the inside one of the tip segment. Press *Ctrl / Command + B* to apply a bevel to these edges. Use the mouse wheel to change the number of bevel segments. 4 seems pretty good. See *Fig 11.42* (B).

7. Select the front-bottom edge of the fingertip segment and give it a more pronounced bevel. See *Fig 11.42* (C).

8. Return to Object mode and enter Top view. Select all three segments of the finger and make three duplicates. See *Fig 11.43* (A).

9. Make sure that you have your pivot point set to **Bounding Box Center** so you will be able to easily rotate the fingers. Set the Pivot Point from the drop-down icon at the top. See *Fig 11.43* (B).

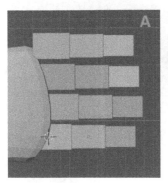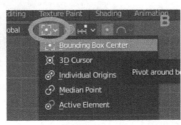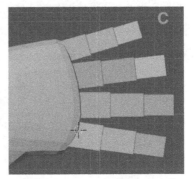

Fig. 11.43 – Creating a more natural finger spread

10. Work on one finger at a time, selecting all of its segments. Rotate, position, and scale them to your taste to create a more natural finger spread; see *Fig 11.43* (C). The little finger will need the most scaling.

11. To create the thumb, select the two foremost segments of the first finger and duplicate them. Scale the segments up, rotate them, and position them in a way that looks *thumb-thing* like this:

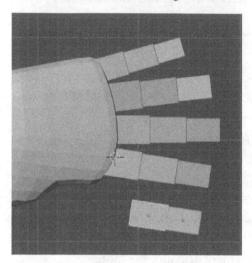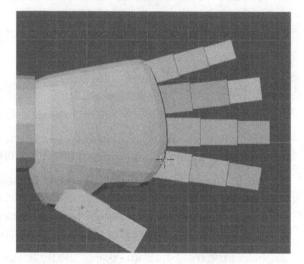

Fig. 11.44 – Thumbs up if you get this right

12. Do yourself a favor and in the Outliner, create a new collection named Hand and move all your pieces into it.

13. Select the base/palm of the hand, that is, the biggest part. Under the Modifiers property tab, go ahead and **Apply** the Subdivision Surface modifier you put on it before.

14. Next, select the hand base and *all* the finger bits. Press *Ctrl / Command + J* to join everything together. What a hand-some hand!

Our time with the hand is finished for now. Time to move on to the lower extremities.

The Leg

There will be three sections to the marine's leg: the upper leg, the lower leg, and the foot. We will create ball joints for the hip and the knee.

The Upper Leg

Let's build out from the torso by creating a hip joint:

1. In the side view, set your 3D Cursor to the approximate location of the joint (*Shift + right-click*). See *Fig 11.45*.

2. Create a UV Sphere with 16 **Segments**, 16 **Rings**, and a **Radius** of .1. Position it using the Front and side views. See *Fig 11.45*:

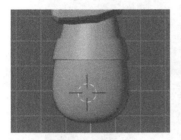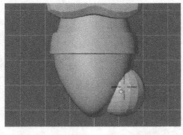

Fig. 11.45 – Set the 3D Cursor then eyeball the hip to position it in the Front and side views

3. Next, create a Cylinder with 16 **Vertices**, a **Radius of** .08, and a **Depth of** .36.

4. Enter Edit mode and turn on X-Ray. With [*V mode*], select the top vertices and scale them out. See *Fig 11.46 (A)*. Be sure you get all the vertices!

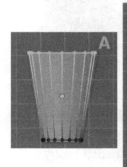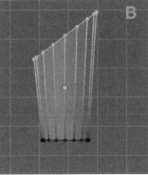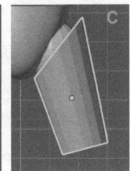

Fig. 11.46 – Scale the top vertices, rotate them, and rotate the leg from the Front and side

5. Rotate the top vertices. See *Fig 11.46 (B)*. Again, be sure you get all the vertices!

6. Back in Object mode, rotate and position the upper leg from the Front and the side. See *Fig 11.46 (C and D)*.

7. Duplicate the hip sphere (*Shift + D*) and scale it by .9. Stash this off to the side for a second.

8. Join the sphere of the hip with the upper leg with *Ctrl / Command + J*.

Down, down we go. Soon we'll be at the bottom! Hurry! Shake a leg!

The Lower Leg

We'll start with a knee joint, just like how we started previously with a hip joint:

1. Take the sphere you stashed and position it at the end of the upper leg using the Front and side views as guides. See *Fig 11.47*:

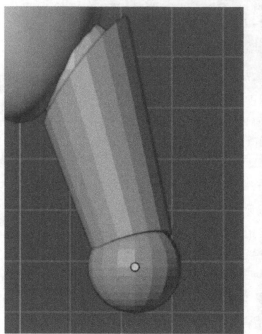 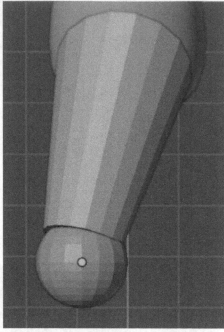

Fig. 11.47 – Position the knee joint using the Front and side views

2. For the actual lower leg, start with a Cylinder with 16 **Vertices**, a **Radius** of .12, and a **Depth** of .37.

3. We are going to treat it similarly to the upper leg, but for variety (and to demonstrate alternatives), we'll manipulate faces instead of vertices. Enter Edit mode with [*F mode*] and select the top face. Scale it to .8 to create a taper; see *Fig 11.48 (A)*.

4. In the side view, rotate the face about to the angle in *Fig 11.48 (B)*.

5. This step may be a little tricky: you are going to alternate between Object mode where you position the entire leg and Edit mode where you are moving just the top face. Refer to *Fig 11.48 (B and C)*. Notice that in the side view (B), the whole lower leg tilts toward the front, so you have to drag the face in that direction. In the Front view (C), the leg is tilted left toward the torso, so drag the top face in that direction. Take your time until you are satisfied with the look.

6. Join the sphere of the knee to the lower leg by using *Ctrl / Command + J*.

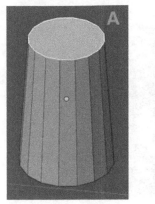
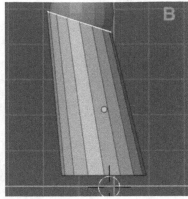
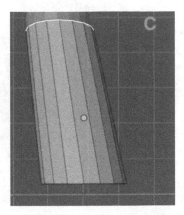

Fig. 11.48 – Taper the top face, rotate it, and then move it in the side (B) and Front view (C)

Finally, the marine has a leg to stand on, but there's one final thing missing…

The Boot

We've reached the bottom. No time to lose. The game is afoot! Let's create the boot…

1. In Object Mode, create a Cube with **Size** . 2. Enter isolation mode with *Numpad /*.

2. Scale the cube on the Z axis to . 7 (shortening the height), and also scale it on the Y axis to 1 . 5 (lengthening it). See *Fig 11.48* (A).

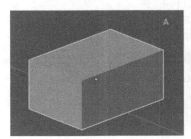
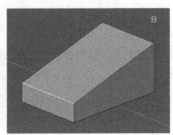
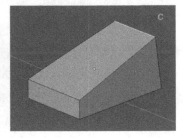

Fig. 11.49 – Scale the box on Y and Z axes, then lower the front edge and scale the rear top edge to pinch it

3. Refer to *Fig 11.49*. In Edit mode, with [*E mode*], select the front edge and drop it on the Z axis (B). Select the rear top edge and scale it in (C).

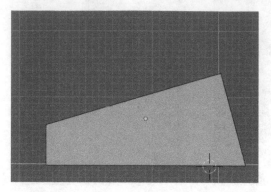 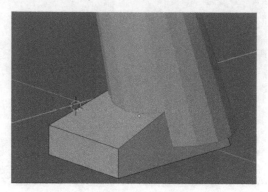

Fig. 11.50 – Reshape the side profile, then position the boot under the leg

4. In the side view, grab the top rear edge and pull it forward (left) to change the overall profile shape. Exit isolation view, then back in Object mode, correctly position the boot under the leg.

How does that song go? "These boots are made for walking"? You bet they are. That was the last bit of marine modeling for this chapter! Let's do some final tasks and then we are out! Woot!

Touchups

Here are a few miscellaneous things that we might have missed before:

- Be sure the shoulder ball and upper arm are joined. Rename this `arm_upper` in the Outliner.

- Have the elbow and forearm joined. Call this `arm_lower`.

- Join the hip ball and thigh. Call this `leg_upper`.

- Join the knee and lower leg and call this `leg_lower`.

- Select all four of these. Right-click to **Shade Smooth**.

- In the Object Data properties, check **AutoSmooth**.

There's one more basic thing we need to do after this touchup…

Parenting

We need to create a hierarchical relationship between the body parts. This is not rigging yet, but it is ensuring that all the parts of the marine move together.

To parent something, you first select the child and then select the parent, and then press *Ctrl / Command + P* and choose **Set Parent to Object**. Do this for the following parts:

- Parent the foot to the lower leg, the lower leg to the upper leg, and the upper leg to the torso.

- Parent the hand to the lower arm, the lower arm to the upper arm, and the upper arm to the torso.

- Parent the head to the torso.

If you can't select something, make sure you didn't make it unselectable in the Outliner!

Finalizing the Model and the File

Okay, we're almost all set, but our marine is looking a bit lopsided. Let's fix that. What we are going to do is select all the objects that currently only appear on the right side, duplicate them, and then mirror them on the other side.

The first thing to do is let Blender know the point we want to mirror around:

1. Press *Shift + S* and choose **Cursor to World Origin**.

2. Next, go to the top middle of your screen and select the dropdown for setting the pivot point:

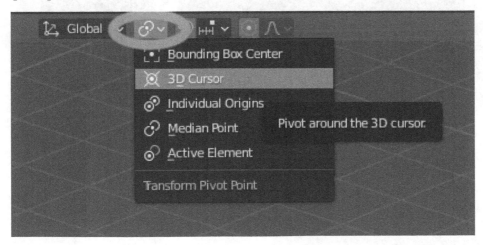

Fig. 11.51 – Set the pivot point to the 3D cursor

3. Now, you need to select all objects (arms, legs, hand, foot) that need to be mirrored. You may want to hide or make unselectable the torso and the head since they don't get mirrored.

4. You are going to duplicate these objects, but hold off for a moment. When you duplicate something as soon as it is copied, its position is under mouse control, but we don't actually want to move what we copy. So, when you duplicate, be prepared to immediately cancel the movement with a right-click. Ready? Duplicate your parts with *Shift + D*. Now, right-click!

5. With the duplicates now selected, on the upper-left dropdown menu, choose **Object | Mirror | X Global**. You should see the parts appear on the other side. Notice how the parent-child relationship have been duplicated too!

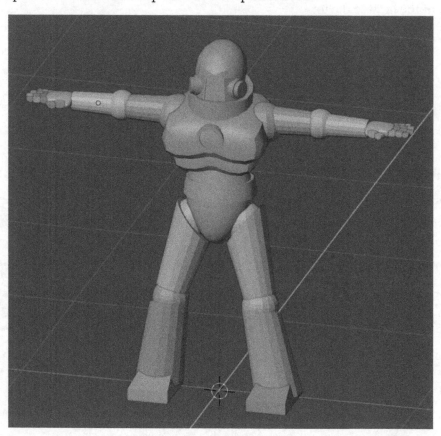

Fig. 11.52 – Ready for anything

6. Awesome! Now for the final bit. Make sure all your objects are selectable (including the head and torso). Now go ahead and select everything with the *A* key.

7. With everything selected, choose **Object | Apply | Rotation and Scale**.

8. If parts of your model now look very strange, it's because their normal got messed up. Do the following: Enter Edit Mode. Select All. Choose **Mesh | Normals | Recalculate Outside**. That should fix it.

And that, as they say, is that!

Summary

Semper Fi! Awesome work! You have brought our marine into existence. What a chapter!

After reviewing some of the Blender basics we covered in earlier chapters, we spent a short amount of time preparing for the main event by previewing the final model and learning some tricks with the Outliner.

After that, we did a deep dive into marine modeling from head to toe: head, torso, arm, hand, leg, and boot. Each part had its own unique challenges. Along the way, we combined tools that we previously learned about with new tools and techniques, such as vertex/edge sliding and object mirroring.

There are about 10 million ways we could improve the marine—hopefully, your head is bursting with 5 million of those. We've got to move on for now, but as you learn more, don't be afraid to revisit your work. Tinker tinker tinker!

Now, if you're tired of looking at the untextured marine (I know I am), in the next chapter, we'll get him UV Unwrapped with some textures applied to him. Fall in, marine, there's more work ahead…

12
It Was Rigged!: Character Rigging

"Marines come in two varieties, big and mean, or skinny and mean."

—Rear Admiral "Jay" R. Stark

Okay, the name of this chapter is a bit misleading, because we have a big first order of business to take care of before we get into rigging our character, and that is UV unwrapping and texturing. So, there are really two main objectives for this chapter, but I couldn't come up with a catchy chapter title that covered both! Anyway, the main sections are:

- UV-Unwrapping and Texturing the Marine: We will quickly review the process of unwrapping and texturing, then go part by part, head to toe, and get the marine fixed up.

- Rigging the Marine: Here, we will cover what rigging is and the process involved. Then, we will try to figure out the smartest way to rig our character.

- Exporting the Marine: We have already done a bunch of exporting from Blender, so we will quickly get our marine shipped out and ready for action in Unity.

- Secret Weapon #3: There is a pleasant surprise here but telling would ruin it.

By the end of the chapter, our marine will be looking a lot better and ready to get animated in the next chapter! Ready? Of course you are. Let's go!

Technical Requirements

This chapter will take place entirely in Blender. It will make use of a texture I created called `marine_texture.jpg`, which is available on the GitHub repository for this book.

The supporting files for this chapter can be found here: `https://github.com/PacktPublishing/Mind-Melding-Unity-and-Blender-for-3D-Game-Development/tree/main/Chapter12`

The code in action video for this chapter can be found here: `https://bit.ly/30sZtzz`

Just One Thing...

Okay, this is more related to rigging than UV-unwrapping, but we might as well get it out of the way since it needs to get done at some point.

Remember from the last chapter how we parented all the marine pieces together and then duplicated them from the right side to the left side?

Well, very shortly we are going to want to differentiate between the right and left sides, so we need to do some renaming. Basically, we will go through the parts and append an `_R` to the name to indicate the right side and an `_L` for the left. Ready? It's tedious but easy. Let's go:

- Append an `_R` to the right-side foot, lower leg, upper leg, lower arm, upper arm, and hand.
- Now, switch sides and append an `_L` to the same pieces.

That's it! We're good to go.

UV-Unwrapping and Texturing the Marine

It has been quite some time since we discussed UV unwrapping and texturing back in *Chapter 5, On the Level: Making Modular Scenery* , so let's remember how the basic process goes before tackling the marine.

UV Unwrapping Refresher

In order to unwrap an object, you need to select it and then switch to the UV Editing view from the view choices at the top of the screen. There is no need to follow along right now. Just recall how this works. The view has two panes. On the left is the 2D **UV Texture Space**. On the right is the regular 3D view we have been using all along:

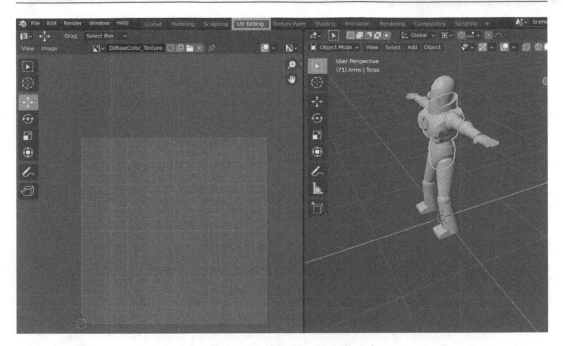

Fig. 12.1 – UV Editing view selected

First, we load a texture image into the UV space. Then, we pick a part of the model to unwrap by entering Edit mode, which gives access to the UV menu. There is a handy function called **Smart UV Project** that we use. ("Project" as in "projection," not as in "the project is late, Smithers!")

You will then see the model unwrapped in the UV space. This is where most of the work takes place. Recall that you can select from four element editing modes. The three familiar ones are vertex, edge, and face. The last one (which we will use a lot) is for editing **UV Islands**, which are basically just groups of elements that are treated as a single thing.

The UV space is 2D, but you can still perform the basic transformations you are familiar with in 3D: scale, move, and rotate. A big part of the process is manipulating the elements into the right places so that they align well with your texture.

To see your texture on the object, you need to add a material slot to your object and add a material that has your texture image. Lastly, you need to switch to **Material Preview** mode in the 3D view.

Is this process coming back to you? Don't worry if it's hazy, we'll go step by step. Here we go.

Loading the texture image into the UV space

The first thing to do is get our texture loaded into the UV space. To do that, follow these steps:

1. Switch into the **UV Editing** mode if you are not in it already. See *Fig 12.1*.

2. At the top of the UV pane, select **Open** (*Fig 12.2*) and navigate to where you stored `marine_texture.jpg`. Select the file and press **Open Image** in the popup.

Fig. 12.2 – How to load your texture into UV space

3. It is very likely your image will appear huge. Use the scroll wheel to reduce it to a comfortable viewing size.

> **Tip: Texture sizes**
>
> Most modern-day textures are square and have a pixel dimension that is a power of 2: 1,024, 2,048, 4,096, and even higher (computers can process these sizes faster than non-powers of 2). Basically, the more pixels, the more detail you can get in. The trade-off is that you are using up graphics memory. We are going to use a very small, simple texture for the marine.

While we are at it, let's turn on **Material Preview** mode, so we'll be able to see the results of our work.

4. In the upper right of your screen, there are four sphere icons allowing you to choose a viewing mode (*Fig 12.3*). Select Material Preview mode, which is the third sphere icon you see. You may need to expand your view if you can't see all four spheres. There's also a good little trick: if you move your mouse up to that area of icons, you can actually use your scroll wheel to move the icons left and right if there are too many to display:

Fig. 12.3 – View mode icons

5. Optionally, you can press the *Z* key *when over the 3D view* (only!) and select **Material Preview** from the mode choices.

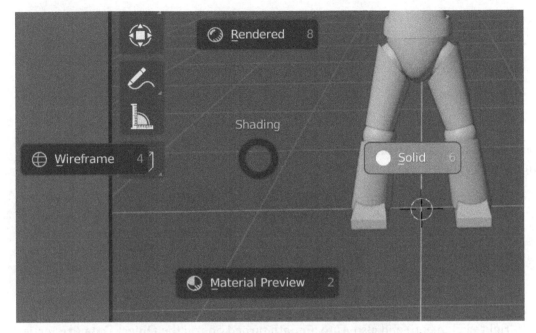

Fig. 12.4 – View mode choices from the Z hotkey shortcut when over the 3D view

Okay, that's a lot of setup out of the way. Let's get into the heart of this process.

Getting started with the Marine

Your marine should consist of the following parts (L and R indicate left and right):

- **Head**
- **Torso**
- **Arm_Upper_L**
- **Arm_Lower_L**
- **Hand_L**
- **Arm_Upper_R**
- **Arm_Lower_R**

- **Hand_R**
- **Leg_Upper_L**
- **Leg_Lower_L**
- **Foot_L**
- **Leg_Upper_R**
- **Leg_Lower_R**
- **Foot_R**

These divisions will make our unwrapping/texturing fairly quick. There's a couple of things you might want to double-check:

- Make sure all your marine parts are in one of the preceding objects. Remember that *Ctrl / Command + J* will **join** objects. In particular, make sure you get all the fingers for the hands. Also, be sure you have *first* applied the **Subdivision Surface** modifier to the base of the hand *before* joining the fingers; otherwise, the fingers will get the modifier, too. This tripped me up a couple of times, so be on the lookout. (This was in the previous chapter but be sure you didn't skip it!)

- While you're at it, check that all your parts have **Shade Smooth** turned on (from the right-click menu) and also **Auto Smooth** turned on (on the **Object Data Properties** tab under **Normals**).

So, we've got 14 marine parts ahead of us. The left/right pairings will let us work efficiently. Let's do it.

Processing the Head

Every body part is going to need a **material slot** that gets assigned a **material**, but we are going to create the material a *single* time while we are working on the head:

1. Switch to Object Mode for a moment. Select the head.
2. Select the materials tab of the property pane on the lower right. See *Fig 12.5*:

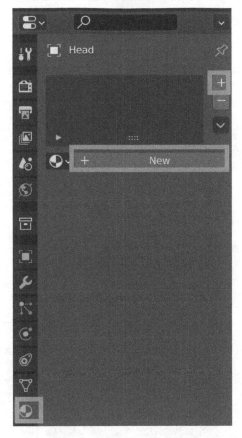

Fig. 12.5 – Specifying material slots and properties

3. Create a new material slot by clicking the plus sign underneath the thumbtack icon on the upper right. See *Fig 12.5*.

4. Create a new material by clicking **New**.

5. Click where it says **Material** and rename the material to `marine`. See *Fig 12.6*.

6.   Click the dot next to **Base Color** and choose **Image Texture** from the pop-up window.

Fig. 12.6 – Rename your material and set its Base Color to an Image Texture

7.   Click the **Open** button (*Fig 12.7*), locate `marine_texture.jpg` again, and choose **Open Image**.

Fig. 12.7 – We only need to create the material one time

Return to the UV Editing layout. Ugh, the head kind of looks like a confusing mess, right? (See *Fig 12.8*.) Let's get busy unwrapping.

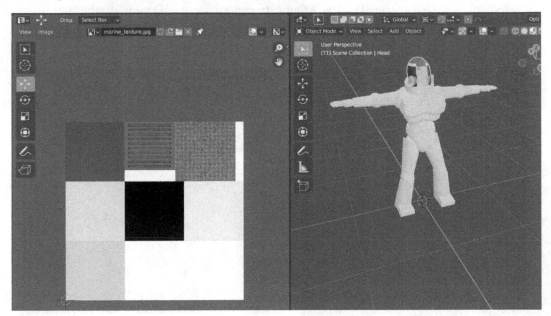

Fig. 12.8 – Time to get the helmet properly unwrapped

8. Press *Numpad /* to enter isolation view, then press *Tab* for Edit mode.

9. Select everything by pressing *A*, then choose **UV | Smart UV Project**. You can accept all the default values and just click **Ok**.

You should now see the elements of the head unwrapped in the UV pane, something similar to *Fig 12.9*. Don't forget that to see things in the UV pane, you have to have elements selected in the 3D View. As an experiment, in the 3D view, double-tap *A* to deselect all and you should see the unwrapping disappear from the UV pane. Go ahead and press *A* to reselect all and see the unwrapping again.

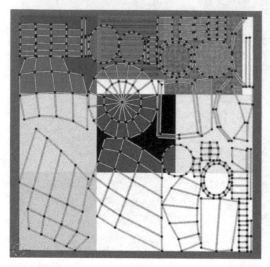 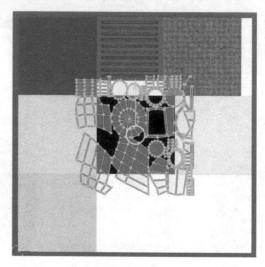

Fig. 12.9 – The result of Smart UV Project, left, and all elements scaled down, right

10. The first thing we're going to do is scale down the unwrapping to make it more manageable. With your mouse over the UV pane, press *A* to select everything and the elements should turn orange. Next, press *S* to scale and move your mouse so it scales down to about half the size. You don't need to be exact. See *Fig 12.9*.

11. Next, let's switch to UV Island selection mode. At the top of the UV pane, click the icon that looks like two rectangles. See *Fig 12.10*:

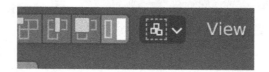

Fig. 12.10 – UV Island selection mode toggled on

Click on different parts of the unwrapping to get a feel for selecting islands.

Unwrapping the helmet grille and visor

Let's start very easy with two simple parts of the helmet: the face grille and the visor:

1. In the 3D view, choose Face select mode with *Ctrl / Command + 3*. Then, select the front two faces that form the grille. See *Fig 12.11*.

    Once the faces are selected, their UV islands will show up in the UV pane.

2. With the cursor over the UV pane, press *A* to select all the islands and use *G* to move the islands over the texture area in the upper right. You can also move them by putting your cursor inside the little gray circle and clicking and dragging. See *Fig 12.11*:

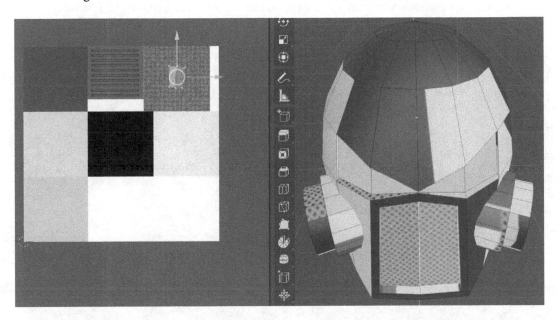

Fig. 12.11 – Select the faces of the grille in the 3D view, then move the islands in the UV view

Only slightly harder are the four faces that make up the visor area of the helmet. I actually got lucky with my unwrap since I want them to be cyan and they just happened to line up that way. But what you should actually do is this:

1. Select the four faces of the visor in the 3D view. In *Fig 12.11*, they are already cyan.

2. In the UV pane, select everything with the *A* key and move them so they are completely in the middle of the cyan area of the texture, which is the middle right. With these and all other UV islands, if they won't completely fit into a texture color area, you may need to scale them down.

So far, so good, right? Let's keep taming the confusion.

Unwrapping the side cylinders

Moving up in complexity, let's tackle those things that stick out of either side of the helmet:

1. In the 3D view, select a face of one of the cylinders. Doesn't matter which one. Press L to select **linked** faces and the rest of the cylinder faces should select.

2. Add to your selection by holding down *Ctrl / Command* and selecting a face from the cylinder on the other side. Pressing L again should select all faces of the other cylinder, so you should now have both cylinders selected. See *Fig 12.12*.

3. In the UV pane, select (A)ll islands and move them into the gray area of the texture on the middle left. See *Fig 12.12*. You may have to move them a few at a time and, as I said, it's possible you may need to scale them down. As a side note, it is okay for UV islands to overlap:

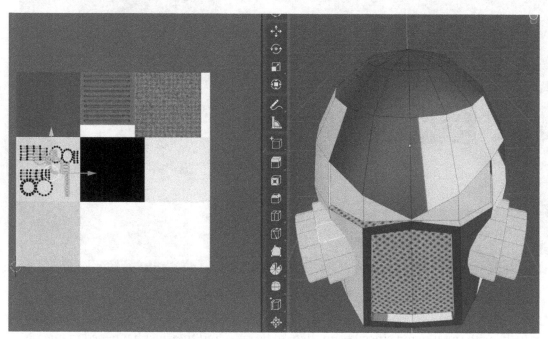

Fig. 12.12 – The two side cylinders selected and their islands positioned

Now on to the last step of completing the head/helmet/whathaveyou.

Unwrapping the rest

Actually, that last step might have been the hardest one for the head. We'll do the rest of the parts in a bit of a quick and dirty way, but we still have a lot to cover. The basic plan is that everything we have not already processed we want to move to the dark-blue area in the upper left. To get started, follow these steps:

1. In the 3D view, select (A)ll.

2. In the UV pane, select any islands you *haven't* already moved and move them to the dark-blue area.

3. Inspect the head in the 3D view by tumbling your view, looking for faces you might have missed that are the wrong color. If you find one, select it and you'll see its island appear in the UV pane, so you can then move it.

4. If you select (A)ll in the 3D view, you should now have something that looks approximately as in *Fig 12.13*.

5. Exit isolation mode with *Numpad /* and return to Object mode with *Tab*.

6. Get into the habit of saving your work.

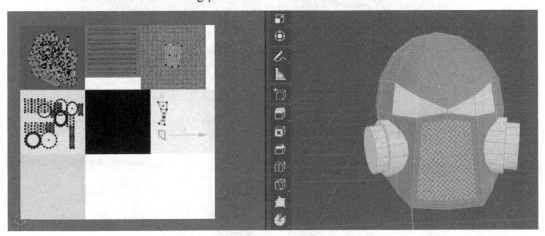

Fig. 12.13 – The helmet with final unwrapping

That's it for the head. Good job! The other parts of the marine will go through a very similar process.

Processing the Torso

So, here we go; after doing the parts of the head, this process should seem very familiar:

1. Select the torso in Object Mode, press *Numpad /* to enter isolation view, then press *Tab* for Edit mode.

2. As before, in the materials properties pane, add a new material slot with the plus (+) icon. This time, however, you don't need to create a new material; you can choose it from the dropdown. See *Fig 12.14*:

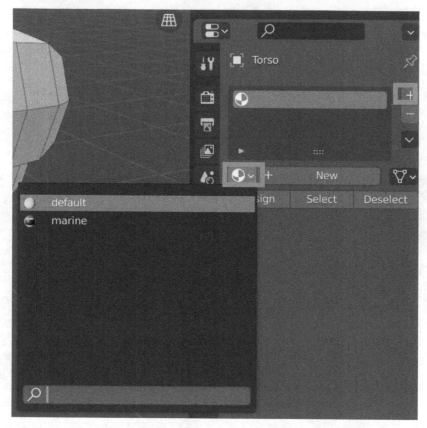

Fig. 12.14 – Create a new material slot, then click the dropdown and select the marine material

3. Select everything in the 3D view by pressing *A*, then choose **UV | Smart UV Project**.

4. Whoa! Once again, the size is out of control and there are a lot more elements than the head, so it's hard to see what's going on. In the UV pane, reselect UV Island selection mode if it got deselected. Refer to *Fig 12.10* if you forgot how.

5. Press *A* to select all islands and then *S* to scale. Just reduce it a little bit; you can get more detailed later.

6. The majority of the torso will be dark blue, so go through all the islands and move them into the dark-blue area. This is a little bit of work and we will wind up re-working some of this for some of the features, but it gives us a good place to start. You can select groups of islands to move them if they are small enough.

Unwrapping the collar and the chest ring

The collar is relatively straightforward and gives us practice selecting face loops. Follow these steps:

1. In 3D view, make sure you have Face selection enabled. *Shift + Alt* + left-click a face of the collar and that whole section of the collar will be selected: front, top, and inside. Continue to *Shift + Alt* + left-click until you have selected all the faces of the collar.

2. In UV view, select (*A*)ll islands and move them to the black area of the texture. See *Fig 12.15*:

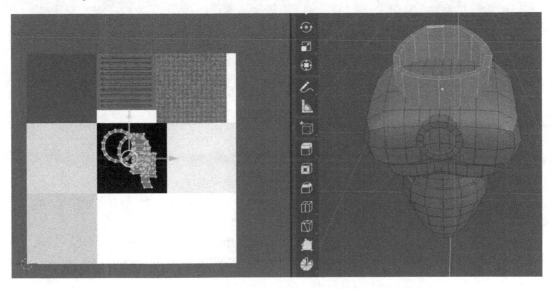

Fig. 12.15 – Collar selected and UV islands moved to black area

The process is nearly identical for the chest ring. Let's look at it:

1. In 3D view, deselect everything by double-tapping *A*.

2. Select a face of the chest ring, then press *L* to select linked faces. This should get you the whole ring.

3.   In UV view, select (*A*)ll and move everything to the black area as well (*Fig 12.16*). Or choose a different color area. Up to you.

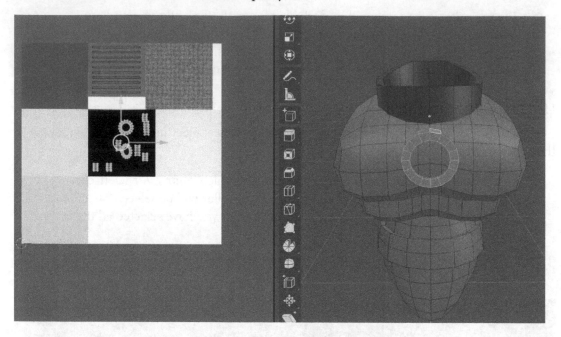

Fig. 12.16 – The chest ring processed

Can you guess what comes next after the *upper* torso? (Hint: it's not the pinky toe.)

Unwrapping the lower torso

This is going to be really easy and familiar:

1.   In 3D view, deselect everything by double-tapping *A*.

2.   Select a face of the lower torso, then press *L* to select linked faces. This is also going to get the belt area, but that's okay, we'll fix that soon.

3.   In UV view, select (*A*)ll and move everything to the black area. Hmm, maybe most of the torso is black and not blue. I lied. You can complain to my secretary.

Unwrapping the belt

The belt is slightly different but still pretty easy:

1.   In 3D view, deselect everything by double-tapping *A*.

2.   Select a face loop of the belt with *Alt* + left-click. In order to select a loop going around the belt and not vertically, you need to click *near the left or right edge* of the face.

3. The belt is two faces high. Use *Shift + Alt* + left-click to add in the other loop of the belt.

4. In UV view, select (*A*)ll and move everything to the blue area.

5. Exit isolation mode with *Numpad /* and return to Object mode with *Tab*.

Fig. 12.17 – The belt is processed. The torso is complete

That's it. The remaining parts are very straightforward and have a similar process.

Processing the Arms

The basic plan here is that the ball joints will be black and the armor dark blue. We can actually get a little more efficient here since you can edit multiple objects at once:

1. In Object mode, use *Shift* + left-click to select the upper and lower parts of both arms, so you will have four things in your selection. Enter isolation view (*Numpad /*) and then *Tab* for Edit mode.

2. Enter the UV Editing layout. Select everything in the 3D view by pressing *A*, then choose **UV | Smart UV Project**.

3. Use the Outliner panel to select each of the four parts, one by one. Just as we did for the other parts, add a material slot in the materials properties tab. Assign it our marine material that we created. See *Fig 12.14* if you forgot how.

4. Still in 3D view, select a face of one of the four ball joints. Press *L* to select the linked faces of the ball/sphere. Sometimes it seems like you need to press *L* again to "nudge" Blender.

5. In the UV pane, select (*A*)ll the islands and move them to the black area. Always remember to check whether you are in island selection mode.

6. Return to *step 4* and repeat this process until you have done all four spheres.

7. The process is the same for the limb parts. In 3D view, select a face of one of the limbs. Press *L* to select the linked faces of the limb.

8. In the UV pane, select all the islands and move them to the *dark-blue* area.

9. Return to *step 4* and repeat this process until you have done all four limbs.

10. Exit isolation view and *Tab* back to Object mode.

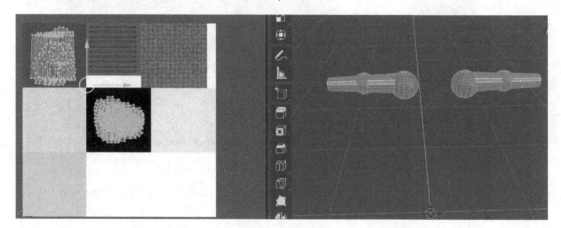

Fig. 12.18 – Working on all four arm parts at once

That's it for the arms. After all this work, you should—(*urge... so strong... must... resist...*)

You should (*can't... resist...*) give yourself a hand.

Processing the Hands

Assuming that each hand is now a single object (because you joined all the fingers), the hands are going to be super easy, because they are just supposed to be black gloves:

1. In Object mode, use *Shift* + left-click to select both hands. Enter isolation view (*Numpad /*) and then *Tab* for Edit mode.

2. Enter the UV Editing layout. Select everything in the 3D view by pressing *A*, then choose **UV | Smart UV Project**.

3. Use the Outliner panel to select each hand, one by one. Again, add a material slot in the materials properties tab. Assign it our marine material. Refer to *Fig 12.14* if you need to.

4. Here's where it gets super easy. In the UV pane, select (*A*)ll the islands and (*S*)cale them way down. Move them (*G*) into the black area. That's it! See *Fig 12.19*.

5. Exit isolation view and *Tab* back to Object mode.

6. This is a good time to save your work if you haven't done so in a while.

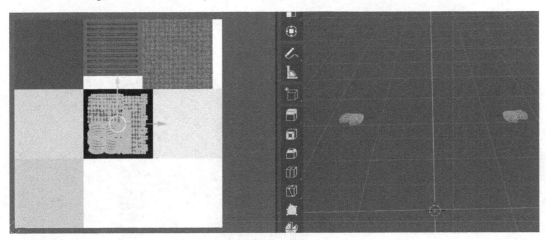

Fig. 12.19 – We really got our hands dirty!

Is this process starting to become second nature to you? Or at least predictable? I hope so. The legs are basically identical to the arms and the feet similar to the hands.

Processing the Legs

Here we go again. The joints will be black and the rest dark-blue armor. Start in the usual way…

1. In Object mode, use *Shift* + left-click to select the upper and lower parts of both legs, so you will have four things in your selection. Enter isolation view (*Numpad /*) and then *Tab* for Edit mode.

2. Select (*A*)ll in 3D view, then choose **UV | Smart UV Project**.

3. Use the Outliner panel to select each of the four parts, one by one. Add a material slot in the materials properties tab. Assign it our marine material.

4. Still in 3D view, select a face of one of the four ball joints. Press *L* to select the linked faces of the ball/sphere. Sometimes, it seems like you need to press *L* again to "nudge" Blender.

5. In the UV pane, select (A)ll the islands and move them to the black area. Always remember to check whether you are in island selection mode.

6. Return to *step 4* and repeat this process until you have done all four spheres.

7. The process is the same for the limb parts. In 3D view, select a face of one of the limbs. Press *L* to select the linked faces of the limb.

8. In the UV pane, select all the islands and move them to the *dark-blue* area. You may have to do a tiny bit of scaling.

9. Return to *step 4* and repeat this process until you have done all four limb parts. See *Fig 12.20*.

10. Exit isolation view and *Tab* back to Object mode.

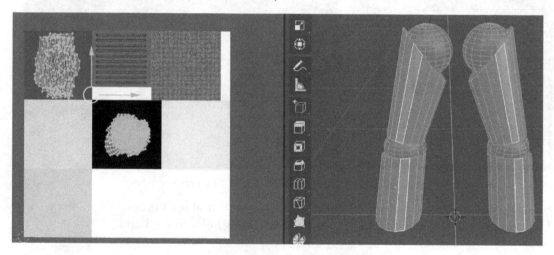

Fig. 12.20 – The legs were identical to the arms

Almost done. Seems like we're inches away, or maybe a few feet…

Processing the Feet

I bet you could almost do this with your eyes closed. The boots are going to be blue:

1. In Object mode, use *Shift* + left-click to select both feet. Enter isolation view (*Numpad /*) and then *Tab* for Edit mode.

2. Select everything in the 3D view by pressing *A*, then choose **UV | Smart UV Project**.

3. Use the Outliner panel to select each foot, one by one. Add a material slot in the materials properties tab. Assign it the marine material.

4. In the UV pane, select (A)ll the islands and (S)cale them way down. Move them (G) into the dark-blue area.

5. Exit isolation view and *Tab* back to Object mode.

6. Save your work again. If you leave UV Editing view and go back to Modeling view or Layout, remember that to see your textured marine, you need to select Material Preview mode *for that view.*

7. This is an important last step. Don't skip it. Sometimes during modeling, the **normals** of different faces can get jumbled, causing the model to display very strangely. Luckily, Blender has an easy fix for this. In Object mode, select (A)ll and *Tab* for Edit mode. Select (A)ll again just to be sure. Now, from the top menu, choose **Mesh | Normals | Recalculate Outside**. That's it. Save your work!

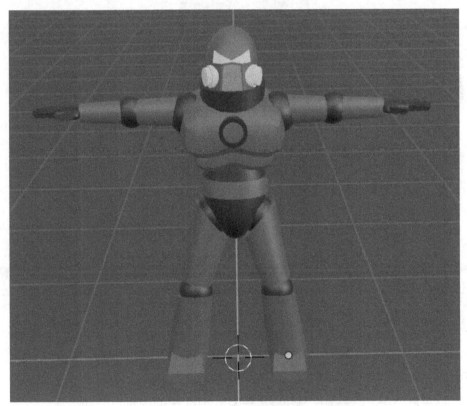

Fig. 12.21 – Ready for action

You made it! We unwrapped and textured all 14 body parts. We learned how to import a texture and also, we made good use of manipulating UV islands, which we hadn't really done before. Our super-soldier is ready for the next phase of his incarnation: getting rigged and preparing for animation. Keep up the good work.

Rigging the Marine

Rigging is the process of creating an invisible "skeleton" for a model, which will be used to control the model for animation. This skeleton, or **armature** if you want to be fancy, is composed of—what else?—**bones**. Although you *can* see it in the view, a bone is not a visible part of the model. Each bone has an influence on different parts of the model and when the bone moves, the corresponding parts of the model mesh will move. Here is what a bone looks like in Blender:

Fig. 12.22 – No, it does not look very much like a real-world bone

Once you have created the skeleton, you can then define the relationship each bone has to parts of the model. You may have heard the term **weight-painting**. This is a sophisticated technique that allows multiple bones to influence the same part of a model with differing strengths.

Rigging is a hugely complex topic—enough to have entire books and courses available to teach it. So, how are we going to rig our character in only one chapter?

The answer?

We are not! Surprise! I fooled you again. Be careful who you trust, human.

Luckily for us, there is a free service on the web provided by Adobe called Mixamo. Mixamo is a fantastic source for free animations and character models, but it also has a stunningly simple visual auto-rigging feature. They will do all the work for us! All we have to do is give our marine to them.

So, let's give them our marine.

Exporting the marine

Do you remember way back when, when we exported the turret and some scenery? It's basically the same:

1. From the top menu, choose **File | Export | FBX**.

2. In the pop-up window, give it a simple name at the bottom, such as—wait for it—marine.

3. Match your settings to *Fig 12.23*. In particular, select only **Mesh** to export. Set **Apply Scalings** to **FBX Units Scale** and tick the three checkboxes below that.

4. Click **Export FBX**.

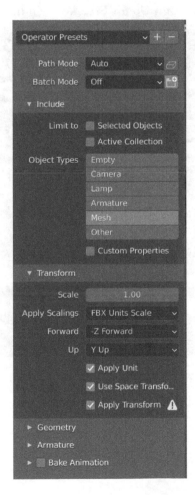

Fig. 12.23 – The export settings for the marine

The marine is ready to roll. And jump or do sit-ups or whatever. Mixamo, here we come!

Getting started with Mixamo

In order to use Mixamo, you need to be able to use Mixamo, are we clear on that?

Okay, what that really means is that you need to have a Mixamo account. And the account is free, as in "no money," *zero dinero. Comprende?*

If you already have a Mixamo account, consider yourself a superior human who will be considered for saving when the time comes (soon).

If you do not have a Mixamo account, get started with Mixamo, with these steps:

1. Use the frontal lobes of your brain to create a free Mixamo account. Go to `mixamo.com` and choose **Sign Up for Free**. You will not be sorry:

Fig. 12.24 – The incredibly confusing Mixamo landing page

2. If you need to sign up, you will be subjected to the following torturous interrogation screen, which you must endure:

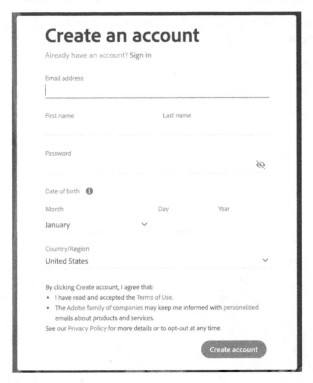

Fig. 12.25 – Normally withhold this information at all costs, but in this case, give it freely

3. If you somehow make it through that process, you will be in good shape. Re-login if you need to and you will be on the home page. Choose to **UPLOAD CHARACTER**:

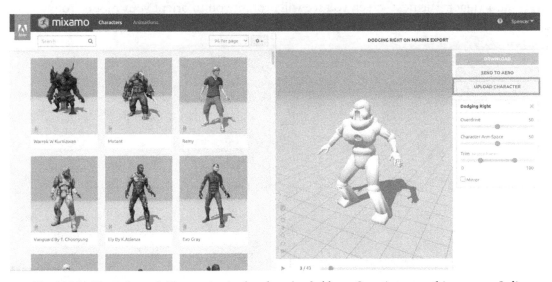

Fig. 12.26 – Yes, I cheated. The marine is already uploaded here. Question everything, young Jedi

4. You will then see a screen prompting you to either drag in your `.fbx` file or click to locate it. Pick one and do it:

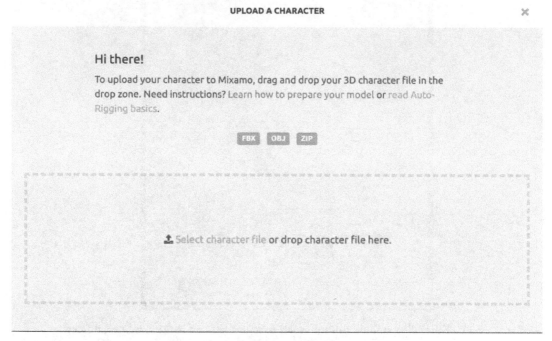

Fig. 12.27 – Pick a way to upload the marine

5. The marine has no rig/armature/skeleton, so you will automatically enter the auto-rigger. The next screen you see will prompt you to orient your model. You should not have to do this, so you can click **Next**:

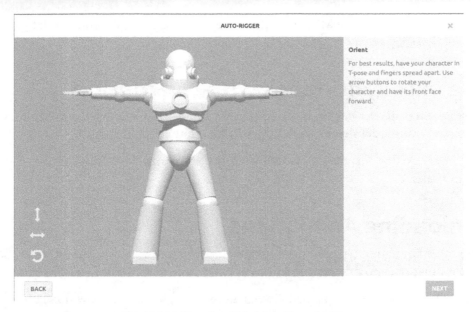

Fig. 12.28 – You should just be able to hit Next

The next screen you see makes rigging seem incredibly easy and should earn Mixamo/ Adobe the **Intergalactic Award for Easy Rigging**. You just visually drag some circles onto the right places of your model. So simple a human could do it!

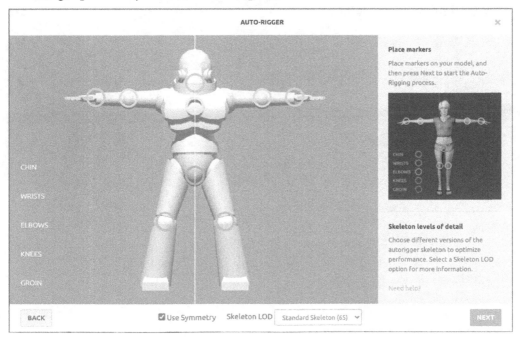

Fig. 12.29 – Drag your circles to match my circles. It's challenging, I know

Next you, er, hit **Next** and give Mixamo a little time to think. When it's done, voilà!
A rigged model. Easy peasy.

Doing excellent things with the marine

Do you see the marine moving on Mixamo? Okay, I don't know about you, but I think it's
so cool to have our model already working well with another application.

Notice in *Fig 12.26* that there is a **Characters** tab and an **Animations** tab. Switch to the
Animations tab.

Downloading Animations

There are three animation types we need to download from Mixamo: an idle animation,
a walking animation, and a dying animation.

Later, you will learn how to transition between animations, so you can download other
Mixamo animations if you like, but wiring up those animations will be an exercise for you.

The three animations we will download are `Warrior Idle`, `Walking`, and `Dying`. You
can type the names into the Mixamo search bar to find them. There are actually a lot of
anims that have the name `dying`. It's not critical you get the one I chose, but you can try
to match the thumbnails in *Fig 12.30*:

Warrior Idle   Dying   Walking

Fig. 12.30 – These are thumbnails from Mixamo

To do that, follow these steps:

1. With the walking animation selected, change **Overdrive** to 60 and **Character Arm-Space** to 80. These feel more space marine-like to me.

2. Check the **In Place** box. We do that since we will move our character through code and not **root motion**.

Fig. 12.31 – Tweak the animation settings before downloading

3. Go ahead and download all three animations. To do so for each one, choose to **DOWNLOAD**. The only thing you need to change in the popup is **Format** to **FBX for Unity**:

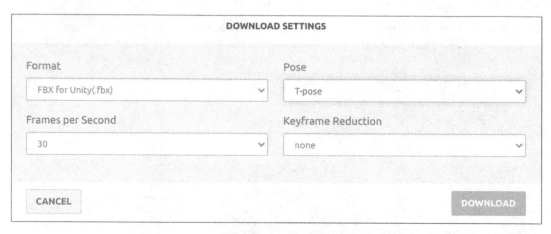

Fig. 12.32 – Only change the format to FBX for Unity

You could actually spend hours now selecting animations to see how the marine performs, have them do situps, dance, and so on. Okay, yes, I did spend an awful lot of time doing this, so go ahead if you want to, but, ultimately, you should come back with the three basic animations.

Just wait for them to download, which should be quick, and… you're done for now!

> **Tip: If you get too excited…**
> If all of this seems too amazing and you think you might pass out, take a deep breath on a count of three, hold it, then breathe out on a count of six. Say out loud: "I am awesome."

Good things lie ahead!

Summary

Let's see what we did in this chapter…

Marine unwrap and texture… check!

Going over the basics of rigging and understanding that a full treatment of rigging would rob you of years of your life… check!

Discovering that Mixamo can give us back years of that wasted life because it helps us with rigging, gives us animations, and is free. As in *free*, costing no money… check!

If you are not absolutely bursting to see the marine start to bust a move in-game, I have no idea what is going to get you jazzed. At any rate, in the next chapter, we start to see the marine move it, move it in Unity!

Section 3:
Assets Assemble! Putting It All Together

Our journey draws to a close, but there is still vital work to be done. Now we will integrate all our assets in a simple mini-game level.

This section comprises the following chapters:

- *Chapter 13, Animation and Movement In-Game*
- *Chapter 14, Endgame: Adding Spit and Polish*

13
Animation and Movement In-Game

"Give my creation…life!"

—Dr. Frankenstein

Now things are going to start feeling a little more fun. We are going to start taking all the pieces we have lovingly crafted so far and put them together into a cohesive whole. It's time for our game to start feeling like a game!

We're going to cover a lot of ground in this chapter, trust me. Specifically, we will do the following:

- Import the rigged marine model and Mixamo animations into Unity
- Create and apply a material to the marine
- Play animations on the marine with an Animation Controller and add footstep sounds
- Add lights to the level and other tweaks
- Script the marine to move with the keyboard
- Follow the moving marine with a Cinemachine camera
- Animate the blast doors and the bridge

See? I told you we'd be covering a lot.

By the end of the chapter, you'll have the marine roving all over the place as both the marine and the level come to life.

Technical Requirements

We'll be back in Unity, finally! You will need the animation files you downloaded from Mixamo. Additionally you will need the marine `texture.jpg` file that we have used before as well as the audio file, `boot1.mp3`, a footstep sound that can be found in the project `assets.zip` file available on the GitHub site for this book.

The supporting files for this chapter can be found here: `https://github.com/PacktPublishing/Mind-Melding-Unity-and-Blender-for-3D-Game-Development/tree/main/Chapter13`

The code in action video for this chapter can be found here: `https://bit.ly/3kLAE9g`

Getting the marine ready for duty

Here we go. Let's get the marine into Unity and ready for the trials that await him/her (it's hard to see through the armor). Follow these steps:

1. In Unity, open your **Textures** folder (you have one, right?) and then select **Assets | Import New Asset** and locate `marine texture.jpg`. Alternately you can just drag it into the **Project** pane.

2. In your **Project** folder, duplicate the marine texture and append `norm` to it. We are going to use it as a quick 'n' dirty normal map.

3. Open your `Models` folder (you have one, right? You're very organized, right? Don't lie!) and import the downloaded Mixamo files. Mine were named `marine export@Walking.fbx`, `marine export@Dying.fbx`, and `marine export@Warrior Idle.fbx`. (When a `.fbx` file has an embedded anim, it is a very common practice to include the animation name in the filename with the @ symbol).

4. Select the three files in the **Project** pane and then, in the **Inspector** under the **Rig** tab, change **Animation Type** to **Humanoid** and click **Apply**:

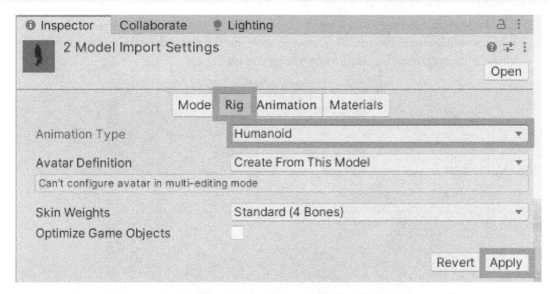

Fig. 13.1 – Selecting the Humanoid Animation Type and clicking Apply

5. In the **Project** pane, rename the idle .fbx model to just marine.

6. Create a new Scene for testing purposes with **File | New Scene**. Go ahead and save the Scene in your **Scenes** folder and name it marine scene.

7. Drag the marine into your Scene view and say hello!

I bet you didn't really say hello, did you? Fine, let's move on to improve the look of the armor.

Creating and applying the marine material

That armor looks pretty flat right now and not very protective. Let's change that. Here's how:

1. In your **Materials** folder, right-click and select **Create | Material**. Name it marine MAT.

2. Select the material and, in the **Inspector** and click **Albedo** and then locate **marine texture** in the popup. See *Fig 13.2*.

3. Set the **Metallic** setting to 0.2 and the **Smoothness** setting to 0.6. These are settings that appealed to me. Play around with the sliders and watch the material in the preview pane. Use whatever settings you like.

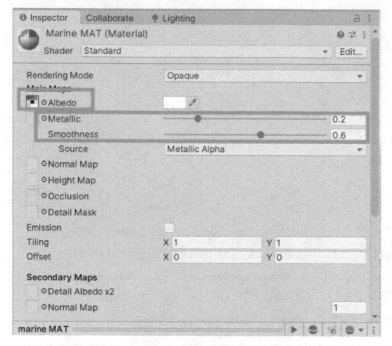

Fig. 13.2 – Setting the Albedo, Metallic, and Smoothness settings

4. In the **Hierarchy** pane, open the marine instance and select all the parts under the torso. (Do not select the rig.) You can twirl everything open by pressing *Alt* + left-clicking the drop-down arrow.

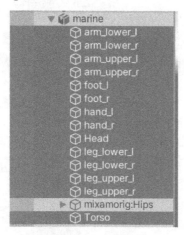

Fig. 13.3 – Selecting everything except the rig

5. In the **Inspector**, find the **Skinned Mesh Renderer** component and twirl open the **Materials** tab. Use the circle selector to set **Element 0** to marine MAT.

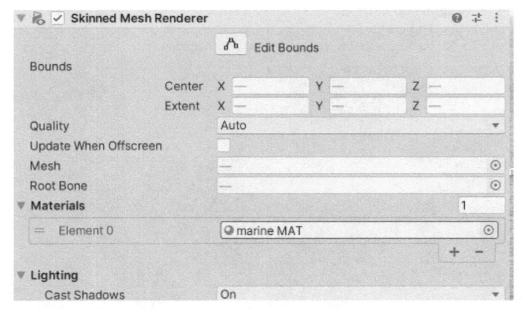

Fig. 13.4 – Be sure you have all the marine parts selected before you assign the material

Your marine should look much shinier now and better protected. Admire your marine from different angles before moving on.

Creating the marine prefab

We want the ability to use the marine in multiple scenes without having to customize it every time so we're going to turn it into a prefab. Follow these steps:

1. In the **Inspector**, set the **Tag** field of the marine to **Player**. Pay attention to uppercasing because this will be used by the turret shooting script.

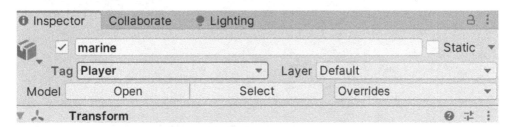

Fig. 13.5 – An uppercase 'P' with the remaining letters in lowercase

2. Add an **Animator** component to the marine with **Add Component** and the search bar. Under **Animator**, check the box next to **Apply Root Motion**.

3. Add a **Capsule Collider** component to the marine. Click the edit button on the component and use the handles to size the capsule around the marine. You don't need to be too precise, but an isometric view may help you.

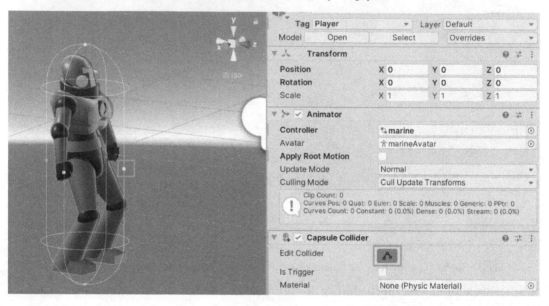

Fig. 13.6 – Press the edit button (on the right) and use the handles that appear (left)

4. Add an **AudioSource** component to the marine. This will be used for footstep sound effects later. Assign it the audio clip `boot1`, which you obtained and imported from GitHub. Uncheck **Play on Awake**.

5. Add a **Rigidbody** component to the marine. Uncheck **Use Gravity** and check the **Is Kinematic** checkbox. We will use this to trigger the doors and bridge.

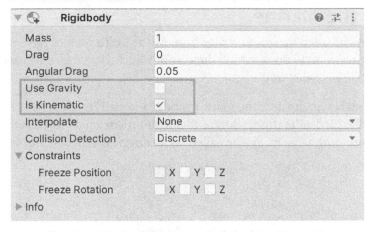

Fig. 13.7 – Unchecking Gravity and checking Kinematic

6. Add a **New Script** component to the marine called `Marine`. We'll leave it empty for now, but will end up using it for movement and other stuff later.

7. If you still don't have the marine object twirled open (*Fig 13.3*), twirl it open. Create an empty GameObject that is a *child* object of the marine and call it `muzzle`. This is the point where the marine's shots will emanate from. We want to position it exactly on the ring in the chest armor. It may help to use an isometric view to position it.

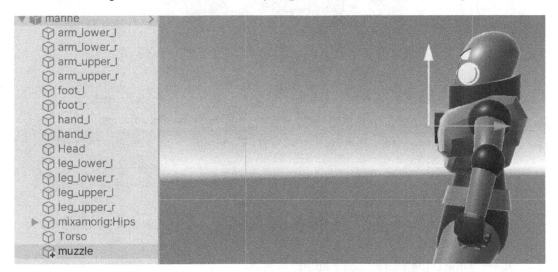

Fig. 13.8 – Positioning the muzzle object on the chest ring

8. Drag the marine from **Hierarchy** into the **Prefabs** folder in your **Project** pane. Choose **Original Prefab** in the popup.

There you go. Your marine is now "prefab-ulous!"

Animating the Marine

Recall that you downloaded three .fbx files from Mixamo. These files have embedded animations. What we want to do is *extract* these anims into .anim files so we can use them more freely. This is what to do:

1. In your **Models** folder, select the marine model and twirl it open. Scroll down to find the embedded animation, which will have a little triangle icon next to it. It may have a meaningful name or just be called mixamo.com. Select the anim.

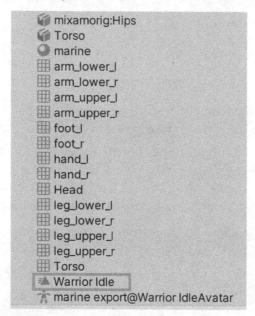

Fig. 13.9 – Opening the marine model and selecting the embedded animation

2. With the anim selected, duplicate it with *Ctrl / Command + D*. Rename the new anim file idle.

3. Do the same thing to extract the animation from the walking and dying .fbx files. Rename the first anim walking, and the second death.

4. Select the walking anim. In the **Inspector** window, check the boxes for **Loop Time** and **Loop Pose**.

5. Do the same thing for the idle anim.

6. Move the three anims to your **Animation** folder.

> **A Note about the Marine's Rig and Avatar…**
>
> I have seen some weirdness where Unity suddenly started giving warning
> messages about the avatar after having been fine with the conversion in the first
> place. If this happens to you, I was able to get rid of the warnings by changing
> the model's rig back to **Generic**, hitting **Apply**, and then changing the rig back
> to **Humanoid** and hitting **Apply** again. Software is strange.

7. Drag the `death` anim onto the marine GameObject in your **Hierarchy** pane. This
   will have the effect of creating an Animation Controller component for the marine
   (*Fig 13.10*) and populating that controller with the `death` anim. I will explain this
   in more detail shortly.

8. For the **Avatar** setting, choose `marineAvatar`, which was created when you
   created a humanoid rig.

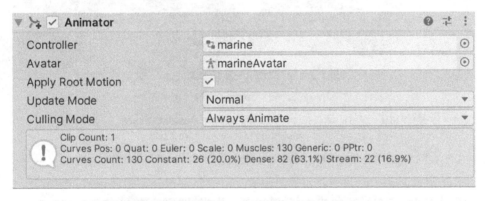

Fig. 13.10 – Your marine needs a controller and an avatar

9. Move your Scene view so that you can clearly see your marine.

10. Select the **Main Camera** object and choose **GameObject | Align With View** from
    the top menu. This way, when you run your game, the camera will see what you're
    seeing in the Scene view. If you didn't know this trick, remember it! It's great!

11. Run your game. You should see your marine stagger and fall. Fantastic!

12. In the **Inspector** double-click the controller. This should open up an **Animator**
    window. Another way is to go to **Window | Animation | Animator**. Dock the
    window if you need to.

13. Drag the `idle` anim and the `walk` anim from your **Project** pane into the **Animator** pane's main area. This will create two new states named after the anims.

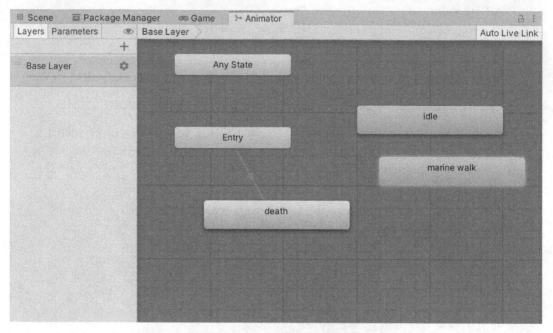

Fig. 13.11 – Dragging the anims into the Animator pane

14. Right-click the idle state and select **Set as Layer Default State**.

Triggers and transitions for the animations

If you are not familiar with the basics of the Unity Mecanim animation system, in a nutshell, you create a state for each animation and then you create logic for how the GameObject will **Transition** into and out of that state:

1. To help create logic for the state transitions, we are going to create three variables, or **parameters**, named `isWalking`, `isIdle`, and `isDead`. (Be careful with the upper- and lowercasing). Switch to the **Parameters** tab of the Animator and use the plus (+) icon to create the three variables of the `Trigger` type.

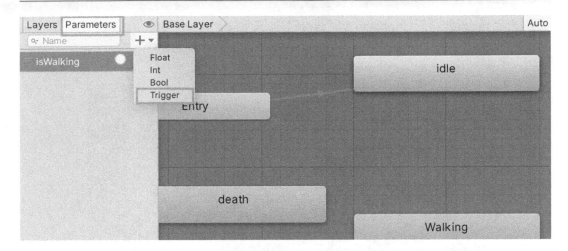

13.12 – Creating the isWalking and isDead triggers

2. To create a transition from idle to walking, right-click on idle and drag the line that appears onto walking. Create a transition from walking back to idle. Then, create transitions for idle > death and walking > death.

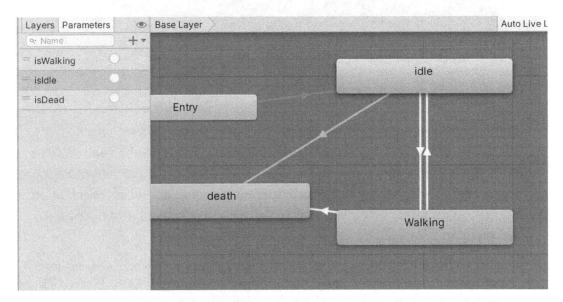

Fig. 13.13 – Transitions between our animation states

3. Click on the transition line pointing from idle to walking. In the **Inspector** window, uncheck **Has Exit Time** (meaning that it will keep looping).

4. Click the plus (+) button and add `isWalking` as the condition.

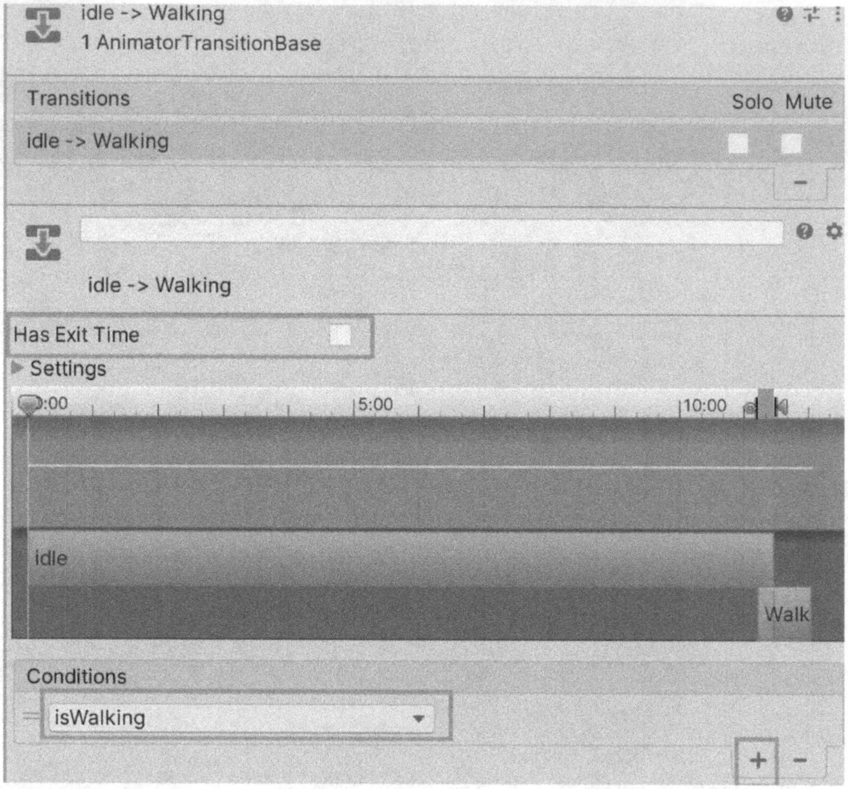

Fig. 13.14 – Unchecking Has Exit Time and adding isWalking as the condition

5. Select the `walking > idle` transition, uncheck **Has Exit Time**, and add `isIdle` as the condition.

6. Select `idle > death`, uncheck **Has Exit Time**, and add `isDead` as the condition.

7. Similarly, select `walking > death`, uncheck **Has Exit Time**, and add `isDead` as the condition.

You can check your work by moving your Game window somewhere where you can see it at the same time as the Animator window. Run your game. Refer to *Fig 13.12*. If you click the circle next to a parameter name, it will fire that trigger. So, for instance, while in the default `idle` state, click the `isWalking` trigger and you should see your marine switch from `idle` to `walking`. You should learn how to do this in order to be able to test the next section.

If your marine's walk and idle anims aren't looping, make sure you didn't skip *step 4* in the preceding *Animating the Marine* section.

Adding footstep sounds to the animation

We want to be able to hear our marine stomping around, right? Here's how to do that:

1. Open up the script file `Marine.cs` to edit it. You can do this from the Project window **Scripts** folder or the **Inspector** window with the marine selected.

2. Create a variable to hold references to the **AudioSource** you will use. Also, in the `Start()` method, assign the reference to **AudioSource**:

```
using UnityEngine;

public class Marine : MonoBehaviour {
    AudioSource audioSource;

    void Start() {
        audioSource = GetComponent<AudioSource>();
    }
```

3. Add two methods called `Boot1()` and `Boot2()`. Basically, we will alternate them and vary the pitch so as to avoid monotony in the footstep sounds:

```
public void Boot1() {
    audioSource.pitch = 1f;  // normal pitch
    audioSource.Play();
}

public void Boot2() {
    // varied (deeper) pitch
    audioSource.pitch = .9f;
    audioSource.Play();
}
```

4. Save the script and return to the Unity Editor. Now we have to call those two methods at the right places in the walking animation.

5. With the marine GameObject selected, open up an **Animation** window by selecting **Window | Animation | Animation**. Note that this is different from the **Animator** window you already have open. Confusing, I know! **Animator** lets you work on animation state flow, while **Animation** lets you edit the keyframes of a single anim.

6. Select the `walking` anim from the dropdown and turn on **Preview** mode
    (*Fig. 13.15*). Get a good viewing angle on your marine and press the play arrow
    to see the walk. Stop the animation. You can also drag the playhead to scrub
    the animation:

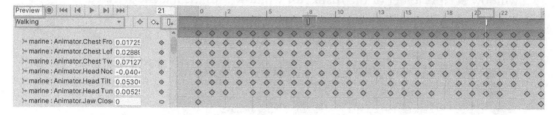

Fig. 13.15 – Selecting the walking anim from the dropdown, turning on Preview, and scrubbing the anim
and add events

What we will do is add **animation events** above the keyframes. These let us call
functions on the object that has the animation. Remember that you must have the
marine object and the walking anim selected to do these edits.

7. Scrub the anim to find the point where the first boot solidly hits the ground.

8. Refer to *Fig 13.15*. Click the **Add event** button, which looks like a tall lozenge with
    a + next to it. This will place an event marker above the keyframe area.

9. Select the marker and, in the **Inspector** window, set **Function** to **Boot1 ()**.

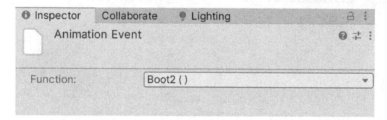

Fig. 13.16 – Setting the first event to Boot1 () and the second event to Boot2 ()

10. Scrub the anim to the point where the other boot contacts the ground.

11. Add a new event there and set **Function** to **Boot 2().**

12. You can't hear audio in the animation preview. Test your work by running your
    game and triggering `isWalking` in the Animator window.

13. Be sure to apply your overrides to your marine prefab.

We covered a ton of ground in this section, starting with giving the marine a humanoid rig, setting its texture, and giving it a collider. Next, we added in animations and created transitions between states with an Animation Controller. Finally, as a nice touch, we added footstep sounds for the marine's boots.

Clomp! Clomp! Clomp! Good to go!

Adding lights to the level

Let's continue to improve our game-level layout. Now we'll add some lighting. And what alien base would be complete without some weird, floating green lights, right? Well, coming right up. Here's what we're going for:

Fig. 13.17 – Floating lights. Note the transparency

To get this effect, we are going to use a sphere with a point light inside it. Just follow these steps:

1. Open your level layout Scene.
2. First, let's create a mostly transparent material with emissive lighting for a glow effect. In your **Materials** folder, right-click and create a new material named Green Glow MAT.

3. Change **Rendering Mode** to **Transparent**, set **Metallic** to 0, and **Smoothness** to 0.51. Refer to *Fig. 13.18*:

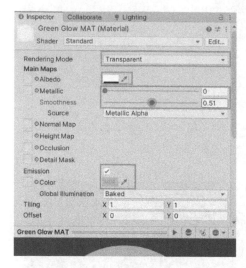

Fig. 13.18 – Settings for the glowing material, the Albedo values, and the Emission values

4. Click the color swatch next to **Albedo** and set the (**A**)lpha transparency value at the bottom to 11. Close the popup (*Fig 13.18*, middle).

5. Tick the checkbox for **Emission**. Click the color swatch and set the (**G**)reen value to 145. Close the popup (*Fig. 13.18* right).

6. In your **Hierarchy** pane, create a new empty object and name it ==Lights==. This will be a good way to keep all our lights together.

7. In the new folder, create a 3D object/sphere and name it BallLight. Raise it up on the *y* axis at something like head height.

8. In the **Inspector** window, open **Mesh Renderer** and **Materials**. Assign your Green Glow MAT material to **Element 0**. You should now be able to see through the sphere.

9. Create a point light as a *child* object of the BallLight sphere (with **Light | Point Light**).

10. Set **Range** to 11.66, **Color** to RGB values (0, 255, 35), and **Intensity** to 2.39. You should be able to tell the light is working now. Toggle it on and off to see the difference, but leave it enabled when you are done.

11. Drag the `BallLight` object (which has the light as a child) into your `Prefabs` folder to create a prefab.

12. Go nuts!

13. Well, what I actually mean is duplicate (*Ctrl / Command + D*) the light in your **Hierarchy** pane and start placing lights around your level. This is a matter of taste. Try varying the height of some of them. This is an overhead view of my placement:

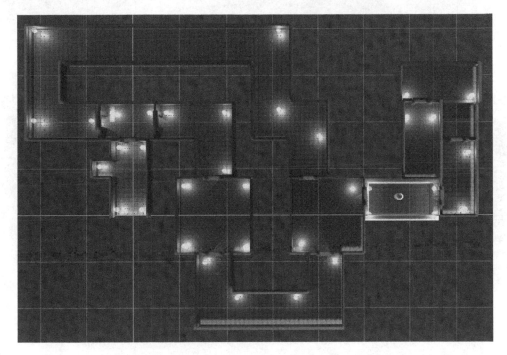

Fig. 13.19 – This is my light placement. Your mileage may vary

Hmm, the only thing I can think of that's missing right now is the marine. Let's fix that!

Marine movement and Camera Control

When we last left the marine, we were learning about transitioning between animation states. Now let's get the marine moving. A full-blown character controller is beyond the scope of this book, but we can still have a lot of fun using the arrow keys for control. The keys we will set up are *Up Arrow* to move forward, *Left Arrow* to rotate left, and *Right Arrow* to rotate right. There's no backing up because marines never retreat!

Here's what to do:

1. Drag an instance of your marine prefab into area A of your level layout. For fun, run your game. You should see your marine performing the idle animation.

Fig 13.20 – Come get some!

2. Stop the game and open up the Marine.cs script in your code editor.

3. Previously, we had one variable that was a reference to **AudioSource**. Add these variables below that:

```
Animator animator; // component ref
bool isMoving;
public float speed = 3.5f;  // walking speed
int rotSpeed = 5;  // rotation speed
RaycastHit hit; // to detect walls
float lookAheadDistance = .25f; // also for walls
public GameObject muzzle; // where we are shooting
                              // from
```

4. In the existing `Awake()` method, add the line below the existing code that sets the **AudioSource**:

```
// … existing code here
animator = GetComponent<Animator>();
```

5. Add an `Update()` method to the script. Remember to be careful with the difference between an = (assignment) and an == (testing):

```
void Update() {
    // are we turning ?
    if (Input.GetKey(KeyCode.RightArrow))
        DoTurnRight();
    else if (Input.GetKey(KeyCode.LeftArrow))
        DoTurnLeft();

    // if the move key is pressed
    if (Input.GetKey(KeyCode.UpArrow)) {
        if (isMoving == false) {
            animator.SetTrigger("isWalking");
            isMoving = true;
        } else DoMove();
    } else { // no movement
        // still in move state but no key
        if (isMoving &&
            !Input.GetKey(KeyCode.UpArrow)) {
            animator.SetTrigger("isIdle");
            isMoving = false;
        }
    }
}
```

Here is what's going on in `Update()`: the basic scheme is to test for keys that are being held down. The left and right arrows are the simplest. They rotate the marine by the value in `rotSpeed`. The Up arrow means that you are walking. We treat the first time you press the arrow especially because that's when we trigger the walk state in the Animator. If no movement is happening, you return to the idle state.

6. Add in the two rotation methods:

```
void DoTurnLeft() {  // counter clockwise
    transform.Rotate(new Vector3(0, -rotSpeed, 0));
}


void DoTurnRight() { // clockwise
    transform.Rotate(new Vector3(0, rotSpeed, 0));
}
```

7. The method we are still missing is DoMove(), which performs the actual Raycast to prevent walking through walls. Let's add this method now. Note the debug line, which is commented out. DrawRay() is a handy tool for visual debugging. When you run your game, it will draw a line in the Scene view (not the Game view!):

```
void DoMove() {
    var moveDistance = Time.deltaTime * speed;

    Ray ray = new Ray(muzzle.transform.position,
                      transform.forward);

    // Debug.DrawRay(muzzle.transform.position,
    //               transform.forward, Color.red);
    // cast a ray forward. if it hits an object tagged
    // as a wall, don't move
    if (Physics.Raycast(ray, out hit,
        lookAheadDistance) &&
        (hit.transform.gameObject.tag == "Wall")) {
            // Debug.Log("wall blocking");
    } else {
        // move the marine
        transform.position += transform.forward *
            moveDistance;
    }
}
```

8. Back in the editor, populate the **Muzzle** property of the script by twirling the marine open in the **Hierarchy** pane and dragging the muzzle object over to the slot in the **Inspector** window.

Fig 13.21 – Populating the muzzle property with the correct GameObject

9. Be sure your wall prefabs are tagged with `Wall`. We did this a looooooooong time ago.

10. And I do believe we skipped this step back then. Open up your wall prefab and give it a **Box Collider** component.

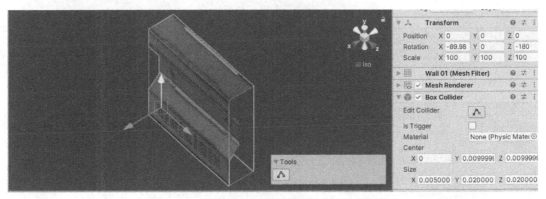

Fig 13.22 – Your wall should be tagged "Wall" and have a BoxCollider component

11. Run your game. You should be able to turn and move your marine, but not through walls.

Things are really heating up now. There's just one problem. If our marine moves too far, we lose sight of him. We want the camera to track him and that's exactly what we'll work on next.

Camera Tracking with Secret Weapon #4: Cinemachine

I bet you're almost getting tired of secret weapons at this point, aren't you? Well, you have to check out just one more.

Cinemachine is a Unity package that basically acts as an AI cameraman and does a whole lot of creative and technical stuff for you.

For what we want to do, we *could* just parent the camera to the character (many projects do this), but that is a stiff and uninteresting view of the game. We want something with a bit more pizzazz. Enter Cinemachine.

Installing Cinemachine

These are the steps to get Cinemachine into your project:

1. In the **Package Manager** window, choose **Unity Registry** from the dropdown to see the built-in Unity packages.

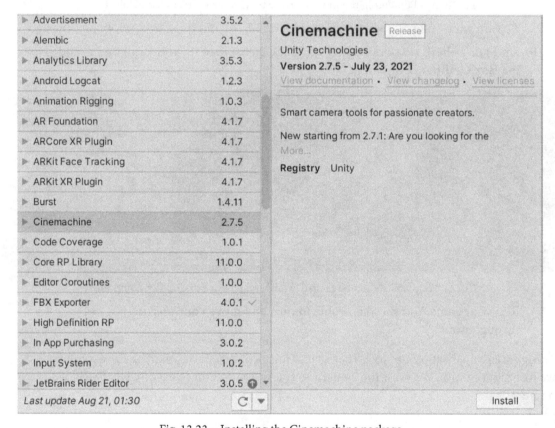

Fig. 13.23 – Installing the Cinemachine package

2. Find **Cinemachine** and choose **Install**.

3. In your **Hierarchy** pane, create a new virtual camera by choosing **Cinemachine | Virtual Camera** from the top menu.

Fig. 13.24 – Using the basic type of camera

When you create the vcam, it will also install a script on your main camera called **Cinemachine Brain**. We don't have time to get into what that's all about, but that's where the magic happens. All of the virtual cameras really just manipulate the main camera through the brain.

4. With the vcam object selected, drag the marine object into the **Follow** slot in the **Inspector**. *Fig 13.25*.

5. Drag the marine's head object into the **Look At** slot on the vcam. See *Fig 13.25*:

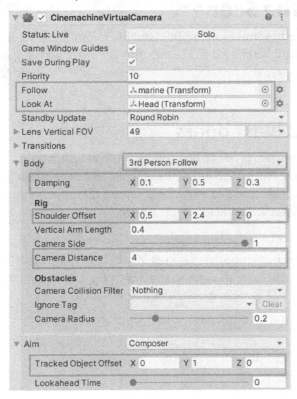

Fig. 13.25 – Virtual camera settings

Set the additional settings on the vcam according to *Fig 13.25*.

6. Set the **Body** type to **3rd Person Follow**.

7. Set **Damping** to 0.1, 0.5, 0.3.

8. Set **Shoulder Offset** to 0.5, 2.4, 0.

9. Set **Camera Distance** to 4.

10. Set **Tracked Object Offset** to 0, 1, 0.

11. Run your game. The camera should now follow the player! Note: If you have the vcam object selected in the **Hierarchy** pane, you will see an overlay in the *Game* view. Deselect the vcam to get rid of this.

12. You may have to tweak **Shoulder Offset** and **Tracked Object Offset** to get the camera to your liking. Use the Game view to preview what you will see at runtime.

How exciting! You can now wander all over the level! Now, let's get more of the scenery to work.

Animating the Scenery

Finally, we're going to add some more motion and life to our level. We'll take the two blast doors we created and animated in Blender and get those working in Unity, and we will learn how to trigger the prism bridge we created with ProBuilder and animated with Timeline.

Animating the Blast doors

You'll remember we have two types of blast doors, which I will cleverly call door1 and door2. Each has its own embedded animations, which we defined back in *Chapter 7, Prep Work: Materials, Grids, and Snapping*. Let's extract their open animations the same way we did with the Mixamo characters. Here's how:

1. In your **Models** folder, select the door1.fbx file and twirl it open. Select the **open** animation you created in *Chapter 7, Prep Work: Materials, Grids, and Snapping* (animations have the little triangle icon; refer to *Fig 13.9*). Now, duplicate it with *Ctrl / Command + D*. For clarity, rename it door1open.

2. Repeat the process for door2, but call that anim door2open.

Working with door prefabs

We'll be placing a bunch of doors so it makes sense to have them as prefabs, so if we make changes, they propagate to all doors. You should already have two textured door prefabs that you created in *Chapter 7, Prep Work: Materials, Grids, and Snapping*. If not, now is the time to create them. Recall that you can drag an instance from your **Hierarchy** pane to your **Prefabs** folder and choose **Create Original Prefab** when prompted. Any rotation problems can probably be fixed by rotating -90 on the X axis.

So now I will assume you have two prefabs to work on:

1. Drag them into the Scene to work on them. It doesn't really matter where.

2. Select door1. Add a **Box Collider** component. Check the **Is Trigger** checkbox, and then click the **Edit Collider** button:

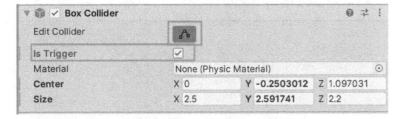

Figure 13.26 – Check Is Trigger and then click the button to edit the collider

3. Use the handles on the collider in the Scene view to reshape the box. Give a generous amount of room in front of the door. You can also set the size numerically in the **Size** property. See *Fig 13.26*.

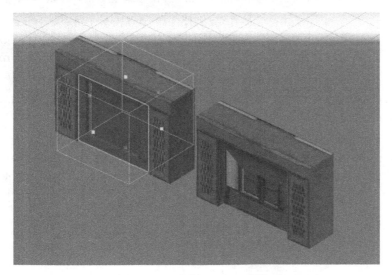

Fig. 13.27 – Editing the collider

4.   Stop editing by clicking the edit button again. Now, add and shape a collider for door2. It may be easiest to enter numeric values.

> **Box Collider Weirdness**
>
> I encountered some weirdness in editing the Box Collider for door2 where the collider shape was wildly off and too big. Don't panic. Just by reducing the size of the box with the editing handles and keeping the center at 0, 0, 0, you can get it to the right size. I've said it before; software is strange.

You can apply changes made to an instance and back to a prefab by clicking the **Overrides** button in the **Inspector** and then clicking **Apply All**.

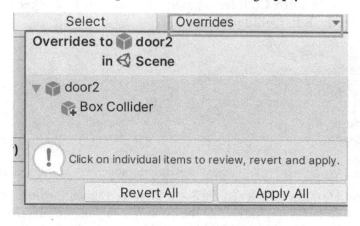

Fig. 13.28 – Changes to instances can be saved back to the prefab

5.   Drag your door1 open anim onto **door1**. This should have the effect of adding an Animator component with a controller. Note: I had an issue with the door animation displaying the wrong side of the door. *If you see your prefab is rotated on Z -180, set the rotation to 0.*

6.   Drag the door2 open anim onto **door2**. Again, this should have the effect of adding an Animator component with a controller.

7.   Just before you try to run your game, add an **AudioSource** to both doors and set its audio clip to **One_Shot_Doors_Electric_Open** or something else that you prefer. Uncheck **Play on Awake**. We do this so that the script doesn't throw an ArgumentNullException.

8. Run your game. If door1 is animating sideways, look at its Animator and check **Apply Root Motion**.

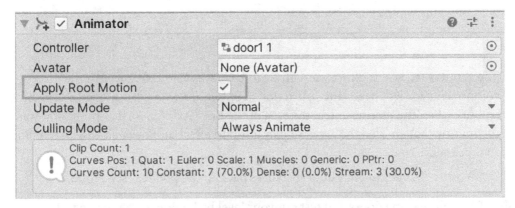

Fig. 13.29 – Root motion can fix some rotation problems

9. *Disable* the Animator for both doors by unchecking the box next to **Animator** (see *Fig 13.29*). We will turn them back on through code.

10. Stop your game and create a new C# script called `Door.cs`. Be sure to add this to *both* door prefabs. Open the script up for editing.

11. Enter the following code:

```csharp
using UnityEngine;

public class Door : MonoBehaviour {
    Animator animator;
    AudioSource audioSource;
    bool hasTriggered = false;

    void Start() {
        animator = GetComponent<Animator>();
        audioSource = GetComponent<AudioSource>();
    }

    void OnTriggerEnter(Collider other) {
        if (hasTriggered) return;
        if (!other.CompareTag("Player")) return;
```

```
        hasTriggered = true;
        animator.enabled = true;
        audioSource.Play();
    }
}
```

The script is fairly straightforward. In `Start()`, we store references to the components we will need. The real action happens in `OnTriggerEnter()`, which will fire when the marine enters the area of the Box Collider. At that point, if it was the marine that entered the area, we play a sound effect and re-enable the Animator so it can play.

12. Apply your changes to your door instances back to the prefabs (see *Fig 13.27*).

Go ahead and place some doors and test out your level by having your marine walk toward them. You should be able to get pretty far!

Full disclosure

I've had to do the process of getting the door from Blender into Unity and animating it several times. There are enough fiddly little bits that it's easy to miss a step and get very frustrated (this has happened to me!). Therefore, I am including a checklist here:

- Export your doors from Blender with the following settings: **Limit to Selected Objects**: on; **Object Types: Mesh only**; **Apply Scalings: FBX All**, **Forward**: **Z Forward**; **Apply Unit**: off; **Use Space Transform**: off; **Apply Transform**: off; **Bake Animation**: on; **NLA Strips**: off; **All Actions**: off.

- Import your door in Unity with the default settings.

- Define the open anim clip as described earlier. Duplicate the clip and rename it as outlined earlier.

For each door, do the following:

- Drag it into the Scene.

- Add an audio source with the clip defined and uncheck **Play on Awake**.

- Add the Door script.

- Add a Box Collider that you shape. Check the **Is Trigger** checkbox.

- Drag the appropriate clip onto the door. Locate the new Animator component. Check Root Motion. Disable the Animator component.

- Turn it into a prefab.

You can watch the Code in Action for this chapter if you are lost in space.

Animating the Bridge

Now for the final piece of the puzzle—the bridge. The scheme for animating this is slightly different from the doors since we want to trigger a Timeline and also there is no single object to attach a script to, at least not yet. Here's what to do to get going:

1. Create a cube and scale it to 4 in X, Y, and Z. Name it `Bridge Trigger`.

2. Add a Box Collider just like we did with the doors (or don't if there is a pre-existing one). Check the **Is Trigger** checkbox.

3. Disable or delete the **MeshRenderer** component so basically, we have one big trigger area. Position this at the front of the bridge.

Fig. 13.30 – Creating a cube and deleting the Mesh Renderer

4.   Create a new script named `Bridge.cs` and add it to **Bridge Trigger**:

```
using UnityEngine;
using UnityEngine.Playables;  // don't forget this

public class Bridge : MonoBehaviour {
    public PlayableDirector timeline;
    bool hasTriggered = false;

    private void OnTriggerEnter(Collider other)     {
        if (hasTriggered) return;

        if (! other.CompareTag("Player")) return;

        hasTriggered = true;
        timeline.Play();
    }
}
```

In order to get this to work correctly, you need to populate the Timeline variable.

5.   Back in the editor, drag `Bridge TL` onto the script component or select it with the circle selector:

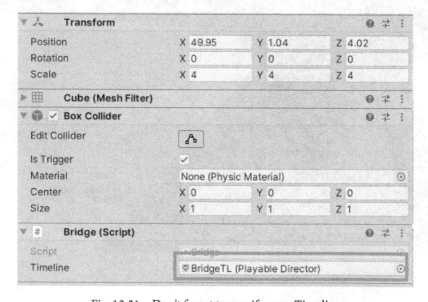

Fig. 13.31 – Don't forget to specify your Timeline

6. On the Timeline object *itself* (Bridge TL), change the **Update** method to **DSP Clock**. This gives better synchronization with sound effects.

7. Go ahead and test your bridge animation. It's so fun to get all this scenery animated! You can save your marine some legwork by positioning your Scene camera somewhere close to the bridge, selecting the marine in the **Hierarchy** pane, and choosing **GameObject | Move to View**.

8. Another full disclosure: your marine can actually walk off the bridge and not fall, but as I noted earlier, full-blown character controllers are beyond the scope of this book, so that will be left as a challenge for you. There are, however, a million resources out there to help you.

And that, as they say, is that. In this section, we got the prefabs of the doors into better shape and then we added scripts to them and the bridge. The scripts all work in similar ways, with Box Colliders acting as trigger zones for the scripts.

Play around with your level. If you disabled your **SoundManager** object earlier, turn it back on. It's fun to have music playing while the marine stomps around!

Summary

What a difference one chapter makes. Now our game seems alive.

We covered a ton in this chapter. First, we got our marine down from Mixamo and into Unity. Then we got him/her all nice and shiny by creating and applying a material.

We extracted the animations from the .fbx files and set up an **AnimationController** with different states and transitions. We also learned how to add events to an animation to create footstep sounds.

Next, we got the marine moving with the keyboard and we enlisted the help of Cinemachine to have a camera follow right along. Last, but by no means least, we got the doors and bridge working when the marine is in the proximity.

Oh, yeah, and we added creepy lights in there somewhere. That's quite a list.

We have one more chapter to go and it's all about adding pizzazz and game mechanics. We'll finally bring back the turret and let the shooting begin! Pew pew pew!

14
Endgame: Adding Spit and Polish

"Fly me to the moon. Let me drift among the stars."

—*Frank Sinatra*

Well, now. It has been quite the journey. You have done well, young grasshopper. This adventure is hopefully just the first of many that you go on to expand your capabilities and have immense fun and share that fun with others.

In this chapter, we will tie up several loose ends, add some pizzazz, and leave you in a good position to expand the game in many new directions.

In this chapter, we will cover the following:

- Getting the marine to shoot and—gulp!—die
- Getting the turret and missile to explode
- Creating a quick-n-dirty health meter
- Creating a main menu screen
- Building your game for distribution
- Adding postprocessing effects
- Adding touches to the final area

That's quite a bit to cover in this last chapter, so without further ado, let's get crackin'…

Technical Requirements

This chapter will take place entirely within the Unity environment. We will make use of some free third-party visual and sound effect assets available on the asset store. The appropriate links will be given when the assets are called for.

The supporting files for this chapter can be found here: `https://github.com/PacktPublishing/Mind-Melding-Unity-and-Blender-for-3D-Game-Development/tree/main/Chapter14`

The code in action video for this chapter can be found here: `https://bit.ly/3CrPKXA`

Make with the shooting already

We are going to waste no time and get our marine rootin', tootin', and shootin'. Or at least shootin'. Similar to the turret, we're going to use a LineRenderer for the blaster beam. Here's what to do.

Preparing to Shoot

First, we will create some components that are part of the shooting process:

1. Open the marine prefab in your `Prefabs` folder.

2. In the Hierarchy, find the `muzzle` game object you created right in the middle of the marine's chest. Be sure you have created a **Muzzle** tag (capital *M*) and applied it to your object:

Fig. 14.1 – Be sure you apply the tag after creating it

3. Next, go ahead and add a **LineRenderer** to the muzzle.

    Whoa! You'll see a lot of magenta going on. This is because the component doesn't have a material assigned to it.

4. In your `Materials` folder, create a new material called `marine laser MAT`. Be sure to have **Shader** set to **Unlit/Color**:

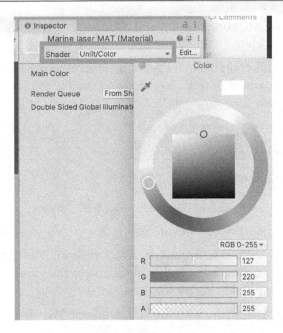

Fig. 14.2 – SetShader to Unlit/Color and pick a color

5. Select a **Main Color** you like. I chose a light blue.

6. Reselect the muzzle object on your prefab and assign your new material to the **Materials Element 0** line renderer. You may need to scroll down to have access to the Materials Selector:

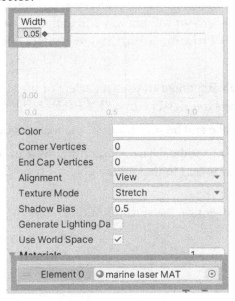

Fig. 14.3 – Set the material at the bottom, then double-click at the top to enter a width value

7. Double-click the number under width and choose 0.05. You should see the width change in the Scene view.

8. We are done with this component for now, so we want to disable it because you don't start the game shooting. Go ahead and disable the **Line Renderer** by unchecking its box:

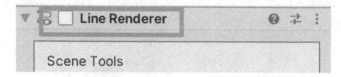

Figure 14.4 – Disable the LineRenderer for now

9. Go ahead and collapse the component. Now let's work on some muzzle flash.

Add a Light component to your same muzzle object. It should be a point light by default. Choose a color for the flash that is close to the LineRenderer color. (Unless you are being weird, excuse me, "*creative*".)

10. Disable the light just as we did with the LineRenderer. We will enable it at the appropriate time.

Visuals are just half of the equation. Let's beef up the sound.

Adding Sound to the shooting

Sound just makes everything better. It's hard to describe. But when you add sound effects to your game—even placeholders—it will not just add one new feature to your game, it will amp everything up 500%. Prove me wrong. Sound is vitality. To add sound, follow these steps:

1. Add an **AudioSource** component to your muzzle. For the clip, I chose **Gun 3_4** from Mikael Vanninen's free **Sci-Fi Guns SFX Pack** on the Asset Store.

2. Uncheck **Play On Awake** and be sure **Loop** is unchecked as well.

3. While we are dealing with audio, let's make another little improvement. Add an **AudioListener** component to the marine object. This will be used for 3D spatialized sound.

4. On your main camera, remove the existing AudioListener, since only one is allowed in a scene.

Scripting the Shooting, Part I

To get shooting to work, we are going to create one new script, as well as modifying the existing `Marine.cs` script. Here, we focus on the new script:

1. Create a new C# script *on the muzzle object* named `MuzzleShootAction`. (I know. Where do I get these great names, right?)

2. `MuzzleShootAction` is going to inherit from `CooldownAction` that we created in the past. Truthfully, it is mostly going to duplicate the `ShootAction` class we made in the past, but I am going to treat it as something brand new, because cutting and pasting code can lead to horrible bugs—worse than those in Starship Troopers.

3. Delete the default `Start()` and `Update()` methods and make the class inherit from `CooldownAction`:

```csharp
using System.Collections;
using UnityEngine;

public class MuzzleShootAction : CooldownAction {
    public int damage = 3;
    public float range = 25f;

    Light glow;
    LineRenderer beamLine;

    Ray ray;
    RaycastHit hit;

} // end class
```

The variables we declare should hopefully be self-explanatory, but nevertheless, I will explain: we declare an `int` to hold how much damage a shot does, and we declare a float to represent the shot range in units. The next two variables, `glow` and `beamLine`, are for visual effect and the ray and raycast hit are used to determine whether you hit an enemy.

4. Now that we have declared those variables, below that, add two simple methods, `DoAwake()` and `EnableEffects()`. The first one stores a reference to two components, while the second either turns them on or off based on the parameter value:

```
protected override void DoAwake() {
        beamLine = GetComponent<LineRenderer>();
        glow = GetComponent<Light>();
}
```

```
void EnableEffects(bool show) {
    try {
        beamLine.enabled = show;
        glow.enabled = show;
    } catch { } // we don't care if these error
}
```

5. Two more methods to go. Add this short one, which calls the coroutine that is the final method:

```
protected override void Triggered() {
        StartCoroutine("Shoot");
}
```

6. Now for the final and most complex method of the class. We will break the `Shoot()` method down into different sections. Create the shell of the method:

```
IEnumerator Shoot() {
    // all coroutines must return an IEnumerator
}
```

7. Inside the `Shoot()` shell, add these lines to trigger the audio/visuals:

```
    // play sfx and vfx
    audioSource.Play();
    EnableEffects(true);
```

8. Below that, add the following code, which gets ready to do a raycast to see whether
    you hit an enemy. This script will be on the muzzle object, so that is what the
    transform will be:

```
var pos = transform.position;
ray = new Ray();
// Set the ray so that it starts at the muzzle
// and points forward.
ray.origin = new Vector3(pos.x, 1.35f, pos.z);
beamLine.SetPosition(0, ray.origin);
ray.direction = transform.forward;
```

9. The following code, to be added below the previous block, is the heart of the
    method. It casts out a ray and tests for a hit with an object tagged as Foe. If there
    is a hit, it damages the enemy. Lastly, we set the endpoint of the blaster beam based
    on the results of the hit:

```
// Perform the raycast against gameobjects
if (Physics.Raycast(ray, out hit, range)) {
    if ((hit.collider.gameObject.tag == "Foe")) {
        Turret turret =
    hit.collider.gameObject.GetComponent<Turret>();
        if(turret != null) {
            // we haven't written this yet!
            turret.Damage(damage);
        }
    }
    // Set the second position of the beam to
    // raycast hit point.
    beamLine.SetPosition(1, hit.point);
} else {
    // set the second position of the beam to the
    // full range.
    beamLine.SetPosition(1, ray.origin +
                        ray.direction * range);
}
```

10. Lastly, we close out the method with two simple lines for the audio/visual stuff. We pause to let them play and then hide them:

```
// let fx play
yield return new WaitForSeconds(.2f);
EnableEffects(false);
```

And that is it for the first part of the marine shooting. The chest gun will actually fire. Now we need to add a way to trigger the shooting, and after that, we need to make sure the turret can take damage.

Scripting the Shooting, Part II

Next, we will revisit the `Marine.cs` class to add code for shooting, but while we are at it, we will add some code to handle the marine dying as well:

1. At the top of the class, add some new variable declarations:

```
// ...previous declarations

MuzzleShootAction muzzleShootAction;

public int hitPoints = 30;      // new

public float deathPause = 5f;   // in seconds

GUIStyle style; // for health display

public bool isDead;
```

2. The `Awake()` method now checks that you have plugged in a reference to the muzzle object, and that there is a Missile script on the muzzle. It also sets up the style for our simple health display:

```
void Awake() {
        audioSource = GetComponent<AudioSource>();
        animator = GetComponent<Animator>();

        if (muzzle == null) Debug.Log("NULL muzzle");
```

```
            muzzleShootAction =
                muzzle.GetComponent<MuzzleShootAction>();
            if (muzzleShootAction == null) Debug.Log("NULL
                shoot action");


            style = new GUIStyle();
            style.normal.textColor = Color.red;
            style.fontSize = 26;
        }
```

3. Modify the Update() method slightly to account for shooting:

```
    void Update() {
        if(isDead) return;


        // … previous existing code


        // are we shooting?
        if (Input.GetKeyDown(KeyCode.Space)) {
            // spacebar
            muzzleShootAction.Trigger();   // fire away!
        }
    } // end of Update()
```

Note that at the very end, we are triggering the MuzzleShootAction we previously coded.

Don't worry if the compiler is complaining about (that is, reporting errors for) a missing method on the Turret script. We will write that soon. Meanwhile, let's get the marine to die!

4. Add a method for taking damage. We will use something similar for the turret:

```
    public void Damage(int amount) {
        if (isDead) return;
        // subtract from our current HP
        hitPoints -= amount;
        if (hitPoints <= 0) {   // death check
```

```
        hitPoints = 0;
        DoDying();   // if no HP, then die!!!
    }
}
```

5. Next, add a super simple method that just starts a coroutine:

```
public void DoDying() {
    StartCoroutine("Die");
}
```

6. And finally, at long last, we get to display the dying animation we got from Mixamo. We signal the Animator with this coroutine method:

```
IEnumerator Die() {
    isDead = true;
    animator.SetTrigger("isDead");
    yield return new WaitForSeconds(deathPause);
    UnityEngine.SceneManagement.SceneManager.
    LoadScene(0);
}
```

The Die() method waits until the death anim is done and then loads the main menu, which we will later create, as the scene at build index 0.

7. Lastly, we will display the marine's health onscreen in a very simple fashion:

```
private void OnGUI() {
    GUI.Label(new Rect(15, 15, 100, 20), "Health: " +
        hitPoints, style);
}
```

For your game, you will probably want something fancier, such as a health bar. There is a simple free one on the Asset Store if you search ProgressBar Pack or follow this link: https://assetstore.unity.com/packages/tools/gui/progressbar-pack-120981. Additionally, there are many tutorials available for health bars on the web.

A Marine Checklist

We are about to move on to dealing with the turrets, but just before we do, make sure your marine is ready for action by going through the following checklist:

1. Open up your marine prefab and select the muzzle object. Make sure the following properties are set:

Fig. 14.5 – Properties for the muzzle object

2. Make sure you have created and applied a Muzzle tag for the object.

3. Assign a sound effect for shooting. I chose **Gun3_4** from the free **Sci-Fi Guns SFX Pack** on the Asset Store.

4. Assign the muzzle object to the target field of the shoot action. You can do this by dragging it directly from the **Hierarchy** into the field.

5. Now switch to the topmost object in the prefab, called **marine**. It should be the one with the Marine script on it. Check its properties:

Figure 14.6 – Properties for the marine object

6. Make sure you have created and applied a **Player** tag for the object.

7. Check that you have assigned the muzzle object to the script exactly as you did in *Step 4*.

Once you've completed the checklist, the marine is good to go! We've accomplished a lot so far. We created a **MuzzleShootAction** that was a kind of **CoolDown** action and we created a bunch of other infrastructure code to allow shooting and dying. Now the turrets will get some much-needed love.

Making the Turrets Go Boom

It has been quite some time since we paid much attention to the turrets. That's about to change. In order to get things exploding nicely, we will need to change three scripts: `Turret.cs`, `LaunchAction.cs`, and `Missile.cs`. None of the changes are all that complicated or things that we haven't seen before:

1. Let's start with `LaunchAction.cs`, which is on the turret object at the top of the turret prefab. At the top of the class, we'll add three new references to the existing ones:

```
    public GameObject lid;
    public AudioClip lidSFX;
    private float lidLiftTime = 1.5f;


    // new - object to instantiate
    public GameObject missilePrefab;
    // new - the instantiated object
    private GameObject missile;
    // new - the script on that obj
    private Missile missileScript;
```

2. Next, we'll slightly modify the existing `Triggered()` method:

```
protected override void Triggered() {
    if (target == null) {
        Debug.Log("launch action 'target' not set to
                  missile spawn pt)");
    }
    RaiseLid();
    CreateMissile();
}
```

3. We can create a missile with the following code:

```
void CreateMissile() {
    missile = Instantiate(missilePrefab,
                          target.transform);
    // new
    missileScript = missile.GetComponent<Missile>();
```

```
    if (missileScript == null) Debug.Log("null missile
        script");
    missile = missileScript.gameObject;
}
```

4. We will leave the existing `RaiseLid()`, and `OnRaiseComplete()` as is.

5. Next, we will modify this one like so:

```
void LaunchMissile() {
    PlaySFX( actionSFX );

    var player =
        GameObject.FindGameObjectWithTag("Muzzle");
    missileScript.Launch(player);
    StartCoroutine("OnLaunchComplete");
}


IEnumerator OnLaunchComplete() {
    yield return new WaitForSeconds(2);
    LowerLid();
}
```

6. We will leave `LowerLid()` and `OnLowerComplete()` alone.

    So much for the `LaunchAction`.

    Next, we will turn our attention to `Turret.cs`. The declarations at the top contain
    some new references for audio/visual effects as well as health:

```
    AudioSource turretAudio;


    State state = State.IDLE;


    CooldownAction scanAction;
    CooldownAction shootAction;
    CooldownAction launchAction;


    bool isDamaged;  // new
    public int hitPoints = 9;  // new
```

```
public ParticleSystem smokeVFX;  // new
public ParticleSystem explosionVFX;  // new

public AudioClip explosionSFX;  // new
```

7. The `Start()` method is largely unchanged except for listening for the launch to complete:

```
void Start() {
    isDamaged = false;  // new
    turretAudio = GetComponent<AudioSource>();

    scanAction = GetComponent<ScanAction>();
    scanAction.OnEnded.AddListener(ScanEnded);

    shootAction = GetComponent<ShootAction>();
    shootAction.OnEnded.AddListener(ShootEnded);

    launchAction = GetComponent<LaunchAction>();
    // new
    launchAction.OnEnded.AddListener(LaunchEnded);

    StartScan();  // new
}
```

8. Next, we have two short methods for damaging the turret. They are very similar to what we did in the `Marine` class:

```
public void Damage(int amount) {
    if( isDamaged == false ) {
        // start smoking if any damage...
        smokeVFX.gameObject.SetActive(true);
    }
    isDamaged = true;
    hitPoints -= amount; // subtract from current HP

    if (hitPoints <= 0) { // if no HP then die
        StartCoroutine("Die");
```

```
        }
    }

    IEnumerator Die() {
        turretAudio.clip = explosionSFX;  // set sound
        turretAudio.Play();  // play sound
        yield return null;
        // show vfx
        explosionVFX.gameObject.SetActive(true);
        // wait 1.2 sec, then destroy turret
        Destroy(gameObject, 1.2f);
    }
```

9. We won't touch the existing methods: ScanEnded(), StartShoot(), ShootEnded(), and StartLaunch().

10. Lastly, add this method so that the scanning process begins again after a launch is over:

```
    void LaunchEnded() {
        StartScan();
    }
```

We're really cooking now! The last thing remaining is to take care of the missile:

1. Create Missile.cs and add it to the top missile object of your missile prefab.

2. To begin with, create an empty shell for the class and declare its variables. We will add Start() and Update() back in, but it's okay to start clean:

```
    using UnityEngine;

    [RequireComponent(typeof(AudioSource))]
    public class Missile : MonoBehaviour {
        public GameObject explosionPrefab;
        public AudioClip explosionSFX;

        AudioSource audioSource;

        public int damage = 20; // how much dmg it does
```

```
    float speed = 20f;   // in units per second
    bool doMove;


    Vector3 targetPos; // where we're aiming
} // end Missile
```

3. Next, we have two very short methods to help launch the missile:

```
void Start() {
    doMove = false;
    audioSource = GetComponent<AudioSource>();
}


public void Launch(GameObject target) {
    targetPos = target.transform.position;
    doMove = true;   // Update() will start moving
                     // missile
}
```

4. The heart of this class is contained in the last two methods. Update() moves the missile once launched and Explode() displays effects and destroys the missile once it is close enough to its target:

```
private void Update() {
    if (!doMove) {
        return; // hasn't launched, do nothing
    }
    // move towards target
    transform.position =
        Vector3.MoveTowards(transform.position,
            targetPos, Time.deltaTime * speed);
    // explode if close enough
    if( Vector3.Distance(transform.position, targetPos)
        < .1f ) {
        doMove = false;
        Explode();
```

```
        // hide the missile
        gameObject.SetActive(false);
    }
}
```

5. As mentioned, the final method is `Explode()`:

```
public void Explode() {
    audioSource.clip = explosionSFX; // set the sfx
    audioSource.Play();   // play it

    // make an explosion object at same location
    GameObject explo = Instantiate(explosionPrefab);
    // set to missile position
    explo.transform.position = transform.position;
    // player near enough, damage it!
    var player =
        GameObject.FindGameObjectWithTag("Player");
    float dist = Vector3.Distance(transform.position,
        player.transform.position);
    if (dist <= 1.5f) {
        Marine marine = player.GetComponent<Marine>();
        marine.Damage(damage);
    }

    Destroy(explo, 1.2f);  // wait, then destroy
                           // explosion

    gameObject.SetActive(true);
}
```

There's still one important thing missing from the turret's lethality: it can shoot, but the shooting does no damage! To correct this, open up the ShootAction script. Add the following at the top, right after the other declarations:

```
public int damage = 3; // or whatever you like
public float range = 40f;   // in units
```

Then, down in the `Triggered()` method, add the following two lines in between the existing code:

```
// prev code
beam.SetPosition(1, pos);


var marine = player.GetComponent<Marine>();
marine.Damage(damage);    // reduce hitPoints


// existing code
iTween.ValueTo(target, iTween.Hash(
```

And that's it for turret scripting! But there were lots of steps, so let's review...

A Checklist for the Turret and Missile

Just as we did with the marine, go through this checklist and make sure everything is ready for showtime:

1. Open your turret prefab and make sure the top-level object is tagged as **Foe**:

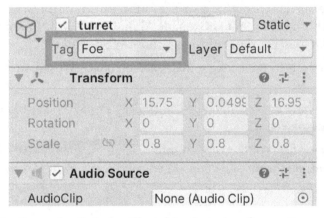

Fig. 14.7 – Remember that you still need to select a tag after creating a new one

2. Add a BoxCollider to the top-level object. *Make sure it is very tall* so that the marine's raycast hits it!

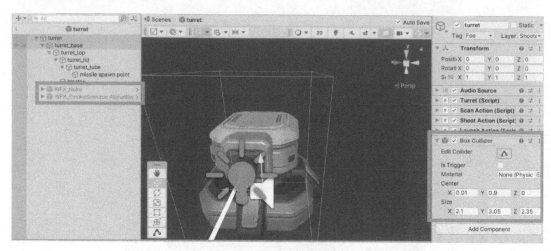

Fig. 14.8 – Add a box collider and some particle systems

3. Add two particle systems to the top-level object at 0, 0, 0. One will be used for smoke when the turret is damaged and the other when it is destroyed. I chose the free **War FX** package by Jean Moreno on the Asset Store: https://assetstore.unity.com/packages/vfx/particles/war-fx-5669. For the smoke, I chose **WFX_SmokeGrenade AlphaBlendBlack**. I found I had to rotate it -90 on the **X** axis. For the explosion, I chose **WFX_Nuke**.

4. Disable both effects by unchecking their enabled boxes. We will turn them on through code.

5. Make sure you have created an empty missile spawn point on the turret_tube object.

6. Populate the new fields of the LaunchAction. Drag the missile spawn point into the **Target** field, get the missile prefab in your Project view, and drag that into the **Prefab** field.

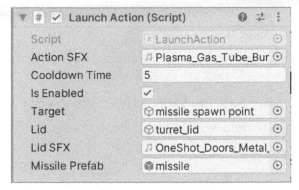

Fig. 14.9 – Populate the target and prefab fields

I know, I know. So many little details to take care of. But it's coming together, and we are almost done.

7. On the turret's AudioSource, set the **Spatial Blend** to .75. This lets the sound seem to be in 3D space relative to the marine.

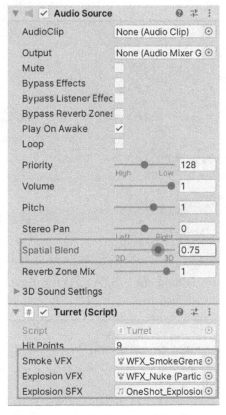

Fig. 14.10 – Change the AudioSource and the Turret components

8. Drag the two particle systems into the slots on the Turret script. Fill in an explosion sound effect. I chose **OneShot_Explosions_7**.

9. Just before we leave the turret, open the ShootAction script. In the `Triggered()` method, change this line to look for **Muzzle** instead of **Player**:

```
var player = GameObject.FindGameObjectWithTag("Muzzle");
```

The muzzle is at chest height whereas the origin of the marine is on the floor.

Okay, one last thing before we test…

Prepping the Missile

This bit is short and sweet. Let's get started:

1. Open up the missile prefab. Make sure the top-level object is tagged as **Missile**.

Fig. 14.11 – Fill in the fields for the Missile script

2. Fill in the fields for the visual and audio effects. Using the same War FX pack as before; I chose **WFX_ExplosiveSmoke Small** for the explosion VFX and using the free Sci-Fi SFX pack we used before, I chose **OneShot_Explosions_4** for the audio.

Okay, we have added code so the marine can shoot, take damage, and die, and we have added code so that the turret can shoot, launch missiles, take damage, and explode. All that's left is to make sure everything is working.

Debugging the Mayhem

And that is everything involved with shooting, exploding, dying, and all that fun stuff! It is a lot to get working together. I have tried to make everything as simple as possible, but almost certainly some bugs will have crept into your code. Don't panic.

Create a simple test situation such as the marine starting very close to a turret in the first area.

The first step before running and testing your game is to get rid of any compiler errors. Begin with whatever error is reported at the _top_ of your debug console. This is because one error might cause *phantom* errors further on—meaning that solving the first will take care of others.

Read the error message very closely. Do not guess at the problem. See what the compiler is actually reporting. Then go and examine the code that is being referenced in the error. Compare it carefully to the code listings in the book. Be especially careful to check things such as getting the equals operator correct (==) and not skipping over the not/negation operator (*!*). When there are strings involved, make sure you have matched cases; for example, be sure that you have created a **Muzzle** tag and that you are testing for `Muzzle` with the same capitalization.

When you have fixed all compiler errors, it is time to run and test your game. Again, it's pretty likely a bug or two has crept into your code. Be methodical. Make a plan, such as first test the turret, and then all the features of the turret one by one: does scanning work? Does shooting work? Does launching work? Can the turret die? and so on. After the turret, test the missile. Then the marine. There is no sequence that is the right one. Just be slow, thoughtful, and methodical.

Don't be afraid to liberally sprinkle `Debug.Log()` messages throughout your code to see what is happening. Also, you may find you need to comment out sections of code to test certain features. If you do so, be sure to write a comment to yourself to add it back in later: `// TODO add back in!`.

Another thing you might want to do in debugging is add in some temporary code. For example, to test the turret, you might add a `Die()` call at the end of the `Start()` method so that the turret immediately dies. If you do this, again, add a comment to remind yourself to remove it.

I hope you don't have many bugs and that you enjoy having the marine shoot and get shot once you solve them. The default hit point values I have supplied let the marine take a lot of damage before dying. You may want to change that for testing.

(Don't forget to turn your sound manager back on if you have disabled it.)

I'm sure you realize that listing different debugging techniques can fill up books, and you should know that the pro way to debug is to use the built-in profiler, but the techniques here can certainly get you through the code in this code.

Creating a Main Menu

Now that we have some game play, let's add in a little more organization by adding a main menu. This will make use of Unity's uGUI system. (Unity also has the legacy immediate-mode GUI, as well as the new UIElements system.) Our GUI will have a little bit of life with some animation and sound:

1. Unity itself gives us a great free starting package. Go to the Asset Store and download and import the **UI Samples** package by Unity Technologies.

2. To see what we are dealing with, find the scene at **Unity UI Samples | Scenes | Menu 3D** and run it. We will modify it for our purposes.

3. Duplicate the scene and rename it to **SE MainMenu**. Store the duplicate in your project's Scenes folder (*not* **UI Samples | Scenes**).

4. Select the tab for your **Game** view. There is a drop-down menu at the top of the Game view that allows you to set the screen dimensions for game play. Select the **16:9 Aspect** choice. There is nothing magical about these dimensions. You might choose different ones depending on your game:

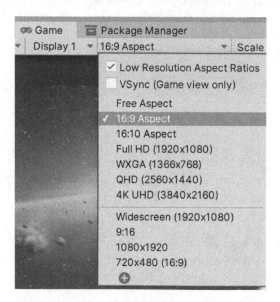

Fig. 14.12 – This ratio is also called "widescreen"

5. Switch back to your Scene view and load your new duplicated scene (but don't play it). Switch into 2D editing mode by clicking the 2D button at the top of your scene view:

Figure 14.13 – Switch to 2D editing mode

6. In your Hierarchy view, you will see you have a Canvas object. You can double-click to focus on it and then you might want to use the mousewheel to zoom in a bit closer.

Changing the menu text

When you twirl open the Canvas in the Hierarchy and drill down to the Window object, you will see five child objects representing the title and button elements of the menu:

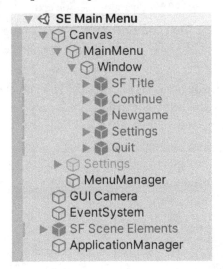

Fig. 14.14 – Look at the children under the Windows object

Follow these steps to change the text:

1. Changing the title is extremely easy. If you twirl open **SF Title**, you will see the **TitleLabel** element. Go ahead and select it.

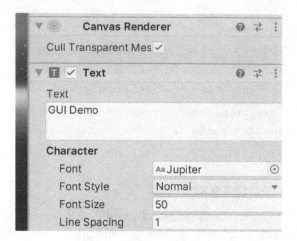

Fig. 14.15 – Changing the title text

2. In the Inspector, locate the **Text** component and change the actual text from GUI Demo to Space Escape. I found I had to add a few spaces at the beginning to make it look right.

3. Next, open up the **Continue** button and drill down so you can view the **Label** in the Inspector. Change the text color to a light-ish gray and change the text to Surrender. The button, by default, is not selectable, therefore failure is *not* an option.

4. Select the top-level parent **Continue** button object. It has an **Animator** component on it. Open that up in the Inspector and you will see a field for **Controller**. This will be set to SF Button. Open the circle selector next to that and scroll to the top of the list to choose the **None** option:

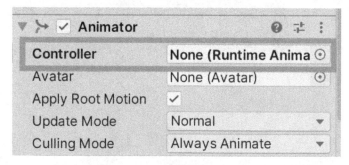

Fig. 14.16 – Set the animation controller to None for the Continue button

5. Go ahead and save your scene and then run it. The menu window should swing into view and the bottom three buttons should be clickable and highlighted when they are hovered over.

Adding audio to the menu

We will use audio from a free package on the Asset Store. You may have already downloaded it. If so, move ahead. The package is called Sci-Fi SFX Package by Chris Markert. You can search the Asset Store with **Sci-Fi SFX**. This is the direct link: https://assetstore.unity.com/packages/audio/sound-fx/sci-fi-sfx-package-184029:

1. In the Hierarchy, select the **Window** object (the child of **Canvas | Main Menu**). In the Inspector, add an **AudioSource** component.

2. Set **AudioClip** to be **OneShot_Doors_Electric_Open**. Leave **Play on Awake** checked.

   This will give a nice, hefty sound to the menu appearing.

3. Next, we are going to write a short C# script to handle the button audio. I will explain it after showing you the code:

```csharp
using UnityEngine;
using UnityEngine.EventSystems;


[RequireComponent(typeof(AudioSource))]          // 1
public class MenuButton : MonoBehaviour,
IPointerEnterHandler, IPointerDownHandler {          // 2
    AudioSource audioSource;       // 3
    public AudioClip rolloverSound;
    public AudioClip clickSound;


    void Start() {     // 4
        audioSource = GetComponent<AudioSource>();
    }


    public void OnPointerEnter(PointerEventData ped)
    { // 5
        audioSource.clip = rolloverSound;
        audioSource.Play();
```

```
        }


    public void OnPointerDown(PointerEventData ped)
    {   // 6
        audioSource.clip = clickSound;
        audioSource.Play();


        if(gameObject.name == "Newgame") {  // 7
        UnityEngine.SceneManagement.SceneManager.
        LoadScene("SpaceEscape");
        }
    } // end OnPointerDown
} // end of MenuButton
```

Let's break down this code:

- At // 1 in the code, we are using the RequireComponent attribute, which will add an AudioSource if there isn't one on the object.

- At // 2 in the code, we have the class declaration for the script. We can see that MenuButton inherits from MonoBehaviour, but that it also promises to implement two **interfaces**: IPointerEnterHandler and IPointerDownHandler. Getting into interfaces is beyond the scope of this book, but they are an essential concept to master. There are many learning resources to help out there. For instance, on YouTube.com, you could search for brackeys interface to get a good one. The direct link is https://www.youtube.com/watch?v=IQpss9YAc4g.

- At // 3 in the code, we are declaring three reference fields. We are going to have to remember to fill in the AudioClip fields when we are back in the Inspector.

- There is no mystery to point // 4. In the standard Start() method, we simply store a reference to the AudioSource component that will be on the same object as this script.

- The next two points, // 5 and // 6, are methods that basically accomplish the same thing: when the button state changes, play a sound effect based on whether it is highlighted or clicked. Note that we do not have a choice in the names of these methods. They are required by the interfaces we promised to implement.

- The code at point // 7 will load the game scene (once we've added it to the Build settings). There are some things to watch for here: **Newgame** is the exact name of the button in the Hierarchy. Spelling matters. **SpaceEscape** is the name I gave to my main scene. If your name is different, change it to that. And again, remember, spelling matters.

- Section // 7 is also a hack in the interest of brevity. A more robust approach would be to create individual click handler methods that you would add to each button's OnClick() list in the Inspector.

4. Save your code now and return to the editor.

5. Select the **Newgame** button and press the arrow to its right to edit its prefab:

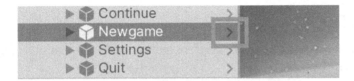

Fig. 14.17 – Enter prefab editing mode

6. In the Inspector, add your MenuButton script to the button prefab. Notice how it automatically adds an AudioSource:

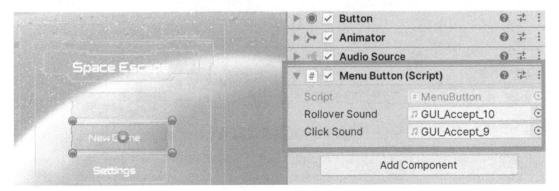

Fig. 14.18 – Add the script to the button prefab

7. Fill in the two sound effect references. The two I liked are **GUI_Accept_10** for highlight and **GUI_Accept_9** for click.

8. Exit prefab editing with the little arrow to the left of the prefab name in the Hierarchy:

Fig. 14.19 – How to exit prefab editing mode

If you absolutely can't wait, you have permission to run the game and hear the effects. The Newgame button will not do anything yet, however.

Setting Up Scene Loading

To get the process of scene loading working, we have to add the scenes to the project's Build Settings. Here's how to do that:

1. Go to **File | Build Settings**.

2. Drag in your menu scene and then your main game scene. Be sure to put the menu first because this is the scene that runs on startup. The numbering starts at zero, so the menu will be index 0:

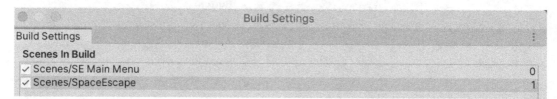

Fig. 14.20 – Add your scenes to the Build Settings list

3. With those two scenes added, you can close the **Build Settings** window and run your game. Choosing **New Game** on the menu should now load your main game. Cool!

One sci-fi UI ready to go!

Adding Post Processing

Postprocessing effects add that little extra something that can set your game apart. Technically, they are beyond the scope of this book, but we can do a super-fast visit just for fun.

Recall that there are things called **scriptable render pipelines**. Currently, by default, Unity supports what is called **built-in pipelines**. Also available are the **Universal Render Pipeline (URP)** and the **High Definition Pipeline (HDP)**. We are using a built-in pipeline. Eventually, URP will become the default, but that is a tale for another day:

1. Firstly, in the Package Manager, under Unity Registry, import the Post Processing package.

   In order to add postprocessing effects, at a minimum we need to create what is called a **Post-Process Volume** and we need to add a **Post-Process Layer** to our main camera. So, let's add this last bit of polish.

2. Create an empty object in your Hierarchy and call it PP.

3. Create a new layer called PP and assign the PP object to that layer.

4. Add a **Post-process Volume** component to the PP object. Be sure **Is Global** is checked.

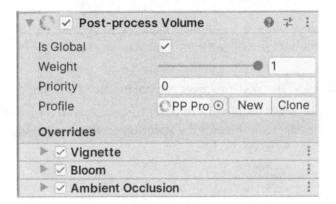

Fig. 14.21 – Add a Post-process Volume, then we will add effects

5. Select your main camera object and add a **Post-process Layer** component. Set its layer to the PP layer you just created. Also set **Mode** to **Temporal Anti-aliasing**.

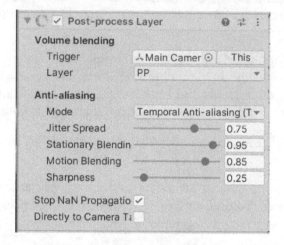

Fig. 14.22 – Add a Post-process Layer to your camera and set Anti-aliasing

Okay, that is the basic setup for postprocessing effects. Like many topics we have touched on, you can take this as far as you like. For example, you can assign different effects to different parts of your level. Imagine an icy area where everything has a bluish tinge. That is a poor example, but you get the idea.

Now what you do is add any postprocessing effects you want to the PP object you created. I will start you off with some basics, but you can play around to your heart's content.

6. On the PP object on the Post-process component, click **New** to create a new Profile.

7. Next, choose **Add Effect** and then **Vignette**. This effect adds a nice darkening effect around the edges and focuses the attention on the screen. Adjust **Intensity** to around 0.5, or whatever you like.

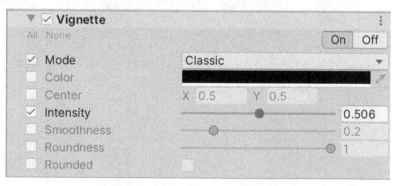

Fig. 14.23 – This is a nice, subtle effect

8. Next, add a **Bloom** effect, which causes a dramatic effect around light sources. I set **Intensity** to `7.6` and **Threshold** to `0.68`. Adjust the values to what you like.

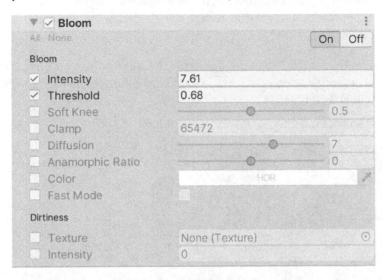

Fig. 14.24 – Bloom effects add a lot of character

9. Lastly, add an **Ambient Occlusion** effect. This is another subtle effect that affects areas where shadows naturally fall.

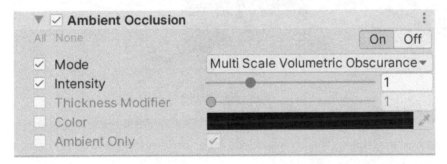

Fig. 14.25 – Ambient Occlusion is another subtle but AAA effect

So, we've just had a whirlwind tour of the amazing world of postprocessing. You learned that at a minimum you need a PP volume, a PP layer, and a postprocessing component on your camera. Postprocessing is a hugely powerful tool that can actually completely change the character of your game.

That's it! If you run your game, I think you will agree that the look has greatly improved.

Creating the Final Room

Now the moment we've all been waiting for, the moment the marine has been desperately striving for: the teleporter pad to get off the planet with the secret plans. Here's how to get it going:

1. In the area on the far side of the bridge, create a Cylinder named `Dais`. Set its **Scale** to 4, 0.1, 4, so it is large and very flat. By default, it comes with a Capsule Collider. Be sure to check **IsTrigger**.

2. Set the dais so that it barely sticks out of the floor.

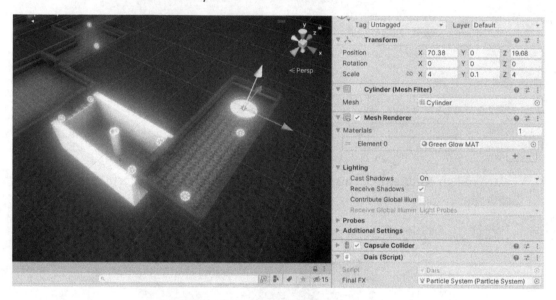

Fig. 14.26 – Create a dais for the final room

3. Apply the **Green Glow MAT** material you previously created.

4. Create a new script on the object called `Dais.cs`. Create the shell of the class:

```csharp
using System.Collections;
using System.Collections.Generic;
using UnityEngine;

public class Dais : MonoBehaviour {
    public GameObject finalFX;
    GameObject marine;
} // end class
```

5. The class only has two methods. Here is the first. It tests whether the player has entered the collider and, if so, triggers a corountine:

```
private void OnTriggerEnter(Collider other) {
    if (other.tag != "Player") return;
    finalFX.gameObject.SetActive(true);

    var player = other.gameObject;
    var scaleTo = new Vector3(.1f, .1f, .1f);
    StartCoroutine(ScaleOverSeconds(player, scaleTo,
                1.0f));
}
```

6. And here is the coroutine it triggers:

```
public IEnumerator ScaleOverSeconds(GameObject
objectToScale, Vector3 scaleTo, float seconds) {
    float elapsedTime = 0;
    Vector3 startingScale =
        objectToScale.transform.localScale;
    while (elapsedTime < seconds) {
        objectToScale.transform.localScale =
            Vector3.Lerp(startingScale, scaleTo,
                (elapsedTime / seconds));
        elapsedTime += Time.deltaTime;
        yield return new WaitForEndOfFrame();
    }
    objectToScale.transform.position = scaleTo;

    Marine marine =
      objectToScale.gameObject.GetComponent<Marine>();
    marine.DoDying();
}
```

7. Be sure to fill in the finalFX field on the dais. For this, I chose **3D Games Effects Pack Free** by Creepy Cat. I chose **Effect_08** in the Prefabs folder and dragged it into the field on Dais.cs.

Go ahead and run your game. Navigate your marine all the way to the end and walk on the dais. The marine should shrink down and—oh dear!—he seems to have confused the coordinates of a teleporter with that of a waste disposal unit. Hmm. Well, you don't think an advanced alien race would let a primitive human escape with their plans so easily, do you?

MUHAHAHAHAHAHA...

Summary

Can you believe it? We made it to the end. We started with nothing and we wound up with a lively mini-game level where we created just about everything ourselves. We created scenery and a character from scratch in Blender, then we UV-unwrapped and textured those elements. We laid out a level in Unity and learned several ways to animate items, including with the Animator and Timeline.

Let's see, what else? We learned about rapid prototyping with ProBuilder and we briefly got introduced to Cinemachine smart virtual cameras.

We found that Mixamo is a godsend in terms of rigging characters and providing high-quality animations.

Lastly, we learned to always double-check the coordinates of any teleporter we want to escape through.

Where can you take the game from here? To infinity and beyond! We have barely scratched the surface of so many things. The techniques in this book can be applied to so many different styles of games: FPS, topdown, you name it.

Hopefully, you are experiencing a whole new level of creative freedom: you now have the choice to use third-party assets as is, modify those assets, or create your own.

Well done. Mission accomplished!

`Packt.com`

Subscribe to our online digital library for full access to over 7,000 books and videos, as well as industry leading tools to help you plan your personal development and advance your career. For more information, please visit our website.

Why subscribe?

- Spend less time learning and more time coding with practical eBooks and Videos from over 4,000 industry professionals

- Improve your learning with Skill Plans built especially for you

- Get a free eBook or video every month

- Fully searchable for easy access to vital information

- Copy and paste, print, and bookmark content

Did you know that Packt offers eBook versions of every book published, with PDF and ePub files available? You can upgrade to the eBook version at `packt.com` and as a print book customer, you are entitled to a discount on the eBook copy. Get in touch with us at `customercare@packtpub.com` for more details.

At `www.packt.com`, you can also read a collection of free technical articles, sign up for a range of free newsletters, and receive exclusive discounts and offers on Packt books and eBooks.

Other Books You May Enjoy

If you enjoyed this book, you may be interested in these other books by Packt:

Blender 3D By Example - Second Edition

Oscar Baechler, Xury Greer

ISBN: 978-1-78961-256-1

- Explore core 3D modeling tools in Blender such as extrude, bevel, and loop cut
- Understand Blender's Outliner hierarchy, collections, and modifiers
- Find solutions to common problems in modeling 3D characters and designs
- Implement lighting and probes to liven up an architectural scene using EEVEE
- Produce a final rendered image complete with lighting and post-processing effects
- Learn character concept art workflows and how to use the basics of Grease Pencil
- Learn how to use Blender's built-in texture painting tools

Blender Quick Start Guide

Allan Brito

ISBN: 978-1-78961-947-8

- Manipulate and visualize your 3D objects in Blender
- Use polygon modeling tools such as extrude, loop cut, and more
- Apply precision modeling tools like snapping and the 3D Cursor
- Render a scene using the real-time engine Eevee
- Create materials for Eevee and Cycles
- Render a scene with the Eevee real-time engine
- Use PBR textures to craft realistic surfaces such as wood with the Shader Editor
- Add motion and animation using keyframes
- Create animation loops using curves and modifiers

Packt is searching for authors like you

If you're interested in becoming an author for Packt, please visit authors. packtpub.com and apply today. We have worked with thousands of developers and tech professionals, just like you, to help them share their insight with the global tech community. You can make a general application, apply for a specific hot topic that we are recruiting an author for, or submit your own idea.

Share Your Thoughts

Hi!

I'm Spencer Grey, author of *Mind-Melding Unity and Blender for 3D Game Development*. I really hope you enjoyed reading this book and found it useful for increasing your productivity and creativity with Unity and Blender.

It would really help me (and other potential readers!) if you could leave a review on Amazon sharing your thoughts on *Mind-Melding Unity and Blender for 3D Game Development* here.

Your review will help me to understand what's worked well in this book, and what could be improved upon for future editions, so it really is appreciated.

Best Wishes,

Spencer Grey

Index

Symbols

2D UV Texture Space 322
3-Button Mouse 12
3D objects
  animating, ways 148
3DS Max 8
3D View Commands
  about 280
    numpad commands 281
    View, navigating 280, 281
.blend files 79

A

abstract base class 88
Adjust Last Operation 68
Analytics tools 7
animated blastdoors
  creating 158
animation
  basic concepts 148
  downloading 348-350
  mistakes 156
  Timeline, using for 255
animation events 368

armature 342
Asset Store
  about 23, 24
  homepage 24
  reference link 396
  searching 25, 26
  URL 24
  using 23
audio
  adding, to menu 413-416
Audio Assets
  about 36
  Ambient Sound 37
  Music 36
  references 36, 37
  SFX 36
  UI Sound Effects 37
  Weapons 36
Audio Effects
  adding 219-221
auto-keying 157
avatar system 255
Axes Gizmo, Blender 46
axis
  excluding 52, 53

B

Binding Poses 285
blastdoor doorframe
  creating 159-163
blastdoors
  creation scheme 158
  texturing 178
Blender
  about 7, 32, 40, 121
  Animation workspace 149-152
  Layout workspace 41, 42
  navigation and hot-keys 121
  numpad 122
  splash screen 41
  using, reasons 8, 9
  view modes and tools 46
Blender Command Review
  3D View Commands 280
  about 280
  Edit Mode Commands 282
  Faster Command Access 283
  miscellaneous 3D View Commands 282
Blender interface
  Axes Gizmo 46
  Editor and Mode selection area 44
  header menu bar 45
  Outliner Panel 48
  Pivot, Snap, and Proportional Editing 44
  Properties Panel 48-50
  reference link 45
  Status Bar 50
  Toolbar 42, 43
  Zoopancamper 47
Blender Units 52, 53
blue colored options, ProBuilder Toolbar
  about 238

Grow Selection (Vertex/Edge/
  Face mode) 239
Orientation (all modes) 239
Rect (Edge/Face mode) 239
Select by Colors (Vertex/
  Edge/Face mode) 239
Select by Material (Face mode) 239
Select Edge Loop / Edge Ring
  (Edge mode) 239
Select Edge Ring (Edge mode) 239
Select Face Loop (Face mode) 239
Select Face Ring (Face mode) 239
Select Hidden (Vertex/Edge/
  Face mode 239
Select Holes (Vertex/Edge mode) 239
Shift (Vertex/Edge/Face mode) 239
Shrink Selection (Vertex/
  Edge/Face mode) 239
book requirements
  about 10
  hardware prerequisites 12
  knowledge prerequisites 10, 11
  software prerequisites 11
box select 162
bridge
  activating 247-251
bridge animation, with Timeline
  Animation Track, creating 265, 266
  audio, adding 274-276
  finishing 271-273
  infinite clip, recording 268
  performing 263
  plan for bridge 267
  previewing 270, 271
  prism walkway, animating 268, 269
  Timeline, creating 263, 264
built-in pipelines 417
Built-In Render Pipeline 19

C

channels
  about 154
  state colors 155
Cinemachine
  about 375
  installing 376-378
clips 254
code checklist 110
community forums, Unity
  URL 13
complex door
  animating 173-176
  bottom, texturing 181
  creating 166, 167
  middle parts, texturing 182, 183
  texturing 181
  top parts, texturing 182
constraints 149
Constructive Solid Geometry (CSG) 231
cubes
  creating 56

D

Digital Content Creation (DCC) 8
Door Animations 190-193
door bottom
  animating 177
  finishing 171, 172
doorframe
  texturing 178-180
door middle
  animating 176
  creating 167-171

doors
  exporting 183
drivers 149
DRY principle 87

E

edge 58
edge actions, ProBuilder Toolbar
  Bevel 243
  Bridge Edge 243
  Connect Edges 243
  Cut Tool 243
  Extrude Edges 243
  Fill Hole 243
  Insert Edge Loop 243
  Offset Edges 244
  Set Pivot 244
  Subdivide Edges 243
edge slide 169
Edit Mode 57
Edit Mode Commands 282
Editor and Mode selection
    area, Blender 44
enum 86
exposure sheet 150
Extrude command 68

F

face 58
face actions, ProBuilder Toolbar
  Bevel 244
  Conform Normals 244
  Cut Tool 245
  Delete Faces 244

Detach Faces 244
Duplicate Faces 244
Extrude Faces 244
Flip Face Edge (Turn Edges) 244
Flip Face Normals 245
Merge Faces 244
Offset Faces 245
Set Pivot 245
Subdivide Faces 244
Triangulate Faces 244
face normals 172
Faster Command Access 283
FBX Exporter package
  installing 32-34
Final Room
  creating 420-422
first-person shooter (FPS) 22
first-person-style (FPS) 118
flat shaded 295
frame rate 153

G

GIMP
  URL 11
Godot 5
grayboxing 234, 235
greebles and nurnies 119
green colored options, ProBuilder Toolbar
  Center Pivot 241
  Conform Normals 240
  Export 241
  Flip Normals 241
  Freeze Transform 241
  Lightmap Uvs 241
  Merge Objects 241
  Mirror Objects 241

ProBuilderize 241
Subdivide Object 241
Triangulate 241

H

hardware requirements Blender
  URL 12
hardware requirements Unity
  URL 12
header menu bar, Blender 45
head, marine
  helmet grille 331
  rest 333
  side cylinders 332
  visor 331
High Definition Pipeline (HDP) 417
High Definition Rendering
    Pipeline (HDRP)
  about 19
  reference link 19

I

In-App Purchases 7
Infinite Animation 256
Isometric view 260
iTween 84, 148

K

keyframes
  about 149
  tip, for disappearing keyframes 157
  working with 154, 155
keying set 156

L

latest version, Blender
   URL 11
latest version, Unity
   URL 11
LaunchAction
   creating 106-110
   testing 110
layout
   creating 120, 121
learning site, Unity
   URL 6
level
   laying out 210
level layout
   Area A 212
   Area B 212
   Area C 213
   Area C2 213
   Area D 214
   Area E 214
   Area F 215
   Area G 216, 217
   tips 211, 212
Lightweight Render Pipeline (LWRP) 19
linear interpolation 84
LineRenderer 98
Local view mode 167
loop cuts 162
loop select 163
low-polygon modeling 58
low-poly models 59

M

made-in-Unity first-person-shooter
   example 4

Main Menu
   creating 410, 411
marine
   animating 362-364
   arms, processing 337, 338
   camera control 371-375
   camera tracking, with secret weapon 375
   colors, randomizing 286, 287
   exporting 343
   feet, processing 340, 341
   footstep sounds, adding to
      animation 367, 368
   hands, processing 338
   head, processing 326-330
   legs, processing 339
   lights, adding to level 369-371
   material, applying 358, 359
   material, creating 357
   movement, implementing 371-375
   objects, organizing 285, 286
   parts 325, 326
   prefab, creating 359-361
   preparing, for duty 356, 357
   prepping 284, 285
   rigging 342
   torso, processing 334, 335
   transitions, for animations 364-366
   triggers, for animations 364
Marine Checklist 397, 398
marine modeling
   about 287
   arm 306-308
   hand 308-310
   head 288-297
   leg 312
   torso 297-300

marine modeling, boot
  about 315, 316
  body parts, relationship between 317
  miscellaneous 316
  model and file, setting up 317-319
marine modeling, hand
  fingers, creating 310
  thumb, creating 310
marine modeling, leg
  lower leg, creating 314, 315
  upper leg, creating 313
marine modeling, torso
  belt 305
  bottom bits 303, 304
  chest blaster 300, 301
  neck collar 301-303
markers 157
material
  about 132, 326
  applying, to tube 82, 83
  creating, for missile tube 82
materials 101 136
material slot 326
Maya 8
Mayhem
  debugging 409
Mecanim system 255
menu text
  changing 411-413
Mini-Game
  defining 22
  Gameplay Mechanics 22, 23
mirror command 167
mirror modifier 160
miscellaneous 3D View Commands 282
Missile
  checklist 405-408
  prepping 408

Mixamo
  about 342, 344
  account, creating 344, 345
  character, uploading 345-347
modifiers 160
Modular Level Design
  about 116-118
  floor, creating 123-125
  goals, setting 118
  Humble Floor 119
  wall corner, creating 130, 131
  wall, creating 126-129
  walls and corners 119
Monkey-corn
  creating 59-62
MonoBehaviour 86

N

n-gon 58
normals 172
notable options
  Actions 246
  Debug 246
  Dimensions Overlay 246
  Repair 246
numpad commands 281

O

object modifiers 50
objects
  creating, with ProBuilder 234, 235
official Blender support page
  URL 13
official Unity Support page
  URL 13

orange-colored tools, ProBuilder Toolbar
    Material Editor 234
    New Poly Shape 233
    New Shape 233
    Smoothing 233
    UV Editor 234
    Vertex Colors 234
orthographic view 48, 260
Outliner Panel, Blender 48

P

package 27
Package filter
    options 29
Package Manager
    about 27
    areas 29
    list loading lag 30
    using 27, 28
Perspective view 48, 260
Photoshop 11
playhead 151
polygonal modeling 10
Poly Shape tool 234
post processing
    adding 417-419
Post-Process Layer 417
Post-Process Volume 417
Prefabs
    models, turning into 189, 190
prism
    prefab object, creating 261, 262
    prepping 257-261
ProBuilder
    about 225
    history 225

installing 226-232
    versus Blender 225
ProBuilder Toolbar
    additional shape creation tips 237, 238
    blue colored options 232, 238-240
    exploring 232, 233
    green colored options 232, 240, 241
    objects, creating with 234
    orange-colored tools 232, 233
    other options 245
    pre-defined shape objects,
        creating 235-237
    red-colored options 232, 242
project folders
    creating 20, 21
Project Template
    options 18
    reference link 18
    selecting 18
Properties Panel, Blender
    about 48
    Active Tool 49
    Material Properties & Texture
        Properties 50
    Modifier Properties 50
    Object Constraint Properties 50
    Object Data Properties 50
    Object Properties 49
    Output Properties 49
    Particle Properties 50
    Physical Properties 50
    Render Properties 49
    Scene Properties 49
    View Layer Properties 49
    World Properties 49

Q

quad 58

R

ray cast 94
red-colored options, ProBuilder Toolbar
    about 242
    edge actions 243
    face actions 244, 245
    vertex actions 242, 243
retro 2D arcade game
    example 5
RGBA pixel format 136
rigging 342
rotation 53

S

scaling 53
Scene Grid
    color, modifying of grid lines 204-206
    snapping 200-204
    vertex snapping 206, 207
scene loading
    setting up 416
scenery
    animating 378
    blast doors, animating 378
    bridge, animating 383-385
    checklist, for door 382
    door prefabs, working with 379-382
scope
    defining 89
Scriptable Render Pipeline 19, 417

Script Template
    about 111
    on Mac 112
    on Windows 111
sculpting 10
Shape tool 234
Shoot
    preparing 388-390
ShootAction
    about 98
    creating 100-103
    preparing 105
    testing 104
shooting, Part I
    scripting 391-394
shooting, Part II
    scripting 394-396
Sidebar 54
simple door
    animating 165
    creating 164
    texturing 180
skybox
    about 218
    adding 217-219
Smart UV Project 323
smooth shaded 295
sound
    adding, to shooting 390
state-based system 255
Status Bar, Blender 50
struts
    creating 70-72
Subdivision Surface modifier 326
sub-samples 153

T

texture image
  loading, into UV space 324
Texture mapping 132
textures
  references 37
  sizes 324
Timeline
  about 151, 254
  tracks 256
  transport controls 152
  using, for animation 255
Toolbar, Blender
  3D cursor 43
  about 42
  Annotation tool 44
  Measurement tool 44
  Move tool 43
  Rotate tool 43
  Scale tool 43
  Selection tool 43
  Transform tool 43
torso
  about 305, 306
  belt 305
torso, marine
  belt 336
  chest ring 335
  collar 335
  lower torso 336
T-pose 285
tracks, Timeline
  about 256
  Activation track 256
  Animation track 256

Audio track 256
Control track 256
Override track 256
Playable track 256
Single track 256
transforms
  applying 55
translation tool
  using 52
transport controls 152
Turret
  about 399-404
  altering 63
  behavior planning 83
  exporting 34, 35
  flaw, fixing 72, 73
  importing 76-79
  iTween, adding 84
  LaunchAction, creating 106-110
  LaunchAction, preparing for 105
  LaunchAction, testing 110
  launch spawn point, creating 106
  launch tube, creating 67-70
  lid, carving out 64-67
  missile, creating 105
  placeholder player hero, creating 92
  preparing, for gameplay 76
  restructuring 79-81
  ScanAction, testing 96-98
  scanning 93-96
  scripting 85-87
  ShootAction, creating 100-104
  ShootAction, preparing for 98-100
  ShootAction, testing 104
  texturing 81

turret actions
    setting up 87-92
Turret checklist 405-408
turret model 31
tweening 84, 148

U

unit basis 117
Unity
    about 4
    Door Animations 190-193
    Great Stuff, collecting 186
    history 4
    importing into 187-189
    model, turning into Prefabs 189, 190
    ultimate advanced tip 111
    using, reasons 5, 6
Unity Ads 7
UnityEvent 89
Unity Hub
    about 11, 16, 17
    Community 17
    Installs 17
    Learn 17
    Projects 17
    URL 16
Unity material
    about 193-195
    creating 196-200
Unity Project
    about 19, 20
    creating 16
Universal Rendering Pipeline (URP)
    about 19, 417
    reference link 19
Unreal 5

up-sample 153
UV Editing Workspace
    working 137-142
UV islands 136, 323
UV mapping 132
UV mapping 101 132, 133
UV space
    about 323
    texture image, loading into 324
UV unwrapping 132, 322
UV unwrapping 101 133-136

V

vertex 58
vertex actions, ProBuilder Toolbar
    Collapse Vertices 242
    Connect Vertices 243
    Cut Tool 243
    Fill Hole 243
    Offset Vertices 243
    Set Pivot 243
    Split Vertices 243
    Weld Vertices 242
vertex snapping 206, 207
video game engine 4
view modes and tools, Blender 46
virtual keyword 90

W

wall
    texturing 136, 137
    unwrapping 136, 137
wall corner
    texturing 142-145
    unwrapping 142-145
weight-painting 342

workspace
  about 45
  customizing 45

X

X-Ray View 70

Z

Zoopancamper, Blender 47

CPSIA information can be obtained
at www.ICGtesting.com
Printed in the USA
JSHW030525100822
29092JS00003B/26

9 781801 071550